BLACK MAMBA
UNDER MY BED

TAYLOR-MADE ADVENTURES BY
RUTH TAYLOR STOTT

First published by Ruth Stott, 2021

Copyright © 2021 Ruth Stott

ISBN 978-0-620-92495-5 (print)
ISBN 978-0-620-92496-2 (e-book)

Cover Design by Greg Philip Davies
Illustrations by Desmond Martin
Typesetting by www.myebook.online

CONTENTS

DEDICATION

This year my beloved husband Joe turns 90.What on earth does one give a 90 year old male living in a Retirement Village? He does not need "things" to clutter his room or his life. Generous folk love buying treasured items for old folk celebrating milestone birthdays. Unique gifts like a barometer, a tie press, gold cuff links, a cuckoo clock, a silk tie or a ceramic poodle from China that is meant to turn purple when rain is forecast. Joe says no one he knows wears cuff links nowadays. He only wears a tie to weddings and funerals, so he kept his two special favourites. He has enough after-shave lotion and male perfume stashed away to keep him smelling desirable until he reaches 120! He loves his old vests and underpants and still cherishes a 40-year old lambswool jersey his English wife, Jean, knitted for him just before she died.

Joe has weathered many storms in his life. He nursed two terminally ill wives. His first wife died only 7 years after they had immigrated to South Africa from the U.K. He brought up their two school going children and worked long hours as a trombonist puffing away in the orchestra pit at CAPAB. (Cape Performing Arts Board)

Joe did not enjoy being single, so after two lonely years, he chose to marry a South African widow and happily accepted her three children. Having his two grown up sons living and working in England, Joe had suddenly become a father to seven!

Then when he lost his second wife, Grace, also to cancer after a happy marriage lasting just 14 years, Joe was brave enough to marry me, a spinster and a schoolmarm in my mid- fifties!

Here we are now, completing 20 joyful years of marriage and adjusting to life in a tranquil Retirement Village. We have travelled extensively, embarked on exciting adventures and then just two years ago, we shared the tragic loss of Joe's youngest son, Jonathan. He had suffered ill health and debilitating pain since his early twenties and passed away in England having just turned 45.

My pupils chuckled when they heard that I had become an instant granny to eight when I married Joe. Now they gasp in disbelief when they hear that this number has swelled to 18! One sporty young man whom I bumped into recently in our local supermarket said, "Wow, Miss Taylor, that's awesome!
You have gained an entire hockey team of grandkids plus 7 reserves!"

After much thought I decided that the best way to honour my husband on his 90th birthday would be to share my memoirs and life's adventures with him in a light- hearted and humorous way. After all, Joe missed out on the first 55 years of my life. He is a courageous cancer survivor and every day that we spend together, I regard as a precious gift from God. I have written this book in secret, late at night and often by torch light. I hope to hand it to Joe on the morning of his 90th birthday as a small token of my deep appreciation for his love and companionship and to keep alive the adventures we have shared.

INTRODUCTION

My school pupils always said that when I retired I should write a book. One of my greatest joys is meeting past pupils from Treverton, Rustenburg and Pinehurst and it delights me to hear how successful they have become in life. I still believe that teaching is a Calling. I was privileged to enjoy the support of five outstanding headmasters and am thankful to say that I never experienced difficulty in maintaining classroom discipline.

I share from the heart the techniques I practised over many years and which worked for me.

- Be well -prepared and make each lesson relevant to the needs of your pupils.
- Genuinely love your pupils and realize there is untapped potential in every single one, having his/her own peculiar gifts and aptitudes.
- Certain "talents" like collecting cockroaches or pickled earthworms may seem peculiar to you if you think peculiar means odd or weird! It doesn't! Our Latin teacher told us that it comes from the word "peculiaris." It really means "one's own" or "personal."

- Never compare a pupil with one of his/ her siblings. Each of us is a unique individual.
- At times you will need to be a nurse, a counsellor and even a detective! You will wish you were a trained psychiatrist!
- You will earn your pupils' respect and build relationships by showing that you are genuine and really do care about their welfare.
- Never talk down to your pupils and avoid resorting to harsh criticism or sarcasm.
- Learn to Trust those entrusted to your care. Trust brings out the best in them.
- A sense of humour is essential. When you make a mistake, admit it.
- Your pupils will respect you even more if you let them know you are only human too.
- Make every lesson as dynamic and exciting as possible. Use drama and interesting visual aids. Be spontaneous. Children love it when you are able to use different accents.
- Share newspaper cuttings and collect fascinating articles. Keep up to date.
- Never show your shock or disapproval if a pupil chooses to confide in you, even when their stories from home might alarm you.
- Involve your pupils in your lessons and remember you are equipping them for Life.
- Build their confidence and self -esteem and be generous in your praise.
- Visit their homes when you are made aware of severe illness, bereavement or distress.
- Children appreciate it if they feel you are sharing their heartache or an emotional burden. Some children don't feel they can open up to their parents and may turn to a compassionate teacher for support.

I regularly bump into past pupils who introduce me to their own children. It warms my heart to hear them telling their offspring how they still recall Geography and History facts from the exciting travel tales I wove into my lessons. They remember the different accents I used and the objects I hauled out of a little suitcase to capture their attention in morning Assembly talks and at Founders' Day. With much hilarity they even recall the occasion I flung my high- heeled shoe at the blackboard to hammer home a point in one of my grade 7 History lessons!

I thank the hundreds of pupils I taught between 1964 and 2000 who made teaching for me an enriching and deeply fulfilling career.

I am grateful that I still have an excellent photographic memory and am able to recall incidents right back to the age of two. In many cases when I meet a past pupil I can still picture where they slept in the Treverton dormitory, or the desk they occupied in my classroom, or even the house or apartment where the family lived.

So before I get too old, and lose this ability, it is my desire to share my life's adventures. I can honestly say that I don't ever remember a single year of my life being dull or boring and I treasure the wonderful friendships made in so many countries of the world.

Throughout my life I have been a prolific writer of letters and postcards. When my dear old mother died, I discovered hatboxes stuffed to the brim with every single letter I had ever written to my parents, whether I was teaching or studying in another province or travelling overseas. Amongst all the letters was another intriguing find. Mom had stored a bunch of green bananas in a warm dark place to ripen slowly. There they were, long since forgotten, but still intact and recognizable. In fact the bananas were beautifully preserved and thoroughly fossilized for posterity, adding an interesting mellow fragrance to mom's treasure trove of letters!

I too hoarded useful brochures and travel pamphlets. I took hundreds of slides and photographs. These all helped me in my lesson preparation and in the numerous travel talks I have been asked to give. So with these to aid me and with a vivid photographic memory still intact, it is my joy to share my memoirs as they spring to mind. I shall keep the chapters short, light-hearted and humorous. There will of course be some sad and nostalgic experiences to share. They may not all be strictly in chronological order because I have visited some countries several times. I also want to avoid burdening my readers with dates. Some of my memories have been triggered by current world events. We all experience good times and challenging times, but looking back over my 76 years, I am so grateful to God for every single day that I have lived on this amazing planet and as a citizen of our unique and wonderful country, South Africa.

Please sit back now and enjoy the journey with me! At times you may feel you need to tighten your seat belt!

Ruth Taylor- Stott
Pinelands, Cape Town
October 2020

BLACK MAMBA UNDER MY BED

AND OTHER TAYLOR – MADE ADVENTURES

Someone I have grown up admiring was the courageous blind and deaf heroine Helen Keller. I clearly remember going to a play which stirred me deeply as a little girl in the 1950's. Many will recall The Miracle Worker, the inspirational story of Helen, blind and deaf since a toddler, learning to communicate with the world through the unfailing efforts of her devoted teacher, Anne Sullivan. Something Helen Keller stated has stayed with me throughout my life and I have proved it to be true throughout my 76 years.

**LIFE IS EITHER A DARING ADVENTURE
OR NOTHING AT ALL!**

RESCUED, JUST IN THE SNIP OF TIME!

*M*y brother David and I shall be eternally thankful for the adventurous genes we inherited from our parents, Noel and Muriel Taylor. (Nee Liddle) They were both enthusiastic members of the Mountain Club of South Africa. They actually met one Saturday afternoon on a daring rock climb on the face of Table Mountain. My Mom loved to tell us how my Dad could not escape because she had him dangling on the end of a rope!

One of my very earliest adventures happened in infancy at the Booth Memorial Nursing Home in February 1944. I believe I had a very narrow escape when I was just eight days old. There was always great excitement when family members of the Jewish faith gathered for a baby boy's circumcision on the 8th day. I understand that the Torah commands it there, and it's known as a shalom zachor, because at that time, blood clotting substances reach their all-time high, well beyond the amount that will accompany a normal human being for the rest of his life.

Apparently in the midst of all the excitement of guests popping in and out of the maternity ward to admire new infants, the nurse on duty misread my name tag! Thinking I was baby Rael and not baby Ruth, I was bundled up in an exquisite lacy tallit or prayer shawl and taken into an adjoining room. My nurse then handed me to a beautifully dressed Kvatter, the family messenger assigned to deliver the little prized bundle to a special seat known as the Seat of Elijah the Prophet. A Brit Milah blessing was said over my little head by the family's Rabbi and the Mohel (circumciser) deftly slipped his hands under my shawl only to let out a gasp of horror. I shall leave the rest of the story to your imagination but the tale has a happy ending. I was told that baby Rael's family forgave the tearful nurse aid and enjoyed the amusing side of the story once the mistake had been rectified. I am happy to report that baby Ruth escaped unscathed and infant Rael finally got to have his turn!

I was back at the Booth Memorial Hospital at age two to welcome my baby brother David into the big wide world. Our beloved but very eccentric maiden Aunt Florrie was one of his first admirers. She was a fascinating Auntie because she lived all alone in a wooden chalet in a shady glade on a hairpin bend in Camps Bay. She frightened us when we were little because she had curved nails like talons and wore a mangy looking furry cape draped round her lean shoulders! The fur belonged to a poor dead little stuffed fox with a wizened face and beady eyes which seemed to follow us round her house. We expected fleas to jump off the fox and bite us. Auntie Florrie was always shadowed by a cantankerous and manipulative little Pekinese dog called Ming with poppy eyes and a flat little nose. Ming must have been protecting Florrie and her little dead fox because she nipped our ankles if we came too close.

Years later our Mom told us that when Great Aunt Florrie died, Ming was inconsolable and trailed woefully behind the coffin at her funeral and had a very sad look on her little flat face for months, so we hoped that someone kind had adopted Ming and given her a bright future.

Fearing that at aged just two, I might become a jealous, attention-seeking little sibling, Auntie Florrie brought along a gift which she hoped would occupy my attention while I was left to play outside in the garden at the maternity home. It certainly did. It was a fuzzy black cat with evil, glinting eyes and a bright pink tongue which flopped out sideways and waggled in a menacing kind of way. The furry cat had a belly which unzipped and was apparently meant to house my pyjamas. However, I soon discovered I could get my revenge on my newly-acquired feline friend by filling its belly with broken sticks, dead leaves, chunks of glass and dollops of dog poo! My efforts at cleaning the garden were obviously not appreciated because I received two firm smacks on my little bottom when it was time to leave the hospital and I was made to empty the contents of my cat's belly before I was allowed to clamber into the car.

This reminds me that when we were very young, my Mom taught us that there were two kinds of Dirt! Clean dirt and dirty dirt! Ours was a real outdoor kind of family. David and I first went hiking with our parents when we were toddlers. Old photographs show that we were so little that our tiny rucksacks almost dragged along the ground behind us. We slept in a tent and even under the stars from about the age of 2 or 3 and we learnt a deep appreciation of Nature. David and I discovered at a very young age that it's under the stars that night- time produces so much of its own special magic.

Whenever we were outdoors and dropped food or sweets into the sand or onto leaves or pine needles, Mom would say, "That's just clean dirt and it is good food so we don't throw it away." She showed us how to blow off the sand or gently rub away prickles or leaves and reminded us about all the poor starving people in our world who would give anything to have food like ours, even if it had clean dirt on it. We were also taught not to fear lizards, chameleons, cockroaches, bees or locusts but to have a healthy respect for snakes.

As we grew up, we always had to wear shoes when we went to the shops or walked on pavements because my Mom would point out broken glass or people who cleared their throats and spat in the road, or dogs that relieved themselves on the pavement. Mom would explain that we wouldn't want to take those germs back home and onto our carpets or sheets! When David aged just 5, gleefully spied a shiny silver tickey (three pence) lying in the road, he put it in his mouth to keep it safe, but my Mom nearly had a fit and told him to spit it out immediately. She then explained in graphic terms as we walked home, where that tickey had probably been in the last few days and weeks!

Ruth in the garden of our first home

My mom and me

My mom and dad's war time wedding 1941

2

ON THE MOVE

*O*ur family moved around quite a lot in my early days. We lived in some interesting homes. When my Mom brought me home from the nursing home my Dad was teaching at Sea Point Boys' High. The War had ended and he was home after spending over four years lecturing to cadets at the benighted Zonderwater Army Camp, a drab, waterless military base outside Pretoria.

We lived in a school house in a prime spot on the Sea Point beach front. Our home was called Eastbourne House. If our home sounds grand, then the name was a misnomer for the entire house would have fallen down if it had not been shored up with hulking great blue-gum tree trunks. Eastbourne House had been an old Rectory but was derelict and had already been condemned to demolition when the Sea Point Boys' High School annexed it for a boys' Club. My Dad and Mom had been installed there to run the new venture after school hours. I was told that we lived in the double-storey section of the house, calculated to be the first part to collapse! In the single- storey part, a boys' recreational club offered chess, darts, table tennis, an embryo library, art, music and snooker to help entertain boys whose parents both worked and who were normally confined to life in an apartment. They also had the use of cricket nets and a tennis court.

My brother and I grew up hearing that life was challenging in those post war days. As a school teacher my Dad earned twenty seven pounds ten shillings per month of which he paid £8 in rental. Mom said if anyone leaned against a wall inside the house, one would immediately be covered in a shower of red brick dust. Lights swung merrily to and fro in a breeze and the creaking floorboards threatened to give way if one did not tread warily. Eastbourne House was full of odd, creepy nooks and corners and it was amusing to hear how our visitors balked at the stairs ~ 17 of them, high, wooden ones that rose up almost perpendicularly to the two bedrooms upstairs. It was to Eastbourne House that my baby brother was also introduced when he was just one week old.

We were told that on David's first night away from the nursing home a vicious black South Easter sprang up. Its velocity had raised both the roof and the ceiling and was shedding all manner of debris onto his cot. When Mom looked up she saw an angry sky snarling at her through the aperture and sent for Dad to come across from school with a team of boys to help stave off disaster. It was a good thing Dad had been a Queen's Boy Scout because with true Scouting ingenuity, he soon had the school boys screwing cup hooks into the floor and the ceiling! They then joined them up with strands of strong wire. Apparently we all slept on mattresses downstairs after that.

Some two years later my Dad decided to do a Master's degree at Stellenbosch University in the hope of becoming fully bilingual. Leave of absence from his teaching post meant going back to Varsity on quarter pay.

I guess my Mom was grateful for the Eastbourne House necessity for frugality and I think we children began to learn the value of money from a tender age. My Dad moved into a University men's hostel called Dagbreek and my Mom, David and I stayed in two rooms in a portion of a rustic cottage called Gate House. It was at the entrance to a farm in a pretty valley and the farm was owned by a delightful Afrikaans family of warm- hearted, hospitable folk.

Our Dad rode over from the men's residence to visit us each evening and we were overjoyed when we saw him pedalling up the lane on his decrepit old pushbike. He spent an hour walking and playing with us in the beautiful poplar and oak-lined lanes and then helped Mom wash the dishes before returning to his studies. He had to boil a kettle because we had no hot water laid on in our hired rooms. Dave and I enjoyed this rather primitive camp- style way of life. It was almost as much of a novelty as seeing piglets suckling, calves being born, eggs laid and fluffy little yellow chicks hatched.

Stellenbosch is known as the City of Oaks or "Die Eikestad." It is a delightful town, ringed by hills and mountains, with a river running through it between banks of wild creepers and fast-flowing streamlets in some of the gutters. I remember that in junior school our history teacher told us that the streets were made wide enough for a team of oxen pulling wagons, to make a complete U turn. The channels carrying water along the side of the streets were also just wide enough to enable the oxen to lower their heads and enjoy a drink of water after a tiring cross country trek, even with cumbersome wooden yokes slung round their necks.

Once my Dad had graduated, he was offered a teaching post at the local Boys' High School, called Paul Roos Gymnasium. He held this position for two years, before being offered the principalship of Simon's Town Secondary School. Living on a farm gave Mom, Dave and me a wonderful opportunity to learn to speak Afrikaans. To this day we feel comfortable conversing in our second language and have made many wonderful Afrikaans speaking friends down through the years.

BABOONS, PENGUINS & SUBMARINES

*M*oving to a charming old- world cosmopolitan seaport like Simons Town, which was still under British occupation in 1951, was an exciting experience for us all. We lived in "School House" on the school premises overlooking His Majesty's dockyard. King George VI died in our second year there and we had a grandstand view as we watched the flag raising and lowering ceremonies and listened to the strains of the National Anthem drifting up to our balcony very early every morning from the flagship's quarterdeck.

Before our Mom married Dad, she was a journalist and worked for the Diamond Fields Advertiser in Kimberley but in Simon's Town Dave and I enjoyed having our Mom at the school too. All of a sudden they needed her to act as a volunteer secretary, telephonist, relief teacher, counsellor and a netball, gym, tennis and swimming coach! By the end of our first year at Simon's Town, Mom had taught every class in the school from age 6 to 16.

The school went up to standard 8 (grade 10) which was called J.C. or Junior Certificate. In those days many pupils left school after J.C. and went out into the working world.

Our house was always full of interesting people because Mom and Dad had to entertain parents, prefects, staff, priests, inspectors, committee members, politicians, and a Rabbi and an Admiral! Many people came to our Dad with problems to solve. Mom had to carry out some unusual tasks in the secretary's office like popping boils, cleaning cuts and grazes, treating a girl who passed a three foot long tapeworm, a boy who had convulsions in the car park and a terrified policeman who ran into the school building to hide because a burglar chased him and he thought he was having a heart attack. Then there was the little boy who had chewed the sleeve of his blazer and accidentally swallowed the brass button on it and the little Sub A girl who poked a peanut up her nostril and couldn't get it to come down again. Mom often brought sick children to our house to nurse because their parents were at work all day. One day she had to call an ambulance to take a very tubby girl to hospital in Fish Hoek because she weighed 120 kg and Mom couldn't fit her into our car.

School House was situated on a steep embankment above the main road running past the police station and the Naval Dockyard. Our house was right beside the Convent and Dave and I received several spankings for perching in trees above the road and dropping acorns onto the nuns' heads as they walked into town in a most dignified manner. At age 6 and 8 Dave and I felt this naughty deed required a fair amount of skill and precision for we had to allow for the acorns to drop from the height of the tree and land on the nun's veil at the correct moment. A very naughty habit to be sure!

We loved clambering up the cliff behind the house where there were caves and exciting rocky ledges to traverse. The terrain was perfect for playing cops and robbers. There were also several very enticing fig trees to climb and we tucked into the ripe fruit as we scrambled higher and higher. We had several close encounters with Cape cobras on the cliff face and often came face to face with menacing baboons which barked fiercely and flashed vicious teeth at us in an ominous way when we dared to venture onto their turf.

There were so many exciting things to do and see in Simon's Town. Of course a favourite pastime was to visit Boulders beach and paddle with the penguins. As our swimming strokes progressed beyond doggie paddle, Dave and I were able to jump off the rocks and swim back into the delightful little sheltered cove with its smooth flat rocks for sun bathing, soft white beach sand and a picturesque row of brightly coloured wooden bathing boxes. Here the Simon's Town regulars changed into their swim suits or left their fishing tackle. It was lovely to see the locals perched on the steps of their bathing boxes, sipping coffee from Thermos flasks and greeting everyone who walked along the beach. Boulders beach was a delightful, safe haven for us to explore.

Down at the Naval Dockyard we were able to board a submarine and when the door slammed closed and the chief engineer began his explanation, we children felt we were experiencing a real live deep sea Adventure. Of course the engineer made it extra exciting for us by describing war time escapades, showing us real torpedoes and then in graphic terms explaining what damage our submarines could inflict upon any "baddies" who dared to venture into our protected waters.

Sometimes the navy practised shooting at mid- ocean targets in False Bay and the ground under our old School House shook and thundered. There were often massive bush fires when the whole of Red Hill was ablaze and we were terrified lest the flames roared down the mountainside and devoured my dad's school and us!

We loved it when our parents were invited to attend important Naval functions and garden parties at Admiralty House because our mom always brought back a doughnut or a slice of chocolate cake in her handbag for us. My parents met all kinds of dignitaries there and were able to practise speaking Afrikaans when the Nationalist government parliamentarians of that period attended special functions in Simon's Town.

On one such auspicious occasion my Mom was asked by the British Admiral whether she would ask the prime minister's wife in Afrikaans if she would like to go to the toilet before dinner was due to be served. The V.I.P. guests were all assembled on the lawn in the beautiful sunken garden facing the bay and the toilets were up one level, just inside Admiralty House. My Mom was not quite sure how to pose the question tactfully to Mrs D.F.Malan in polite Afrikaans. She approached her demurely and said, "Mevrou Malan wil u miskien bo gaan?"

(Mrs Malan, would you perhaps like to go upstairs?)

Imagine my mom's embarrassment when Mrs Malan without batting an eyelid and quite obviously not "catching my mom's drift" asked bluntly "Om wat te doen?" (What to do?)

Fortunately for the reader, I can't quite remember how my mom handled Mrs Malan's response so I shall leave it to your imagination!

On 26 January 1953 when I was still only 8, the British Naval Ship HMS Bermuda sailed out of Simon's Town harbour. That was the end of an era and many residents of the seaside town waved farewell with moist eyes and heavy hearts.

I still have the article my mom, Muriel Taylor, wrote to the Cape Argus and which was published the day after the ship's departure. It was titled "Farewell Bermuda" and I share this extract....

"For two years she has lain at our very front door ....like some guardian watchdog; a beautiful presence, grey, sombre, brooding.

And like some watchdog, she has wakened to growl from her guns in the mornings. At night she's been there crouched like a log and her pin-pricks of light have danced out to meet us across the black scallop of water that laps at our windows.

Fair weather or foul, we have watched where she lay. We have seen her grey hulk suffused in the red mists of morning when the sun climbed from beyond the Hottentots Holland mountain range and our crescent of Bay was a mirror reflecting the face of dawn. On steamy days too, when a heat-haze shimmered over the placid emerald Bay, we have watched her idly, guns glinting, funnels panting for breath.

At dead of night, we have seen the smooth, silver sheen of her steel in the pale moonlight, and leaning far out of the windows, we have wished we could send out a line with a hot dog and some coffee to the patient officer of-the-watch.

And we have watched in the drizzle, a slender mauve spiral curling up to the clouds from her funnel, when one might have thought, with flag dank and limp at her masthead, that the grey cruiser's spirit was quenched.

And now for the last time, her crew has rolled home at midnight and the band has played "God Save The Queen" to the winds of False Bay.

For the last time, as she throbbed at her moorings, schoolboys have stood up in their desks to make sure she would not slip away without their round-eyed amazement, to follow her proud plume of smoke and the clean gash of bows slicing through the Bay.......and school girls, with womanly want, have dreamed dreams that were not inspired by their geography books.

At night it is lonesome now, and one's imagination plays tricks, for the moonlight throws into relief a dozen small craft, their masts etched in silver, bobbing and dancing just under our windows.

The watchdog is gone....and one feels lost and alone in the dark. Our Bay seems empty now for Bermuda has left us and sailed home….."

4

BUCKETS, BROOMSTICKS & BILTONG!

A favourite holiday destination for our family was at the seldom-frequented Gwayang River mouth near George. My parents had honeymooned there in 1941 and were keen to let David and me explore the magnificent wildness of this unspoilt, natural, rugged paradise where there were just three family owned beach cottages perched on the bushy hillside. The houses were a mere minute away from the shining, amber ribbon of the Gwayang River which flowed down to the aquamarine sea. Across the water, facing the bungalows, was a towering yellow-ochre 120 metre granite cliff which was home to a wonderful variety of birds, as well as to many insects, dassies (rock rabbits) bats, lizards and snakes. At the foot of the cliff there was a vast expanse of beach at low tide. This was a glorious place for children's games, races and for board surfing when the tide rolled in and headed up stream.

We approached this tranquil unspoilt little haven by driving through the picturesque village of Pacaltsdorp. Upon arrival, we always stopped for fresh provisions at Mrs Keyter's little shop known as "Die Algemene Handelaar." (General Dealer) She was also the Post Mistress. She had a teenage son called Henry who always walked barefoot. He showed us the soles of his feet and proved that they were so tough and leathery that he could poke a sharp nail into his feet without flinching. This really impressed us as children, until at age 6 I tried poking a drawing pin into my foot. I very quickly realised that I was not as brave as Henry!

Mrs Keyter wore her thin greying hair in a rather lopsided and squashed looking bun. She fascinated us no end because her lips made chewing movements even when her mouth was empty and her teeth wobbled as she spoke. Her shop was full of interesting smells like curry, tobacco, paraffin, Jeyes Fluid and fertiliser. There was an intriguing array of things for sale like watering cans, garden rakes and enamel potties, horse hair mats, broomsticks and gaudy china jugs which hung from the ceiling on rusty hooks.

In between these fascinating items one caught a glimpse of shrivelled little fishes with parched eye sockets. Crammed next to the dried fishes were leathery strips of ostrich biltong and little cotton pouches stuffed with tobacco.

Mrs Keyter called her smelly little dried fishes by a cute, affectionate sounding name. She referred to them as her tasty little " Bokkoms." She even gave us a free Bokkom as a present because my Dad had just driven all the way from Cape Town in one day, to come to her shop. But Bokkom made our car smell horrible and kept staring at us with a dead look in its dull fishy little eyes, so on the way to the beach cottage we asked Dad to stop the car. Dave and I hopped out and we gave little Bokkom to a stray cat for its supper. The cat looked startled but we thought he deserved it more than we did.

My dad bought some delicious Springbok biltong from Mrs Keyter's shop. There were big long strips drying on a dangerous looking spike above the counter. Mrs Keyter sometimes had to duck in case the biltong walloped the little grey bun perched on her head. The biltong was covered in salt and funny knobbly little lumps which Mrs Keyter said was definitely not dirt but roasted coriander seeds to make it taste nice. Mom said people had probably coughed and sneezed all over the biltong in the shop and might have spread their germs. Great big sticky flies called Blue Bottles may have landed on it to rest their legs, so mom poured boiling water over the biltong and scrubbed it with a stiff brush before we were allowed to eat it.

Mrs. Keyter in her intriguing little shop

Mrs Keyter also sold special sweets like plaited liquorice and big square chewy blocks called Wilson toffees, shocking pink chewy ones called Stars, striped peppermint gobstoppers and Wicks and Chappies bubble gum. There were funny jokes inside the wrappers. There were round black balls about the size of marbles, which changed colour as you sucked them. I think the black balls were called by a different name in those olden days but nowadays we do not use that word. Mrs Keyter stored all the sweets in big glass bottles with bulges at the bottom. Our favourite sweets were called mottos. She sold us 4 mottos for a penny. They tasted like scent and were pink, yellow and white and had messages on them like "I love you," "Please kiss me," "Come back soon! " or "I forgive you." Some even had Afrikaans messages on them and we had great fun getting my British grandmother to read the mottos aloud, especially words containing a "g", because we taught her to practise saying gggggggggg the Afrikaans way and our poor Gran sounded as if she was going to be sick!

At one stage we thought our mom might become addicted to liquorice because she enjoyed it so much and even asked for cough mixture made from liquorice. My brother and I couldn't believe how anyone could like it so much because it makes your teeth turn black and we heard that its Greek name is GLYCYRRHIZA GLABRA!

And to think that liquorice is made by evaporating the juice of a root that is a member of the pea and bean family! South Africans tend to get the name wrong when they call it liquorish instead of liquorice!

Pacaltsdorp, where we stopped to visit Mrs Keyter's shop, is a very interesting little village. It was originally named "Hoogekraal " and the little settlement was established in 1813 by the London Missionary Society. The first occupants of Hoogekraal were the Khoi Khoi people under Chief Dikkop. We are told that the Chief was so impressed with the work of visiting missionaries like Rev Read and Rev Winner, that on his own initiative, he personally went to Zuurbraak by ox -wagon and transported the first resident missionary, Rev Charles Pacalt all the way back to Hoogekraal. The journey took Chief Dikkop four weeks to complete!

In 1818 the name of the Village was changed from Hoogekraal to Pacaltsdorp in honour of the fine pioneering missionary work carried out by the Rev C. Pacalt, who lived in a rustic little mission cottage.

It consisted of sod walls, a thatch roof and a cow dung floor! The little Norman style church was originally built from stone, yellowwood from Knysna, glass and clay. Today these are Historic buildings.

Just opposite the Post Office is a gnarled old tree called "The Tree of Meeting" which is 300 years old. Chief Dikkop's grave has become a national monument and can be seen close to those of the Pacaltsdorp missionaries whose graves are in the mission's acre.

A very dear old family friend of ours, the Rev. John Anderson, served as a beloved teacher and minister for over 50 years in Pacaltsdorp. He was known as the "Father of his people" because of his dedicated contribution towards the upliftment of Pacaltsdorp.

In March 1959 the good folk of the village had a memorial church hall built as a tribute to John Anderson. His family also used to holiday in one of the beach bungalows at Gwayang River Mouth and our two families met there and became firm friends. Rev Anderson's daughters have in fact been two of my closest friends for seventy years and my brother went to school with Rev Anderson's son, George, who pastored a church of his own in Canada!

5

CLOSE ENCOUNTERS!

*M*y Mom taught David and me to swim at Gwayang when we were aged just 6 or 7. The warm Indian Ocean entered at the mouth of the river and mingled with the beautiful amber coloured river water which flowed downstream. We learnt to fish and to dive from the rocks along the beachfront. Our family spent many unforgettable Christmas holidays at Gwayang. The beach bungalows were owned by an elderly gentleman called Mr D.G. Mills, a retired lawyer and a man with a very generous spirit and a passion for youth work. David and I formed lasting friendships there with young friends who came year after year to enjoy their uncle's generosity.

The sea was normally very tranquil by the time it entered the river mouth, merged with the Gwayang River and then flowed gently past the beach cottages perched on the hillside just above the beach. However, early in January when I was just seven and my brother was five, we had a terrifying experience. We were splashing about merrily in the shallows, building sand castles and tunnelling deep into the sand in search of pirates' hidden treasure. My Mom was keeping a close eye on us from nearby.

Suddenly from nowhere, a freak tidal wave roared in from the river mouth, like an express train, gaining speed and strength as it raced towards us. We screamed at the top of our voices. Our Dad dropped the book he was reading on the verandah and charged down to the beach. David and I were swept off our feet and tossed about violently. We swallowed gallons of sea water and kicked and paddled furiously. All these years later, I can still remember the feeling of having our faces ground into the sand and pebbles. We thank God that our Mom was an excellent swimmer and in a miraculous way, she managed to swim powerfully towards each of us, grabbing us by an arm and lifting our faces above the surging water. We took huge gulps of fresh air and continued to kick and splutter for all we were worth. By then our dad had charged into the boisterous waves too and my brother and I were both pulled to safely, looking very bedraggled and feeling exhausted. That terrifying memory has stayed with me for nearly seven decades!

There was a lovely long walk up the river at Gwayang, which passed through shady forests and beautiful stretches of fynbos. There is a very special fragrance which seems unique to that magnificent part of the Garden Route. Whenever we approached our holiday destination as children, we would roll down the windows of the car, inhale that delightful, fresh indigenous fynbos aroma and shout, "Yay, we're nearly there!"

At the end of the up-stream Gwayang river hike there was a very, very deep dark pool called "Osgat." (Ox hole) This ominous looking pool has an intriguing story surrounding it. It is believed that back in the 1830's in the pioneering days of the Voortrekkers, a fully -equipped ox wagon and a team of oxen, plunged over the edge of the lofty escarpment above the pool. Many intrepid swimmers and scuba divers have plumbed the murky depths seeking to reach the bottom of this seemingly fathomless pool to prove the truth of the legend. As children we were enthralled when we heard tales of stout- hearted divers whose flippers had actually touched the spiked horns of oxen or had stood on chunks of splintered wagons and seen bleached Voortrekker skulls and skeletons strewn at the bottom of Osgat!

It was on one of these tranquil family hikes upstream that my brother had another narrow escape at the age of four. We set off early one morning with the usual rucksack, picnic things, a Billy can and a snake bite kit. We both love animals and from a very early age were intrigued by shongololos or songololos (millipedes) scorpions and dung beetles. We had not seen these species in our garden at home. Our parents taught us which ones it's not a wise idea to hug or handle! Unable to sting or bite, shongololos roll up in a tight little ball to protect themselves. My dad taught us that centipedes have one pair of legs on each segment of their bodies and millipedes have two, with some having up to 200 pairs! Imagine having to knit booties for twin millipedes!

We were ambling along a sylvan pathway through a copse of wattlewood when little David with bare feet began to scamper ahead.....

He was relishing all the exciting things we saw along the route to Osgat. He suddenly stopped and bent down to pick up a twisty stick lying in the dappled shadow. Just in the nick of time my Mom yelled, "Stop! Snake! "

We all froze in our tracks and watched as a magnificent and well-camouflaged night adder slithered past his little toes and disappeared into a nearby bush. In a shaky little voice, Dave said, "Mommy, I taut it was a stick till it wiggled and I saw the naughty look in its eye!"

Some hikers have actually mistaken the night adder for the far more dangerous puff adder. The body of a night adder is grey or light brown.

The average length is about 60- 70 cm. They have attractive marking with black diamonds on the body and a V marking on the small narrow head. Night adders have cytotoxic venom. They are not considered lethal but should definitely be treated with respect. A bite from a night added may cause severe swelling and pain.

After this close encounter, we children felt a little shaken so we all looked for a lovely flat rock where we could have our picnic. We asked

Dad to make quite sure there were no snakes basking on it! He then boiled a Billy can of water and Mom made some rooibos tea and we all felt better. On the way back to the bungalow we cooled off in a pretty little pool called "Pepsi Pool" because of the colour of the water and the bubbles and froth made by a tumbling little waterfall. Mom said it would be safe to skinny dip in the gorge because we would only be stared at by the dassies (rock rabbits) and eagles looking down from the cliff.

Playing on the beach before the tidal wave struck

6

A LOO WITH A VIEW!

*B*ack in the 1950's most holiday cottages and even some homes and farm houses had outside toilets. For hygienic reasons, these were usually situated at the back of the house and some little distance from the back door and the kitchen. The word "kleinhuisie" (little house) was sometimes used by our Afrikaans speaking friends to describe a little wood and iron shed used for this purpose. Most toilets were of the deep pit, or long drop variety. The entire pit was covered by a sturdy box- like contraption with a round hole in it, big enough to accommodate the rear ends of users of ample proportions. Little children were often given enamel potties to sit on instead for fear that they might plunge through the large aperture! In urban areas toilet arrangements were usually more sophisticated.

In the long drop version a large enamel bucket was placed strategically under the hole and there was a wooden trap door at the back of the structure.

Once or twice a week the municipality would send brave workers along to empty the contents which were carted off in lorries resembling tankers.

Friends we knew had a little wooden plaque hanging just above their long drop toilet.

It read:

WE AIM TO PLEASE.
YOU AIM TOO PLEASE!

On my gran's first night at the beach cottage, as a new visitor from Cape Town, we passed on all the tips we could possibly think of about using the door-less toilet, safely and fearlessly. My dad saw her on her way down the path armed with a paraffin lantern, a torch (just in case the wind extinguished the flame) stout hiking boots in case she stepped on a night adder, an impressive snake stick for protection and a spare toilet roll. All went well for the first few minutes then there was an ear splitting shriek as she yelled, "Help! Tarantula!" We realized that we had forgotten to tell her that the very spindly Daddy Long Legs spiders Gran might just encounter, are really quite innocuous.

However as my ashen- faced Gran raced from the toilet huffing and puffing, she vividly described the nocturnal intruder which she discovered to her dismay was sharing the toilet seat with her! We realized that our Gran had just had her first encounter, not with a Daddy Long Legs, but with a Baboon spider! With eyes wide, she described an enormous hairy fellow the size of a saucer! Baboon spiders are a common sight along the Garden Route and in the Eastern Cape. The name Baboon spider derives from the hair which is monkey-like, and the little pads on their feet which resemble those of baboons. Although they look fearsome, they are generally not aggressive. In other parts of the world Baboon spiders are known as tarantulas. In South Africa these spiders range in size from 13 to 90 mm and thankfully for Gran, their venom is not deadly to humans.

My Mom once owned up to the fact that as a mischievous nine year old growing up in Kimberley in the mid 1920's, she and her incorrigible little pals, in search of pre- bedtime adventure, had often ventured outdoors just as night was falling. They would tiptoe down the lane behind the row of long drop toilets, trying to spot the occupied ones which had glimmering lamps and candles burning within. Then stealthily lifting the trapdoors as they scampered past, the miscreants would use long ostrich feathers to tickle the bare behinds of those enthroned on the wooden box seats! They would dash home, shrieking with mirth as they heard terrified howls coming from within the toilet cubicles. Tales were told of quaking old dears who had frantically exited the toilets to hobble indoors, as if in shackles, with their knickers still round their ankles! The toilet users' biggest fear having been that their posteriors had been targeted by venomous spiders or traversed by adventurous creepy crawlies.

My Mom's anecdote reminded me that the rickety little toilet structure at the Gwayang beach bungalow was still without a door but fortunately it had its back to the kitchen door. We were told by locals that the door had been stolen by a poor homeless vagrant who used the wood to keep himself warm and to cook his supper. As children we forgave him because we could imagine how cold it would be to doss down under a ledge on the beach!

Because there was no way of knowing whether the toilet was Vacant or Occupied, my Dad thought of an ingenious way to alert would- be toilet users. He banged a broom stick into the soil and then attached a piece of cord to it. On the end of the cord he tied an empty jam tin. The idea was that as you went down the path to use the toilet, you would slip the jam tin on top of the pole. When you had completed your ablutions, you would let the tin dangle from the pole once more. The tin could be seen from a fair distance and so you felt assured of your privacy. To start with, this nifty device worked very well, but over time the novelty wore off, and there were times when some patient soul was seen doing a jig around the broomstick desperately waiting for someone to emerge from the toilet because the jam tin had inadvertently been left lodged in its pivotal position for over an hour!

As you can well imagine, using the long drop toilet always proved a daunting experience for our British Grandmother when she came to visit us at Gwayang. Abandoning the comforts of her little flat in Conifer Road Sea Point, she bravely boarded a Garden Route bus at the Cape Town station and travelled alone to share our holiday adventure for about ten days.

There was no electricity at the bungalow so at dusk our dad would light paraffin lanterns and place them strategically.

We had to boil the big black kettle on the fire or cook a pot on the stove if we wanted to wash in warm water. There was a very old stove in the kitchen called an Esse. It was made of cast iron and warmed the entire bungalow. It baked delicious bread even though it only worked using wood or coal. We children preferred to keep clean by swimming in the sea several times a day. The grownups and the children all slept on creaky wooden bunk beds made of pine. The mattresses were rather hard and lumpy because they were made of coir.

Sometimes bits of mattress floated down from the bunk above and made us sneeze. Dad told us not to worry because firm mattresses are good for our spines and are stuffed with the hairy part of coconuts so we were helping to save the environment.

Each bedroom had a large china bowl and an enormous heavy jug which stood on a special little table called a washstand. The grownups liked to wash in them. Our Gran always said, "Now just remember to wash up as far as possible and then down as far as possible, but never forget to wash possible as well!" There was also a gaudy enamel potty with orange and purple flowers painted on it. It was kept hidden under the bottom bunk because we all felt too frightened to go to the outside toilet alone at night, especially if there was no moon and the wind was howling. Every morning my gran woke up very early and wrapped her potty in an old newspaper and tiptoed outside with it. We never knew why she wanted to hide it because we all know what people use potties for!

7

CAREFREE SCHOOLDAYS

I have never been able to understand why so many people say they hated school and seem to treasure very few fond memories of their teachers. Some folk are indifferent, others are relieved that their educational nightmare is behind them. Somehow a much smaller group seems to have a deep pride and loyalty for their old school and actually look forward with keen anticipation to attending their school reunions. I am happy to say that for me and for many of my close friends, school was a happy, carefree time of friendship and laughter. I attended three excellent junior schools, two being girls' schools and one being a co- educational one. I was sad to leave Rhenish, my first school in Stellenbosch, because of my Dad's occupational move. Similarly at age 9, it was hard to leave a lovely group of friends in Simon's Town and our dear Miss Hicks, the pretty young blonde teacher whom we all adored.

Moving to Rondebosch from Simon's Town I discovered that Rustenburg, my new girls only junior school was famous and full of tradition, discipline and routine. My Mom had enrolled me when I was only one month old! We were taught to behave like ladies. Coming from a co-educational school I tried to introduce some fun into our break times where we were supposed to remain seated under the oak trees to eat our sandwiches. We all carried our lunch boxes in little blue bags and we all wore brown sandals which were only obtainable at Rustenburg Shoe Store, just across the road from the school.

Just because I taught my little group of friends to play soccer on the lawn at break time, using a yellow plastic mug after a classmate's 9th birthday party, the Headmistress suddenly heaved up the old sash window and clapped her hands loudly through the window of her office. In a booming voice Miss Orton summoned me there forthwith. To make matters worse, she became most annoyed because I still had two bites of my banana left in my trembling hand. We respected her authority but were petrified of putting a foot wrong. My friends told me all their mothers quaked in their boots too when they saw her approaching. Miss Zoe Orton knew the name of every single girl in her school and their Moms' names too! I was still very new at the school having come in the second term of standard two and was so embarrassed because the headmistress made me stand outside her office every morning for two weeks, and all because we played four-a-side soccer on the lawn with a plastic mug.

The entire school stared at me as the girls and staff walked past solemnly in single file to attend morning Assembly in the Bleby Hall. There was complete silence except when a stern teacher cast a beady eye in my direction and clucked or tut-tutted under her breath. The school hall was named after Miss Alicia Bleby who became the Founder Headmistress back in 1894 and we were told that her ghost floated round the school corridors at night.

Our std. 2 teacher told me I would have to concentrate in class and work very hard indeed. Having come from a much smaller school in Simon's Town, she considered that I was not as advanced as my Rustenburg classmates. "Good gracious child!" she said embarrassing me no end. "Do you mean to say you still don't know how to cast off in knitting and you haven't a clue about how to do short division?" "What on earth did they teach you in your first term and wasn't your father the principal there?"

So poor little Bev, a real bright spark in arithmetic and in needlework became my tutor and had to stay back at break time until I had mastered these essential skills!

Bev also became famous in our class because she was the first girl to have her ears pierced. We all thought she was very brave. She brought a letter from her mom and was given special permission to wear tiny little gold rings in her ears, but our teacher warned her not to try any ear rings that were too flashy. We all realized that Ms W. was just feeling jealous because she was probably too scared to have her own ears pierced.

There were some very strange things that our teachers did in those days. We all had to line up and our skirts were measured with a wooden ruler to check that they were just below our knees. Then worse still, the staff marched up and down our lines, flipping up our skirts to make quite sure that we were wearing school bloomers. Recently when I was relating this procedure to our grandchildren, one of the teenagers said, "Wow Gran, how disgusting! Those teachers would be arrested if they tried doing that nowadays!

The summer panties weren't too bad because they were made of blue cotton material, but the winter ones were navy and made of thick fuzzy material!

The panties had a dreadful name too. They were called "Regulation Bloomers!" Talking of bloomers, we had to do P.T. (Physical Training) or Gymnastics in our bloomers! It was very embarrassing for the stout girls who often brought "sick notes" to excuse themselves. We had a subject called Eurythmics, and had to leap about in the school hall in our bloomers while listening to piano music. We would have to hold up musical notes made of painted wood as we counted the beats aloud and did our best to master various dainty eurythmic steps.

Desmond.

There was an exciting craze in junior school and everyone rushed out and bought large plastic rings called Hula Hoops and carried them to school by bus, train, bicycle or car. Then we played with the hoops at break times, often making ourselves giddy trying to see who could keep her hoop swinging around her waist or neck for the longest time. We heard that a serious number of spines and necks had suffered dislocation from over-zealous Hula Hoop swinging.

We were very excited when we were allowed to write in ink for the first time in standard 4. We had practised our cursive writing over and over by copying a series of writing cards in our writing lessons every week. We used to get free Afrikaans magazines delivered to our classroom every week called 'Die Jong Span' and enjoyed the handwriting competitions where you could win prizes. Our pens were made of wood and had metal nibs and were called dip pens because we dipped them into ink. I remember having a turn to be Ink Monitor and I had to stay after school and fill up all the little porcelain ink wells which fitted into neat round holes cut into the top right hand corner of our desks. If you pressed too hard on the nib, it split and the ink splattered all over your pages. If anyone lurched into your desk, the ink well became dislodged and ink went everywhere and often ruined your books in the desk below.

What jubilation when we were allowed to buy our first fountain pens when we entered standard six at the high school!

It was at Pamela East's 12th birthday party in Upper Claremont that we all learnt to Bop and do the Twist. I get the feeling that many of us still prefer the music of the Sixties. Who will ever forget the hit songs of that era....Pat Boone singing Love Letters in the Sand, Cliff Richards on his Summer Holiday, Rosemary Clooney with Where will the Baby's Dimple be? And Elvis Presley with Love me Tender and Return to Sender!

Sewing was my least favourite lesson because we created some very strange garments. Miss Bowles came down from the high school and taught us how to darn, using a hardboiled egg inside a sock. You just had to remember not to squeeze the sock as you darned. That lesson has proved very useful because my husband likes his old pure wool socks best of all. The school gave us cotton material called Fasco and we had to make two tone baby bibs in bottle green and khaki! Yuk! Then we ironed on little transfers of cartoon characters. I feared no baby would want to be seen wearing my bib, even with Donald Duck, Pluto or Minnie Mouse smiling broadly, because the colours of the school material were so hideous. Speaking of cartoon characters....

A very happy 90th birthday to the much- loved Mickey Mouse who like my husband Joe, was also created in 1928 and has made our world a happier place.

I'm afraid that my school knitting was also a disaster! I only managed to complete the front of my matinée jacket in standard 4, so when it was time for the end of year exhibition of handwork, mine had to be sewn down onto the table cloth covering the trestle table, so that none of the mothers could see that my little jacket was backless! Thankfully our class teacher put up a big sign next to the display saying PLEASE DO NOT HANDLE THE GARMENTS. I was given a black order mark because I had let the side down and as punishment had to knit a pink square for a blanket for an old age home. The black mark was all because my white wool had become grubby but after all, it only happened after a whole year of knitting. If only we had been allowed to wash our baby garments my matinée jacket would not have looked beige on the display.

Miss van der Merwe told our class that it was an utter disgrace because no baby would want to be seen dead wearing a backless beige matinée jacket!

I shall never forget the day our std. 5 class teachers, Miss Featherstone and Miss Turner, announced that it was a very special day for us all. Those who passed at the end of term would soon be entering Rustenburg Girls' High School. A nurse from the Education Department would be coming along after big break to tell us what happens at age 12 or 13 when you "become a lady and leave childhood behind." The nursing sister duly arrived in a very smart uniform complete with maroon epaulettes and carrying an interesting looking black suitcase with a Red Cross painted on it. She asked us how many of us had already been told by our moms what would happen round about this time of our lives. There were a few sniggers. She said we were soon to embark on an exciting adventure called Puberty. She did a few intriguing drawings on the blackboard and reprimanded the girls who giggled. Sister Mabel said she felt that most of us were old enough to learn some important new "grown up words like adolescence, womb, vagina, ovary and menstruation."

She made us repeat the words twice after her. Then we had to look through the windows and see who could still remember these special words! Eyes were rolled and there were more sniggers! Miss Turner looked daggers at those who giggled.

Then Sister Mabel told us to put our heads down on our desks and not to peep! We all hoped for some exciting surprise to pop out from her black suitcase, but what a let-down..... Instead she asked us to raise our hands if we had already left childhood behind us and had started menstruating. Of course most of us sneaked a quick peep and discovered to our huge relief that only Julia, Sally and Patricia had become ladies already. Sister Mabel ended her lecture by giving us each a free sample pack of Doctor White's sanitary towels in a brown paper wrapper so as not to arouse too much curiosity amongst our younger siblings. Sister Mabel said Miss Featherstone had kindly arranged with Miss Bowles that she would sacrifice part of her sewing cupboard and keep a few little brown parcels hidden there in unmarked shoe boxes, in the event of an "adolescent emergency happening unexpectedly at school!"

An interesting trend developed in mid high school ....by then we had probably all become ladies and wanted to have beautiful golden tans, especially when we pranced about in skimpy tennis dresses. A new product suddenly hit the market. Its name was something like Tantex. It was a liquid and had to be applied at bed time to create a fake Hawaiian tan overnight.

Too good to be true! Unfortunately the recipe was still in its experimental stage and we all pitched up at school with orange lines where our socks or sleeves ended and had mango-coloured foreheads peeping out beneath our Panama hats. The product also became ingrained in our finger nails and on the palms of our hands, which made us appear to be really serious users of nicotine.

When Tantex lost favour, a new craze developed in high school, where girls started using men's Brylcreem.(a popular hair cream for styling) This was smeared generously on arms, legs and faces and girls used it to tan at break times with their skirts raised to a respectable limit. Unfortunately this method of tanning had serious disadvantages. Brylcreem is designed to feed nutrients into hair follicles and to grow new hair, so it was no wonder that girls who used it for tanning suddenly found that they developed very hairy arms and legs and worse still, whiskers on their chins! In later life some of our classmates who virtually fried their limbs at break times, now have to deal with serious sun damage.

The most popular place for sun tanning was on the concrete slabs in the school quadrangle near the hall. It was here that our matric (grade 12) Latin mistress, a retired Headmistress, reprimanded us whilst she patrolled at break time, not for using Brylcreem but rather for parking our posteriors on cold concrete. Her words still ring in my ears. "Mark my words girls, you will all be suffering from haemorrhoids before you turn 30!"

Well, so far, so good Mrs. S!

A frightening moment for all of us came, when upon entering high school, we were advised that the regulation bathing costume for Rustenburg girls was the Speedo! It was no surprise that many girls suddenly became "unwell" on our swimming days! These girls then sat out once a "sick note" had been produced. Our gym mistress' nickname was PO and she supervised our swimming lessons from the comfort of her car and then gave a loud blast on her hockey whistle when it was time to climb out of the pool. Why was she named "PO?" you may well be wondering. Her name was Miss Chamberlain!

Because we had to wear our regulation school bloomers for gym lessons in high school, a humane rule was suddenly introduced by our headmistress, Miss Margaret Thomson. Girls who were experiencing their monthly period would be permitted to sit out if in severe pain or be allowed to wear a navy netball skirt to feel more secure on those days. You can imagine what happened. We all felt far more comfortable prancing about in gym skirts, but this special dispensation appealed particularly to the chubbier girls.

Suddenly there was a spate of "sick notes" on gym days, all excusing girls who were menstruating or asking permission to wear a skirt. We guessed that many of the notes were forged by pupils, so it was not really surprising that on one Monday morning Miss Chamberlain declared in an icy tone, "Girls, I do consider it a very strange phenomenon that in one class we suddenly have 16 girls all menstruating on the same day!"

Looking back now over more than seventy years, so many happy memories are linked to classmates, many of whom are still in my circle of friends.

Incredibly, some of my school, Training College and University friends now live in the same Retirement Village as I do!

We acknowledge with gratitude that we received a first class education from a very fine dedicated team of teachers. Of course there were a few who were eccentric or unprepared for the mammoth task of moulding and nurturing young minds but for most of them, teaching was a genuine Calling.

We were taught in an era long before ballpoint pens, Pritt, Prestik, overhead projectors, pocket calculators, white boards, electric sewing machines, computers or microwave ovens. Imagine life without a cellphone or an iPad for a teenager nowadays! I remember with great excitement when Koki pens first appeared when I was in standard five. (Grade 7) Stockings with seams down the back of the leg, Panama hats and suspenders have all disappeared. Many from the 1950's and 60's will recall how we stiffened our school belts with starch hoping to achieve a wasp waist effect!

Over weekends when we partied, we soaked our gauze petticoats overnight in basins of starch or sugar water, then drip dried and ironed them so that they stood out under our skirts creating a beautiful flared effect. We put up with the scratchy feeling against our legs. Soft, kid glove shoes almost like ballet slippers with flat soles were in fashion and I remember having a pink, a blue and a beige pair to match most outfits. Hardly any ladies wore slacks in our youth, until Helanca stretch fabric was in vogue in the 60's, but full, circular skirts remained popular. Boys wore their school blazers proudly to attend special functions and it wasn't uncommon to see a young lad at the theatre, opera house, in church or even at a funeral or a rugby match, sporting his school blazer and badge.

There was a time when ladies wore hats and gloves whenever they caught a bus or train to go shopping in Cape Town. I distinctly remember when our class at Training College was taken on a visit to Parliament in 1962 that we were instructed to wear hats and gloves. Later it became time to apply for teaching posts upon completion of our training. We were instructed by our College principal, Miss Seeliger, to dress appropriately when visiting any school and particularly when attending an interview with the Headmaster or mistress in question.

An interesting fashion developed in the 50's and 60's when instead of wearing hats to church, ladies started to wear pretty coloured feathers which were attached to a stretchy headband. I was reminded of this trend when I watched the wedding of Prince Harry and Meghan Markle where so many of their guests chose feathers instead of traditional hats! Some of the TV wedding commentators described the feathery adornments as "Fascinators," but I also heard them being called "Hatinators" which intrigued me no end!

This reminded me that I once had a most embarrassing experience during a special church service in the famous old Groote Klerk at the top of Adderley Street in Cape Town. I had turned 16 and my mom had bought me my first "Hatinator!" I had just washed and curled my hair so I guess that being fine hair, it was soft and fluffy when I pressed the stretchy headband and pink feathers into position. Imagine my shock and dismay, when in the middle of the sermon being delivered by a prominent speaker from overseas I felt the headband starting to twitch and slide upwards. Before I could grab it, the head-band had shifted up my scalp and without further warning it sprang into orbit and bounced merrily down the aisle. Imagine my embarrassment when there and then, a dear old gentleman bent down to retrieve it with his walking stick. To make matters worse, he came tottering down the aisle to hand it back to me. The preacher stopped speaking and very graciously allowed the old fellow to tap- tap his way back to his pew! He then twisted round to give me a knowing little wink and a cheery wave! Whew, was my face red!

When I returned to my old junior school to take up a teaching post there in 1980, staff members were still required to wear dresses or skirts and to come to school in closed shoes and stockings. Sandals and bare legs were strictly forbidden. Isn't this a far cry from the way we see some educators reporting for duty at their schools today casually wearing shorts, trainers, track suits or boob tubes!

Ruth aged 9, growing pigtails

Ruth's Std. 5 class at Rustenburg

8

A PIONEERING VENTURE

*I*f anyone had told us that my Dad's life- work would really only begin in 1953, fourteen years after his graduation, we should probably have smiled broadly because Mom, Dave and I all felt we had seen a great deal of what the teaching profession had to offer in the realm of child instruction, parental interest, staff dedication, the moulding of children's characters ~ and sheer, solid hard work, demanding much burning of the midnight oil and little time really for everyday entertainment and trivial pursuits!

While we were at Simon's Town my dad was interviewed, selected and appointed to become Founder Headmaster of a not-yet built Co-educational High School on the highway in the leafy suburb of Rondebosch, just one block away from the Presidential Residence and most of the cabinet ministers' homes. Rondebosch already boasted several top-quality single-sex schools, and close by in the suburb of Pinelands, the First Garden City, Mr Jack Kent had his new school, Pinelands High off to a fine start just one year before, in 1952.

Interestingly enough, the layout of Pinelands is based on the revolutionary Town planning ideas of Sir Ebenezer Howard and was the first attempt at a Town-planned area in South Africa! Over 6 000

Cape Town citizens had succumbed to the 1918 Spanish 'flu epidemic and in order to combat the overcrowding which was believed to contribute to the spread of contagious diseases, Pinelands became the first Garden City in South Africa! My husband and I feel doubly blessed to be living in Pinelands now that we realise what a special suburb it is!

Back to Rondebosch now....

The early Dutch settlers in the Cape couldn't help noticing an abundance of many fertile clumps of round bushes growing in this lovely area, so decided to name it "Ronde Bosjen." Later it was changed to "'t Rondeboschje" and finally, in the last century, it was given the name "Rondebosch."

The site chosen for the new school, Westerford, was blessed with magnificent trees, including age-old chestnuts and oaks, and with its breathtaking Table Mountain backdrop was surely one of the most beautiful in the country. It was this glorious setting which inspired my mom as she accepted the challenge of designing a school uniform, tie and badge. She chose blue for the azure sky and mountain, maroon for the deep red poppies and gold for the setting sun as it illuminated the largest of the giant chestnut trees and the age- old oak trees which we understand were introduced to our country from Europe by Simon van der Stel, the first Governor of the Cape from 1639.

David and I aged 7 and 9, felt proud and excited to be part of Dad and Mom's pioneering efforts. I never dreamt at that stage that in another 6 years, I too would proudly be wearing a Westerford uniform and would be completing my last three years of schooling there. Dave and I found it exciting to come all the way from Simon's Town after school and to run about freely and explore the seemingly vast unkempt grounds while our mom and dad strolled round in deep discussion with Mr. Jim Green who was to be the school architect. It felt so good to beat a path through the waist-high grass, to play beside a tranquil streamlet, lined with poppies and bracken, to paddle on hot days and to watch little tadpoles dart amongst the mossy pebbles and then develop into frogs as the weeks went by. It was fun too, to play hockey with fallen pine cones and broken branches and to collect chestnuts to roast in our fireplace at home.

The only buildings to be seen were an empty, neglected and ramshackle old single-storey homestead and a decrepit coach-house. There was also a disused tennis court without wiring or net and an avenue of oaks lining a rutted lane. Some 250 years before, Dutch immigrants had settled where lions, rhinos, leopards and buck had roamed freely and there had even been hippopotamuses wallowing in the nearby vlei.

The name Westerford, chosen for the new school, had been Anglicized from the Dutch version of "Westervoort" meaning "Western Ford."

It was a momentous day for the first 29 pupils who gathered on the steps of the weather beaten old Homestead in January 1953 for the start of their brand new high school Adventure. The old house had been temporarily repaired to welcome them. Without school uniforms at that stage, they might have appeared to inquisitive passers-by to be a motley crew, but what an extraordinary group of loyal and idealistic learners they turned out to be. They were passionate about their new school and their parents rallied round and supported the new Venture in so many practical ways. In those early years the pupils and parents planted grass for playing fields and lawns. They weeded and laid out attractive gardens, contributing greatly to the magnificent school it is today.

Many of those loyal early pioneers, now becoming octogenarians have not missed a single school reunion or Founders' Day and it's amazing to think that Westerford turned 67 this year (2020) and now has more than 900 pupils! The school has earned its fine reputation for high levels of excellence in many spheres, but most notably for academic prowess. Westerford has always attracted a totally dedicated, talented and skilled Team of educators. Our Dad chose as the school motto "Nil Nisi Optimum" ~ Nothing but the Best! It is therefore not surprising that for several years now the school has been honoured as one of South Africa's Top Performing Public Schools.

For us the saddest part of The Westerford Story has been the absence of our father who would have been proudly watching each new and exciting advancement. On 28 October 1976 when my dad was still in his prime at age 58, he died very suddenly and totally unexpectedly having developed a brain abscess following complications after a sinus operation during the October ten-day school holiday. Our mom Muriel, who had started a Past Pupils' group after the first matriculation class in 1957, soldiered on courageously until she was almost 84, still maintaining contact with many past pupils and their parents from those early pioneering days.

From its humble beginning, how Noel Taylor would have rejoiced to see his vision fulfilled and Westerford pupils benefiting from the Imhoff sports grounds, the Diamond Jubilee Centre (2013) the well-equipped Science and computer laboratories, the swimming pool, the indoor sports centre and of course, the AstroTurf with its superb seating arena and magnificent landscaped area.

Founder Headmaster of Westerford, Noel Taylor

Ruth's dad

Ruth's mom

9

GOODBYE MR. CHIPS!

hat a shame that Teacher Training Colleges were closed down by the new government in the mid 1990's. Back in the day we students received an excellent training from first class lecturers in Primary teaching method and class management, whereas the focus nowadays for those who attend university to become teachers, has been more on subject content and on the academic side. In my 36 years as a teacher I encountered many new young teachers straight out of University, who felt inadequate when it came to basic classroom skills such as how to write on the backboard using an age appropriate script, how to deal effectively with disciplinary problems, or manage a classroom library corner, set up a nature table, mark a class register, motivate reluctant learners, cope with those with learning disabilities, write out lesson notes or plan schemes of work, set examination papers or organize a school camping excursion.

I was encouraged to read in Business Day that our Minister of Basic Education, Angie Motshekga, has set a target for 65,000 bursaries for the education of teachers over the next five years through the Funza Lushaka bursary programme. There has also been a desperate cry from teachers' unions to re-open teachers' training colleges to increase the supply of well- trained teachers in our public schools.

Our College years passed all too quickly. Those were happy, productive years and the teaching aids we were taught to make, proved invaluable for many years. We learnt how to teach Art, needlework and Physical Education and how to coach netball, tennis and hockey. Those who were musical could manage a singing class, train a junior choir and instil a love of music in their kindergarten classes. After regular spells of teaching practice in a variety of schools, where we faced experienced lecturers who sat in on our "crit. lessons," I can honestly say that most of us felt adequately equipped to step out and face a classroom of eager little pupils, nowadays called Learners.

All too soon, the hunt was on to secure teaching posts. To our dismay we discovered that very few posts were available in Cape Town for beginner teachers. Fellow students launched out into new pastures, accepting posts in Knysna, Port Elizabeth and East London. Some even ventured into neighbouring provinces. A friend of mine accepted a post in KwaZulu Natal in a town called Babanango, which none of us knew existed!

On her first morning there, Beryl opened her back door and stared straight into the eyes of a massive hippopotamus grazing on her lawn! She did not go out to introduce herself because she had been warned that these giants can weigh as much as 1 800 kg! (3 968 lbs!) Hippos apparently never eat while in the water and aren't known to graze on aquatic plants. Instead they prefer short grass and green shoots and reeds. One might envy the hippo having a multi-chambered stomach but it would be wise to remain on friendly terms, having been told that the canines and incisors in the front of a hippo's mouth can grow to 50, 8 centimetres!

Imagine my delight when my paternal grandmother telephoned me excitedly and told me of a brand new boarding school called Treverton being opened in the Midlands of Natal, in a delightful little town called Mooi River. You may remember singing a little Afrikaans folk song about a young lady called Sarie Marais who lived near the Mooi River. This little song is believed to date back to the First Anglo-Boer War. Wasn't it wonderful to hear Jim Reeves and Kenneth McKellar on tours to our country actually singing "My Sarie Marais" in Afrikaans! No wonder they received standing ovations!

The new school soon to be called Treverton had an intriguing background.....

While teaching at King's School, Nottingham Road, Natal, a young teacher named Peter Binns, with a burning passion for education and the youth, and who was born in Durban in 1903, saw the opportunity of starting his own Preparatory boarding school for boys in the idyllic little town of Mooi River. His father Percy, was the Chief Magistrate of Durban and his grandfather, Sir Henry Binns, happened to be Prime Minister of Natal in the last century.

Peter Binns' mother had emigrated from Cornwall. As a young lad Peter had spent many happy childhood days on his grandfather's and great uncle's sugar cane farms near Tongaat, north of Durban. The names of the two sugar estates on his mom and grandmother's (Clara Acutt) side of the family were Riverton and Trenance, so it was not surprising that Peter Binns remembered both farms with great affection in deciding to link the farm names and call his new school TREVERTON!

Treverton opened its doors in August 1939 with just 14 boys! The old Anglican vicarage was used to house the boarders and was known as Main House. The main road linking Johannesburg with Durban was still a dirt road and past pupils from that era recall how they were covered in dust and grime as passing traffic thundered by. They tell us how buildings were erected here and there as funds permitted and that boys seldom ate their meals in the same place twice running. Peter Asher gave these impressions, "Cricket was played on the field outside the dormitory, rugby on the golf course and tennis down a steep hill beside Hawthorne Avenue. There was organized chaos, and the intimacy of the small school made it feel very much like a family affair."

The dormitories were given quaint names like The Cavern, The Barn, The Chicken Run, Little Thatch and Koppies.

The small scattered buildings all had thatch roofs and were surrounded by large oak and plane trees from which towards the end of the school year, Christmas beetles produced a deafening chorus. On top of the thatched roofs spider-like twists of wire could be seen. The headmaster put these up as lightning conductors after one of his teachers had a narrow escape when struck by lightning while out walking with a group of boarders. Thankfully he recovered after a spell in hospital.

Mr. Binns was a strict but kindly man and has often been likened to 'Mr Chips.' He was personally involved with every aspect of school life and seems to have been on duty for 24 hours of every day, living, working, eating, playing, swimming and hiking with his boys. We are told that he woke the boys very early for a morning run to encourage hardihood, then lined them up with their toothbrushes and personally squeezed a blob of toothpaste onto every brush! He supervised all their meals, saw that the boys showered daily and put them to bed. He also handled the catering, kept the pocket money accounts and dealt with school correspondence and at the same time we understand he was an outstanding teacher.

The success of Treverton was largely due to Peter Binns' personal supervision of the school and his wholehearted devotion. It is believed that as a bachelor he literally burnt himself out because of his commitment and love for his school. He underwent a very serious operation but never fully regained his strength and very sadly he died on 3 August 1958 when he was only 54.

It was almost as if his beloved school died with him. The Executors of his estate appointed Mr. Douglas Pennington as the new Headmaster. He did a sterling job as Mr. Binns' successor but sadly, rising costs and diminishing enrolment, brought financial distress and forced the Trustees and Administrators to close the school at the end of 1961 with very little warning. This proved traumatic for the staff, parents and pupils. All moveable property was sold to raise money to pay the creditors. The buildings and grounds were cleared and the property was put up for sale.

With the passing of time, the elements and vandalism caused deterioration and dereliction of the empty property. Windows were smashed, trees and shrubs were stolen and Treverton became home to invading colonies of rats and feral cats.

10

A DOOR OF OPPORTUNITY OPENS WIDE

*T*his was the abandoned and run down property which the Rev André Erasmus heard was up for sale at a bargain price of R17 000! At midnight he excitedly wrote to share this good news with a fellow colleague in the ministry, Rev. Sydney Hudson-Reed, who happened to be President of the Baptist Union for that year. He immediately hastened from Port Elizabeth to Natal to see if this unexpected news could possibly give rise to the fulfilment of his dream for the establishment of an independent faith-based Boys' Prep School. Rev Hudson-Reed described what he saw at first glance as "the shell of the living organism of the past."

Hereafter events began to move at an incredible pace…..

The deserted school premises were inspected and proved to be more than adequate to provide accommodation for 200 boys. The property was ideally situated, 140 km from Durban and 480 km from Johannesburg, in a well- wooded, picturesque setting with all the essential facilities.

Hundreds of kilometres were traversed, midnight planning sessions were held, dozens of interviews took place and a flood of letters was sent out. There followed the signing of an intention-to- buy document with the Southern Building Society which considered the "Church" to be a safe and honourable buyer and actually dropped the purchase price from R17 000 to R15 000!

On 24 April 1963 the Treverton Trust came into being, as a non- profit making Company, for the purpose of launching the new school. Guarantors and Trustees who underwrote the purchase of Treverton became the first members of the Trust Foundation and Mr Derek Hudson-Reed, a senior teacher and House Master from St Stithians College in Johannesburg, was appointed as Headmaster of the resuscitated Treverton Prep. School.

The name Treverton was retained, to honour the memory of Mr Peter Binns' school and the new Mission Statement promised to offer boys a balanced all- round quality education based on sound biblical values. The Aim of the Founder Governors was to create a school which would meet boys' educational, physical, social and spiritual needs, so as to send out into our often times bewildering world, children well - prepared and equipped to face the challenges which await them. Ideally, respect for self and for others, compassion, self-discipline, perseverance, honesty and love would permeate campus life. Boys would be free from city distractions. There would be an emphasis on training hardihood, on healthy outdoor activities and there would be a strong sense of community, faith and family.

Applications were being invited from "dynamic, innovative and suitably qualified educators with a pioneering spirit, who love sport, music and the great Outdoors, to fill teaching posts from standards 1 to 4 startling in Jan. 1964."

My grandmother's phone call telling me about the re-opening of Treverton came as a bolt from the blue and seemed an opportunity too good to miss! I ventured to approach my adventurous and spunky College classmate, Lyn Gowar, who loved sport and was a talented musician. We both decided we had nothing to lose and would seize this God-given opportunity to make a meaningful difference in the lives of young boys. So with a fair amount of trepidation we both submitted our CV's and handwritten letters of application via registered airmail and waited and prayed………..

Back in the early 1960's there was of course no access to Skype or video calls so lengthy telephonic interviews with the newly -appointed Headmaster and members of his Governing Body followed. Calls to the little town of Mooi River had to be booked in advance via their Telephone Exchange which operated from behind the post office.

I am suddenly reminded of that hilarious South African TV show starring Miems de Bruyn, which was set in the late 1950's and was called Nommer Asseblief? (Number Please?) where Louna,Obie and Bettie, the three daughters of Willie and Kokkie, worked on the telephone exchanges of Botrivier and Kleinmond, small rural towns in the Western Cape.

The telephone exchange in Mooi River as we experienced it was very similar to theirs! To contact the telephone exchange you had to crank a little handle on the phone. You were then connected to a "live" operator who barked "Nommer asseblief?" (Number please?) He/she wrote down the number you requested and booked your call. Sometimes you were given an estimated time of delay. The duration of each call was recorded and often a gruff or very weary voice would chip in saying, "Drie minute! Eindig asseblief jou oproep!" "Three minutes up. Please finish your call." Sometimes you were lucky and the operator lost track of the time or even dozed off and you got far more than your money's worth!

On some occasions the telephone wires got crossed and you found yourself inadvertently overhearing or joining in the conversations of others! It was not uncommon if imparting exciting news or sharing a secret, to hear heavy breathing or panting on the line and to realize that someone was eavesdropping!

Being in a rural area, Treverton had to share farm lines, called "party lines" and these were wonderful hives of gossip. News of births and deaths and hot events spread like wildfire and we soon discovered that the ladies in the Exchange knew everything about everyone! There was a time when the Mooi River exchange closed at 9pm, so if you

RUTH STOTT

encountered a real emergency, like a friend going into labour at midnight, or a nighbour having a heart attack, you would need to leap into someone's car and hasten to report news of the crisis down at the police station.

The country people were always very kind to the ladies manning the Exchange and on many icy cold June/ July evenings when the temperature dropped below freezing, you might see kind-hearted Mooi River residents stopping outside the post office and running in to drop off hot mielies, freshly baked bread or scones, vetkoek or flasks of hot chocolate to help the ladies keep up their spirits until home time at 9pm. It's hard to imagine how we all survived those freezing nights in the Natal Midlands without air conditioning.

In those days before the advent of faxes and emails, we often received good or bad news in telegrams. Whilst waiting for a young man on a bicycle to deliver the "hard copy" message to your front door in a bright orange envelope, or a gold one if it was a special event like a Golden Anniversary or a 100th birthday, the post office would take the trouble to phone you and read your message to you in case it was urgent. The messages had to be tapped out in Morse code and received by the Post Master. One can imagine that on a busy day with many interruptions mistakes could be forgiven.

One such glaring error occurred when I received news in a telegram sent by a relative living in the county of Somerset in the U.K. but relayed to me initially via the local Mooi River telephone exchange, announcing that very sadly "Our beloved Great Aunt Tina had passed away suddenly but very peacefully in her bath." She was well into her 80's and had enjoyed a full and happy life, but fortunately for her, and for those grieving, a telegram arrived an hour after the phone call and Great Aunt Tina had in fact passed away very peacefully in her sleep in the city of Bath, in Somerset!

Somerset is a beautiful city in the valley of the River Avon. We all knew our dear old Auntie would have much preferred to slip away, decently covered and tucked up in her pink nightie in her own bedroom!

I shall never forget that momentous Red-letter day in October 1963. What joy and excitement when my friend Lyn and I each received telephonic news, confirmed in an accurate telegram, that we had both been accepted as founder staff members and house mistresses of the resuscitated Treverton Boys' Preparatory School! How wonderful that we would be able to undertake the long train journey to Mooi River together in January 1964!

Our Pioneering Adventure was about to start in earnest!

11

ALL ABOARD!

*L*yn and I knew we would not be back in Cape Town for at least three months so we went to Treverton well -prepared. Friends who had visited the Drakensberg had reported that if you blinked when passing through Mooi River, you might miss the town completely as it lies snuggled in a sleepy little hollow. In those days one travelled from Johannesburg on the old main road via Harrismith and Estcourt and from Mooi River, you passed through charming little rural spots like Nottingham Road, Balgowan, Lidgetton, Lion's River, Howick, Merrivale and Hilton. Today these stunning little scenic stops form part of the Midlands Meander, a definite Must Do to include on your Bucket List.

Slip into Balgowan on your way to Durban if like me, you roared with laughter reading the hilarious series of Spud books by John van de Ruit starring Spud Milton, or if you enjoyed the movie Spud 2: The Madness Continues. The books and the film describe day-to-day experiences in Spud's elite all boys' boarding school, staffed by some very eccentric teachers. Michaelhouse School with its magnificent Natal Midlands scenery was the setting for the movie. Wander through the red- brick quadrangle and enjoy the sounds of the chapel bells and the melodious singing of the choirboys, then pop into The Caversham

Mill Restaurant at Lidgetton, just 15 minutes from Howick, before hitting the trail again.

This delightful spot is situated on the banks of the Lion's River and overlooks a waterfall. In the rainy summer months you will be inspired by the powerful rush of the water in such a tranquil haven. I have no doubt that you will be enchanted to discover that you have per chance dropped in on a bird lovers' paradise. As you sip your cappuccino you may have the thrill of seeing a Kingfisher swooping low or a Yellow fish attempting to leap high against the flow of the waterfall.

No one who had previously driven through the Natal Midlands ever mentioned having seen "proper" shops as they flashed by Mooi River en route to Durban. They had noticed that there was a good roadside garage and café on either side of the National Road, so just for safely Lyn and I decided to stock up with sufficient toiletries and stationery to last us for at least two school terms!

At just 19 years of age, leaving home and departing from Cape Town station at 3pm on the Orange Express, later known as the Trans Karoo, was naturally a heart-wrenching experience for Lyn and for me. Neither of us had left home before and we both come from close-knit families. The train was packed and we had been warned that for those passengers travelling all the way to Durban, the trip could become tedious. Seasoned travellers had recommended that we wear old clothes. A kind old lady at church suggested we wear hair nets or beréts because at least 700 miles of our trip would be travelled using a steam engine. Everyone knows that steam trains belch out thick black smoke, cinders and grit. It was going to take the express train operated by S.A.R. and H, (South African Railways and Harbours) 41 hours to travel the 1 300 miles, averaging a speed of 31,7mph!

There would be time spent in stations like Beaufort West, De Aar, Kimberley and Bloemfontein, with passengers embarking or alighting, goods being loaded at the rear end, coaches being shunted back and forth and for some reason, wheels being tapped! Remember those days? Your friend's dad may even have been a skilled wheel tapper in Kammiesvlei or Put-sonder-water!

On arrival at Cape Town station a kindly porter handled our baggage and showed us the way to Main Line platform 17. We spotted our names listed on a tag just beside one of the windows of our dark brown/ ox blood (certainly not orange!) 2nd class carriage. There would be 6 of us jammed into our small compartment. With heavy hearts, we embraced our family members and had to be heaved aboard by our Dads. There was a very sturdy wooden swing door above a short ladder with metal rungs. The door swung outwards towards the platform with lethal force, revealing the corridor leading to a row of 2nd class compartments. Ours was marked F.

A strong smell of disinfectant indicated exactly where the toilet was located. An elderly conductor with an Afrikaans accent ran his ticket clipper along the metal door handles yelling "All aboard," and followed this with an Afrikaans instruction, "Alle kaartjies asseblief! " (All tickets please) A large glass water dispenser in a metal frame and supported by a greasy looking leather strap was riveted to the wall at the far end of the corridor and the floor was already awash as we clambered aboard.

Everyone rushed to book spots closest to a window and leaned far out, waving scarves, jerseys and hats. A sea of sorrowful faces yelled passionate goodbyes in English and Afrikaans. A guard gave one very loud final blast on his whistle, waved a limp, dejected looking little flag and hopped aboard the train rather daringly at the very last minute. We could hear the sound of steam building up....there were a few jerks and splutters and the Orange Express gained momentum as it slid away from the platform. Lyn and I both had lumps in our throats and moist eyes. It had not been easy saying goodbye but now it was time to pull ourselves together. We were brand new teachers, on our way to an exciting new adventure in an unknown destination.

It was also time to turn our attention to meeting our fellow travelling companions. Two of them were going all the way to Durban. One was travelling to Ladysmith and one to Pietermaritzburg. We all wondered how on earth we were going to make room to sleep. The luggage was already occupying all six bunks and one passenger was yet to join us when we reached Bellville. Lyn and I had paid a surcharge because we each had two very large trunks containing our clothes, personal effects and teaching aids stowed in the goods van at the rear end of the train.

Because the two of us were considered young and fairly nimble, our travelling companions asked us to occupy the two top bunks. They informed us that only first class passengers were supplied with ladders to reach the top bunks. We were meant to have thick green leather straps to haul ourselves into bed but our straps were missing. Apparently vandals or delinquent travellers quite often hurled straps and ladders through train windows. Lyn and I were delighted to be awarded the top bunks, although we were very sorry to hear the lengthy list of afflictions and ailments which prevented our companions from climbing up and down! We knew we would have more breathing space above our noses than those below us and we gleefully discovered a little bonus rack up high, at the far end of our bunks where we could store our reading material, toiletries and the "smalls" we would need on our two day journey. We were travelling in casual clothes but had each packed very carefully, in the lids of our suitcases, a set of what we felt would be appropriate clothes for our arrival in Mooi River. After all, we needed to make a good impression seeing we were soon to meet our new Headmaster for the first time.

Our fellow passengers apologized that they didn't speak much English but said if we spoke slowly they would try and understand what we were saying. We assured them that we were happy to chat in Afrikaans and soon there was a happy buzz in the compartment as we all swopped pedigrees!

There were black and white photographs in wooden frames on the undersides of the top bunks which were still strapped tightly against the walls. It helped to break the ice by chatting about the pictures which depicted the Castle of Good Hope, Die Groote Klerk, a Union Castle mail ship, Clifton's Fourth Beach, Lion's Head and the Voortrekker Monument.

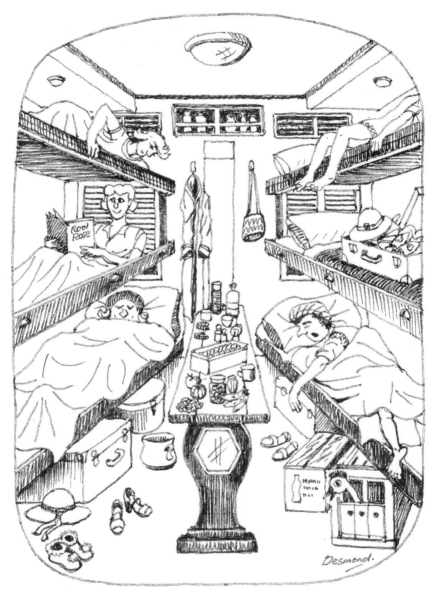

All aboard the Orange Express

Unfortunately smoking was permitted in our second class compartment and within minutes Hettie (Hendrina) in her 40's, had lit up and soon we were all suffused in a wavy blue haze of Camel cigarette smoke which made us choke and splutter. She explained that she needed to smoke to calm her nerves and was on her way to take up a new job and hopefully to find a boyfriend in Durban. We were all relieved when Hettie assured us that she smoked no more than 10 cigarettes a day and never smoked in bed for fear of setting her hair and mattress alight!

Then suddenly desperate chirping, squawking and scratching could be heard coming from a wooden crate parked on the middle bunk. Miss Trudene Cronje, a lean, stern looking spinster of about 60, with a back as straight as a ram rod and a tightly plaited little grey bun perched on her head, owned up and explained that her birds were like her children and depended solely on her. She simply had to take them on holiday to Pietermaritzburg with her because she was going to be away from her flat in Malmesbury for a whole month. Her birds obviously weren't used to train travel or being cooped up in a dark box and hadn't appreciated becoming passive smokers. The squawking persisted and Miss Cronje tried in vain to settle them by humming quietly, then clucking softly and finally by aiming fistfuls of bird seed through the slits in the crate, followed by trickles of water, squeezed from a plastic mug, some of which she hoped would drip down into the saucer she had placed below the crack. Sadly her aim was poor or she misfired because the train was lurching and most of the bird seed bounced all over the floor, making a dreadful mess.

Gerda was the youngest in our compartment but told us her parents were "stokoud," i.e. very elderly (50 and 53!) and were unable to control her, calling her " 'n Probleemkind." (a problem child) and at 16, she was being sent away from the "City and the bright lights of the Strand" to attend a strict boarding school in Ladysmith to "get reformed!" She asked us not to "shove her onto the top bunk" because she wanted to be free to come and go, to explore the train and to "kuier!"(visit) Gerda had boarded the train wearing a gym tunic with a frayed girdle, black stockings, a black blazer with red stripes and austere looking black lace up shoes. But before we had reached Woodstock, she had stripped off her uniform, rolled it into an untidy ball and pushed it under the bottom bunk. Showing no modesty, she pulled on a floral mini skirt, silver stiletto sandals and finally a clingy, bust-hugging black top with sequins. She then yanked up the mirror which formed part of the wooden table covering the wash basin in our compartment, and as we glided through Woodstock station without stopping, Gerda proceeded to apply very heavy make up to cover her teenage acne. We were all fascinated as we watched her curl her eye lashes with a tong -like gadget, before coating them with jet black mascara. Finally out came a glitzy tube of baby pink lipstick and a plastic compact of far-too-crimson blusher, which she swirled round her cheeks with her middle finger, asking us if we thought she had applied it in a heart shape! And then after aiming a quick squirt of a rather sickly perfume, called Purple Moon, down her cleavage, off she went, her silver heeled stiletto sandals clicking down the passage.

The train was packed with rowdy and exuberant Army boys. Most of them were heading for Kimberley and Tempe in Bloemfontein but some we understood were going even further afield to Ladysmith and Durban to embark on intensive training in the South African Defence Force, usually referred to as the SADF.

Upon departure from Cape Town station we had noticed many moms, aunties, grannies and girlfriends weeping openly as they bade farewell to fine young school leavers heading for a compulsory 9 month stint in the Army. In those years we were led to believe that Communist powers were supporting the South West African People's Organization known as SWAPO, the former independence movement in Namibia and that our borders needed to be defended at all cost. Further north there was a Border War raging between South Africa and the Angolan liberation movement UNITA, the Angolan government and army, supported by Cuban forces. So it was these brave young men, some barely out of high school, who were now on the Orange Express and were heading for intensive army training. All too soon some would be having to face guerrilla insurgents and it was a sad and sobering thought that some of these fine young lads might never return to their homes and their loved ones.

12

THE PINK POTTY UNDER THE BUNK

*J*ust half an hour after our departure from Cape Town, the train reduced speed and we were gliding into Bellville station. The platform was jam packed and we wondered how all the extra bodies were going to squeeze aboard. However, it turned out that most of the platform party had come to wave goodbye. Once again many young men with bulging rucksacks and laden tog bags climbed on board, leaving behind sorrowful relatives and sweethearts.

But right now our eyes were on passenger number 6, about to enter our already bursting-at- the- seams second class compartment. Our hearts sank. Tannie Gertie was a lady of enormous proportions. We estimated that she could be in her late sixties. She lumbered along very slowly, grasping the arm of a strapping young man sporting an unruly carrot coloured beard. Gertie van T. was seriously bow- legged and walked with a pronounced limp to her starboard side as if she might soon be requiring a bionic hip or knee.

It took three Army hunks to hoist her up the iron steps and lead her along the corridor to our compartment marked F. Her family members kept shoving more and more boxes, baskets, blankets and excess clutter through the window. She appeared to have as much luggage as the rest of us put together. We were already packed in like sardines and were dreading bedtime. Lyn and I wondered how on earth we were going to find even an inch of floor space in the night if we needed to jump down from our top bunks and slip down the corridor to answer the call of Nature!

We were all invited to call our new travelling companion "Tannie Gertie" rather than Mevrou van T. (Auntie Gertie rather than Mrs van T.) She only spoke Afrikaans and introduced herself in no uncertain terms, providing a complicated medical background. What she said left us gasping. It sounds much better in her own language....

"Mense, ek gaan now heeltemal eerlik met julle wees. Hierdie is nou my permanente sitplek en ek gaan hiersó sit al die pad van Bellville tot in Durban! Ek gaan nie die kompartement verlaat nie. Ek het my eie kosmandjie saamgebring. My bene voel nie lekker nie. Julle kan sien....hulle is baie swak. Ek lei ook aan suikersiekte en ek moet julle waarsku...Ongelukkig moet ek dikwels piepie maak."

"People, I am going to be completely honest with you. This is now my permanent seat and I am going to sit here all the way from Bellville until Durban! I won't be leaving the compartment at all. I have brought my own basket of food along. My legs don't feel so good. You can see. They are very weak. I also suffer from diabetes and I must warn you that I need to relieve myself frequently!"

We all stared at Tannie Gertie with incredulity. How on earth was she going to remain in our compartment for two whole days and nights? Unfortunately we soon found out! We were only about ten minutes out of Bellville when she started scratching about in her luggage. She sunk both arms deep into a battered circular hat box. We feared she was going to lose her balance. As she fished about amongst a fascinating assortment of hats, some fuzzy ones, some with feathers and some knitted or crocheted, the loose skin on her upper arms shook and wobbled. Tannie Gertie muttered to herself as she delved deeper and deeper....

" Waar op aarde het ek dit nou weggesteek? " She muttered ("Where on earth did I put it?")

Trying to be helpful, we asked, "Wat soek Tannie nou?

Kan ons nie miskien vir Tannie help soek?" (We asked what she was looking for and offered to help her search)

Then triumphantly from the bottom of the colourful pyramid of hats, Auntie Gertie held aloft, much to everyone's shock and horror, a bright pink plastic potty which she had tried to camouflage in an OK Bazaars packet!

What follows is still indelibly printed in my memory even after all these years. Upon the appearance of the pink potty concealed in the OK Bazaars packet, Hettie lit another Camel cigarette and became engrossed in her Rooi Rose magazine. Miss Cronje checked that her little grey bun was still intact and perched presentably on her head, grabbed her knitting from the bottom bunk and hurriedly sought refuse in the passage just outside our compartment. Lyn and I were about to beat a hasty retreat too, when Auntie Gertie grabbed my hand and pleaded with us to stay and help her with her ablutions! She said we needed to act on behalf of her daughters whom she had left behind in Bellville. She had to be helped on and off her potty or her legs would give way and she would lose her balance.

Neither of us could believe the undignified task which had suddenly been thrust upon us. Gertie asked whether either of us was "pieperig" (a very descriptive Afrikaans word for squeamish) It would not have helped to reply in the affirmative because we really needed a third helper to assist with the mopping up operations. We desperately hoped that Gertie's next ascent to the pink throne would be when it was our turn to go to the dining car for the first sitting of dinner. But right now with Gertie's business of the day behind her, the matter in hand for Lyn and me, was how to deal with the contents of the pink potty. Thankfully Gertie assured us that this was her task. She travelled to Durban once every year to visit her sister and had worked out that the best disposal method by far was to wait for the train to reduce speed near a piece of open veld. Then as discreetly as possible, she would lower the window and drop the contents. "Staan terug, mense!" she warned. ("Stand back people!") Lyn and I nipped out into the passage for safety. Job done...out came the OK Bazaars plastic bag again and under the bunk went pink potty plus packet until the next call of Nature.

I shall pause here to allow sensitive readers to take a deep breath as Lyn and I desperately needed to do.

Unfortunately our duties weren't over just yet....Gertie told us how she suffered with dreadfully dry skin and flyaway hair and she thrust a large tub of Vaseline into Lyn's hands asking her please to rub her back and to pat her hair into place with Vaseline. Using her comb, Gertie then plastered her hair down and shoved a little striped knitted cap on her head, which made her look rather like a cheerful little round teapot.

Gerda had not yet returned to our compartment and was still chatting to a lively group of Army chaps at the far end of the passage. We were grateful to have had extra space to manoeuvre Gertie on and off her potty. We could hear much mirth and frivolity as the young men and Gerda shared bottles of Coke and a large packet of Simba chips. The noise in the passage became a bit much for Miss Cronje who opened the door and peeped into our compartment before slipping back into her seat alongside Hettie. She heaved a sigh of relief and muttered," Sjoe, vandag se jong mense is baie anderste as ons!" (The young people of today are very different to us!)

Hettie yawned and said she needed to stretch her legs and wanted to buy a drink and enjoy the view from the lounge adjoining the dining saloon. Lyn and I loosened the clasps and let the windows drop wide open. Using our towels, we frantically fanned away her smoke and used her Rooi Rose magazine to flick away the bird seed and ash which seemed to be everywhere. Then we chose to clamber up onto our top bunks to have some peace and quiet and enjoy our books before going to supper.

Gertie was scratching in her luggage again and had hauled out her kosmandjie.(her food basket) It was wrapped in a tartan rug and she seemed to have packed enough food for an army. Because we already had meal tickets, we declined her offer of sandwiches, biltong, prunes, ham, baked beans, hard boiled eggs and pickled onions. We had barely opened our books, when we were required to jump down from above to assist Tannie Gertie who was grunting as she struggled to pull down the rather stiff folding table over the stainless steel washbasin. We helped her spread out her supper on her tartan blanket and poured her Rooibos tea from her thermos flask. She then laid out an impressive line- up of multi- coloured capsules and tablets to deal with all her ailments.

Our sudden movements had unsettled Miss Cronje's birds and loud chirping and scratching was once more heard from the crate under the bunk. At this point we decided to leave her to calm her little feathered friends while we too stretched our legs and explored the coaches between us and the dining car. The dinner gong made a melodious sound as one of the stewards tapped the keys whilst walking the length of the train.

Lyn and I were impressed with the dinner menu and found the Karoo lamb delicious. The waiters were friendly and the service in the dining saloon was attentive and efficient. It amazed us that the railway chefs were able to produce such fine meals in cramped quarters. We shared a table with Angus and Doreen, a delightful old Scots couple from Aberdeen who were visiting South Africa for the first time. I think we were able to share some travel tips and dispel some of their myths about our country, before we headed back to face a night in our cramped sleeping quarters.

Gerda chatting up her army friend

13

THINGS THAT GO CLICKETY CLICK IN THE NIGHT

*J*annie Gertie had decided to keep her clothes on and was rolled up in her tartan blanket on the bottom bunk with her little woollen tea cosy hat pulled over her face and was snoring and grunting very loudly. Miss Cronje came back from dinner shortly after we returned, complaining that the noisy young soldiers were blocking the passages, chatting up young school girls and throwing their empty beer cans into the veld. She reported having seen "our Gerda" sharing one of the young men's cigarettes. Miss Cronje said she was used to her own privacy so she slipped out and changed in the toilet. She came back looking rather ghostlike, having removed all her make up. She had changed into her dressing gown and slippers with pink pom-poms and pulled a rug over herself on the other bottom bunk, but not before she had peeped into the crate and whispered good night to her little feathered friends.

There was no sign of Gerda yet and we guessed that she would sneak back into the compartment after we had put the lights out. Hettie yawned as she puffed at her last cigarette for the night and struggled to pull on a pair of flannel ski pajamas under the sheet on her middle bunk. She popped out her false teeth before giving them a vigorous brush in the washbasin. She then pulled back the folding table across the basin and carefully replaced all the items Tannie Gertie had left parked there for the night, a black rubber torch, a wooden hairbrush, a packet of Ouma rusks, her Afrikaans hymn book called Psalms en Gesange, an enamel mug, a cake of red Lifebuoy soap and believe it or not, her upper and lower dentures!

The bedding porter had started his rounds while we were still enjoying our dinner, so we were grateful that Tannie Gertie had supervised the sleeping arrangements. Seeing that the green leather straps had been lost or stolen, Lyn and I were glad to be able to use the middle bunks for toe holds as we retreated onto our top bunks. It felt so good to have one's own little private space. We snuggled down feeling thankful that we had bought bedding tickets. The linen smelt fresh and clean and the dark blue blankets were warm and fuzzy. The night air was chilly even though it was January and we guessed that the heaters in the compartments had been switched off for the summer months. We were entering the Karoo and by now the train had gathered speed. I clearly remember a Geography teacher telling us that the word Karoo possibly came from the Khoi Khoi word "garo" meaning desert. The Karoo is indeed vast and flat, covering almost 40 % of South Africa's land surface and straddles 4 of the country's nine provinces!

It was a relief after an emotional day of family farewells and new acquaintances, to be tucked up snugly, way up high, above all the boxes, bundles, birds and baggage stuffed below us, which filled every precious inch of floor space. It was a comforting feeling to be rocked to sleep by the gentle swaying movement of our coach, the chooga - chooga- chooga coming from the steam engine and the rhythmic clickety clack, clickety clack of the wheels on the track.

Just as I was drifting off, a new sound came to my ears. A sound I did not recognize and one I had not heard before. I sensed that Lyn too had stirred and was feeling for her penlight in her handbag at the foot of her bunk.

Covering the bulb with her hand to create a dim light so as not to disturb our travel companions, Lyn flashed the light downwards. We soon identified the culprits! It was not Miss Cronje's birds. It was Tannie Gertie's dentures!

They were travelling back and forth on the surface of the table covering the washbasin, making clickety click, clickety click sounds as the train rocked them back and forth between the Ouma rusks, the plastic mug and the hymn book! We did our best to stifle our giggles. Just then Gertie rolled over, passed a very loud wind and gave a throaty grunt which sent us clambering back to the safely of our top bunks.

Now that we knew where the clickety click was coming from, we anticipated each slither across the table and waited for an accompanying clickety click. It became difficult to drift off to sleep so we stealthily dropped our towels down onto the table to smother the annoying little sounds.

It must have been about 3 am when Lyn leaned across from her bunk and tapped my shoulder. Very loud snoring was coming from the middle bunk just beneath me. Gerda must have returned very late and crept into our darkened compartment.

There was a strong smell of cigarette smoke. Hettie promised us she never smoked in bed so we ruled her out as a suspect. I recognized the sickly scent of Gerda's Purple Moon perfume and knew that she was back. Lyn flashed her penlight downwards to make quite certain that Hettie wasn't having a panic attack or a nightmare and hadn't broken her solemn promise to us.

Imagine our abject horror when Lyn and I simultaneously noticed a great big pair of men's Army boots and khaki socks perched on top of Tannie Gertie's wicker kos mandjie!(food basket!) barely three inches away from her pillow and her nose! Then worse still, Lyn's trusty little torch revealed that the loud snoring was not coming from Auntie Gertie this time, or from Miss Cronje, but rather from the wayward owner of the Size 12 Army boots! There he was, bundled into the middle bunk, fully clothed (thankfully!) and squashed in beside "Our Gerda!"

At this point, Miss Cronje stirred so we felt it wise to switch on the lights and send our uninvited guest and his Army boots on his way as speedily as possible. Then feeling rather sleep-deprived, we all rolled over in our bunks again and decided to keep our lecture for Gerda until daybreak.

14

HISTORY ON THE MOVE

*E*arly next morning we seemed to wake in relays. Lyn and I opened our eyes when we heard the gong sounding to summon passengers to the first breakfast sitting. Miss Cronje had already slipped out of the compartment to dress in the privacy of the toilet. Gerda was curled up in her blanket and was still dead to the world after her late night revelry. Hettie had pulled on a tracksuit, lit her first cigarette of the new day and had her nose buried in her Rooi Rose magazine. Tannie Gertie had already located her OK Bazaars packet from under the bunk and had lined up her pink potty ready for action! She was waiting patiently to be helped on and off by one of us, but meanwhile she had been redeeming the time. Her dentures were safely back in place, all ready to explore the contents of her wicker basket again. Her cheeks were glowing having been washed and polished with her invigorating red Lifebuoy soap. The fascinating contents of her "kos mandjie" had been spread out on the folding table. It's strange what some folk enjoy for breakfast! I would never have thought that pickled onions would go with Ouma rusks or fish paste with koeksisters. I thought they were a definite No No for anyone suffering from diabetes. After Lyn and I had helped Tannie Gertie with her ablutions, rubbed her back with Nivea cream and patted her hair into place with Vaseline, she edged closer to the window whilst waiting to dispose of the contents of her potty once the coast was clear. It was still a bit too early to aim for the Big Hole of Kimberley.

Tannie Gertie generously offered to share the contents of her kosmandjie with us. Gerda had just woken, yawned wearily, rolled over and looking rather sheepish, had jumped down from her middle bunk. Unfortunately for her, Miss Cronje was returning from the toilet having dressed and completed her ablutions. She slid the door open and gave Gerda a real tongue lashing, telling her that we could all see why her parents called her a "probleemkind." (problem child) and why they were sending her to boarding school to get some good discipline instilled in her, and then added that she was very thankful that she only had to worry about her birds' behaviour!

By now Gertie had solved her potty problem, had come away from the window and was enjoying a steaming cup of Rooibos tea from her Thermos flask which a kind waiter had re-filled several times. She encouraged us all to sample some of her daughter Magda's koeksisters and koesisters. Lyn and I had always considered them to be one and the same tasty, fattening treat but Gertie soon put us right. For koesisters you drop the "k". It's a Cape Malay treat, rather like a potato-shaped doughnut and spiced with naartjie peel, cinnamon, aniseed and ginger, then deep fried in hot oil and rolled in desiccated coconut. Gertie told us how the children of her Muslim friends would look forward to this special treat on a Sunday morning. In Bo- Kaap certain ladies were known as "Koesister aunties" and children would run to the houses where these ladies lived, to collect a special weekend breakfast treat.

Koeksisters are another delicious traditional Afrikaans confectionery made of plaited dough. They are also deep fried then plunged into icy syrup and left to drain. They have a crispy crunchy crust and are golden in colour, with a liquid syrup centre which tastes like honey. We were impressed with Magda's baking but only sampled one koeksister each because we had already bought meal tickets for the remainder of our journey.

It was about morning tea time and almost 18 hours since we left Cape Town, when we heard the conductor rattling door handles and shouting, "Next stop Kimberley! Kimberley!" A number of folk were already shoving their suitcases into the passage. It appeared there was also to be an exodus of Army lads bound for training at the S.A. Infantry Battalion. Gerda had disappeared earlier and we guessed she was bonding again with her new found Army friends.

I was excited at the thought of seeing the Diamond City, even if only through the train window. Our mom was born and bred in Kimberley and even at the age of 80, she boarded a Greyhound bus from Cape Town to attend the Kimberley Old Girls' School Reunion! A dear old school friend of mom's called Grace Ledger, kept us enthralled with stories of pranks they got up to as boarders in Beit House. Grace was a real inspiration and turned 100 years old on 17 December 2018, only a few years after she decided to stop driving and felt the time was ripe to wear a hearing aid!

It's amazing to think that when Erasmus Jacobs discovered an interesting looking white pebble near the Orange River way back in 1866, it turned out to be an extremely valuable diamond, weighing an impressive 21,25 carats! Three years later an 83,5 carat rough diamond, now known as The Star of Africa was discovered in Hopetown by a Griqua herdsman. The shepherd sold the diamond to a neighbouring farmer for the hefty price of 500 sheep, 10 oxen and a horse!

These exciting finds caused miners to flock to the area from all over the world.

Kimberley gained its name from the rocky Kimberlite pipes where diamonds are embedded. The citizens of Kimberley are proud to boast that their great Big Hole is the largest man made hole on earth! Imagine a pit dug only with picks and shovels actually reaching a depth of 240 meters and covering a perimeter of 1, 6 km! We all leaned out of the train and gasped at the immensity of this vast pit with its turquoise looking water, apparently caused by the presence of algae.

No wonder Kimberley was the site of the world's biggest diamond rush!

I remember hearing a heart-warming story of an adventurous mixed breed female dog which went exploring and fell the equivalent of 50 storeys down the Big Hole and miraculously stayed alive without food for eight days.

Valiant rescue workers risked life and limb to finally bring the traumatized dog to the surface after a 15-hour rescue mission. An incredibly brave Warrant Officer named John Seeley is believed to have supported the exhausted dog which had slipped off a ledge and plunged into the icy cold water. Eventually he and the dog were hauled to safely wearing life jackets and harnesses.

After a most welcome 20 minute stop in Kimberley where many passengers chose to disembark to stretch their legs and stock up on snacks and refreshments, we were soon on our way again. This time our train was bound for Bloemfontein, often nicknamed "Bloem", where we would have a slightly longer stay because most of the Army chaps would be leaving the Orange Express to head for Tempe where the S.A. Infantry Battalion was awaiting them.

No one knows exactly how Bloemfontein was given its name (From the Dutch words for Flower and Fountain.) One legend tells of an ox named "Bloem" (a strange name for an Ox unless he was a bit of a Pansy!) who was owned and loved by a pioneer farmer. Sadly the ox was attacked by a very hungry vicious lion near the fountain.

Another theory is that in about 1840 the wife of an early settler named Johannes Brits planted some beautiful flowers round a fountain frequented by parched, travel-worn pioneers who passed across the central plains.

Then too, there was a Korana Khoi Khoi leader called Jan Blom who lived in the area not far from the fountain, so who knows which version to believe!

What I did not know previously, was that Bloemfontein was the birthplace of the novelist J.R.R. Tolkien, the author of The Hobbit and Lord of the Rings.

But what we all should know is that Bloemfontein is called the City of Roses and is the capital of the Free State province and the judicial capital of South Africa ~ and of course it is Home to the Cheetahs rugby side! That's because the Sesotho name for Bloemfontein is Mangaung, which means "Place of the Cheetahs!"

It is also where Emily Hobhouse, an English lady with a very big heart, carried out wonderful relief work amongst mothers and children in the concentration camps during the Anglo-Boer War. It's heartbreaking to think that an estimated 45, 000 people died there, many of them women and children.

Desmond.

Of great interest to all South Africans is the fact that our current ruling party, The African Nation Congress (ANC) was founded in Bloemfontein in 1912.

Bloemfontein has produced many of our country's famous achievers like Hansie Cronje, Alan Donald, Zola Budd, Ryk Neethling, Francois Steyn and Leon Schuster who was educated there.

For lunch we shared the snacks we had bought at the platform kiosks in Bloemfontein and once again Tannie Gertie produced her kosmandjie and offered her tinned sardines, rusks, gherkins and prunes to anyone still feeling peckish!

The pancake-flat Karoo landscape continued well into the afternoon with scrubby bushes, windmills and quaint railway sidings flashing by. Gertie and Miss Cronje chose to have a nap after lunch. Hettie puffed at her 5th cigarette and opened her new Sarie magazine and Lyn and I read through our Treverton literature once again, trying to visualise what was awaiting us.

The train seemed much quieter now, since two large contingents of Army boys had left us. Soon we heard the welcome sound of the gong echoing through the passages and it was time to clean up for supper in the dining car. There was delicious ox tail followed by malva pudding with hot custard and ice cream. We tucked in with gusto, realizing that very soon Lyn and I would have to adjust to eating boarding school food.

After an eventful first night aboard the train, and with Gertie's ablutions now behind her, (no pun intended!) we were all ready to settle in for an early night. Miss Cronje had returned from changing in the toilet. She complained that she had been held up because she was number six in the queue waiting to brush her teeth.

Gerda had said farewell to her new Army friend at Bloemfontein station and was looking decidedly despondent. She scratched under Hettie's bottom bunk and pulled out the bundle containing her new striped blazer and rather dishevelled looking school uniform. She changed into it reluctantly and decided to climb onto her middle bunk, hoping to grab a few hours' sleep before being met by her new Housemistress at 2am when our train was scheduled to arrive in Ladysmith. The train had speeded up and soon the rocking movement and the rhythmic clickety clack of the wheels on the tracks lulled us all to sleep...

Hettie had stored her new Sarie magazine under her pillow and was purring gently with a scarf wrapped round her head. Tannie Gertie and Miss Cronje were both snoring, one slightly baritone and the other bass. Miss Cronje's little grey plaited bun had slipped sideways and was resting on her left ear. The birds had stopped chirping and scratching and had settled for the night, but only after a few more fistfuls of bird seed had been aimed through the slits in the crate and more droplets of water had been dispensed from Miss Cronje's blue plastic tooth mug. Tannie Gertie had her emergency line up spread out on the table covering our washbasin ~ torch, tablets, Vaporub, a ripe orange and her wooden hair brush, but thankfully this time she had silenced her dentures by popping them into her gloves for the night! It had been a happy day and all was well in Compartment F.

15

THE TALL STRANGER IN THE GREAT COAT

*J*ust before we put the lights off in our compartment, a very friendly conductor rattled our door with his metal ticket punch and knocked briskly to gain access. "Young ladies," he said, speaking in Afrikaans. "Did anyone inform you of your arrival time in Mooi River? You do know that you must be dressed and ready to disembark at 12 minutes past 4 in the morning!"

We shuddered.We had been told it would still be very dark but hadn't realised that our arrival would be at quite such an unearthly hour!

"One brief stop before we reach Mooi River is Hidcote station" he said, " and I will give you a shout and warn you that soon after Hidcote, you must be prepared to jump out with all your luggage."

We reminded him that we both had trunks in the guard's van. He confirmed that statement by consulting his well-thumbed little notebook and assured us that one of the railway guards would be on hand to assist us with our checked baggage.

Both Lyn and I dozed fitfully....

I guess we were both feeling apprehensive. We were soon to meet our new Headmaster in the pitch dark at 4.12 am! Would he approve of us! We felt so young at age 19 to be becoming his founder teachers.

Would we be able to control a whole dormitory of little boys who would probably be even more homesick than we were feeling! What would it be like living in a little country "dorp" (small village) where we didn't know a soul!

Lyn and I both leapt into action even before we reached Hidcote. We had to move swiftly and it was difficult working by torchlight. Our travelling companions were still dead to the world, seeing there was ample time for beauty sleep before they reached Pietermaritzburg and Durban. We knew we needed time to sort out our hairstyles and apply a little make up. Lyn had beautiful thick bouncy hair which only required a quick flick with a comb.

I had endured the torture of sleeping in a few prickly rollers to give my fine hair a lift. We had decided before climbing onto our bunks for a few hours of sleep, that it would not be appropriate to meet our new Boss dressed in our fuzzy old hockey tracksuits. After all, our mothers had set a fine example in their own style of dress whenever they had attended smart occasions, like going into Cape Town by bus or train to do shopping. So being part of the hat and gloves era of the 60's, we too felt we should not let the side down!

Looking back now, more than 50 years later, Lyn and I must have looked a fine sight as we jumped off the Orange Express at that unearthly hour of the day! By the time the conductor came to alert us to the fact that the train was passing the Hidcote siding at a very fast rate, we had already dragged our luggage into the corridor and were both fully dressed in our smart attire. We had washed our faces and cleaned our teeth by flickering torchlight, then followed up with a quick dash down the passage to peep in the toilet mirror to apply a little lipstick and adjust our hats to the correct angle! Yes, there we were dressed as if to attend a wedding!

Our companions were still in the dark. Tannie Gertie was a great big motionless mound on her bottom bunk. She was in a deep, deep sleep, with her head under the blankets and was snoring full throttle. Hettie and Miss Cronje had stirred in the darkness of our compartment and whispered "Totsiens, en alles van die beste! Sjoe, maar julle is uitgevat om julle skoolhoof te ontmoet!"

("Cheerio and everything of the best! Whew, you two are all togged up to meet your new Headmaster!")

We seemed to have whizzed through a tunnel or mountain cutting because a blast of cold air suddenly whipped through the length of the carriage. We hung onto our hats for dear life. Lyn's pale blue- brimmed hat matched her ice blue suit beautifully and she looked elegant in her 5 inch white sling back stilettos. I was wearing my water melon pink sailor suit with a little anchor embroidered on the pocket to give the outfit a jaunty nautical look. My mom and I had found a very pretty pink hat in a pillbox style at Henshilwoods Outfitters in Claremont and my mom had added a satin bow in a deeper shade of contrasting pink. I also wore a brand new pair of white shoes with pointed toes and elegant 5 inch stiletto heels.

At last the train began to decrease speed. The brakes squealed on the tracks. As we peered through the inky darkness, we spotted a few pinpricks of light from farm houses dotted amongst the rolling countryside, then all of a sudden, the lights of a small town popped up to the right of the train track as if stirring from a sleepy hollow. The station signs flashed into focus, confirming that after two long days of travel, we had finally reached our destination, Mooirivier! One of the biggest Adventures of my entire life was about to start!

I felt my heart pounding. We came closer and closer and finally the platform glided past our carriage. It felt as if we were never going to stop, but then with a sudden jerk, our carriage ground to a halt. As promised, our friendly conductor, Meneer Stoffel van Wyk, was on hand to help us handle our baggage and exit the train safely. We were relieved to see that our trunks were being lowered from the goods van.

By now we had both donned white gloves to complete the picture! One of our College lecturers had reminded us that the "first impression" is actually only a seven second window period upon first meeting someone! This for us meant that we had better keep our hats and gloves on even though it was still the middle of the night!

A shock awaited us as we jumped down the metal rungs of the steps at the far end of our carriage. Our second class coach was towards the rear end of the train and had unfortunately run out of platform! It was drizzling slightly and the soil beneath us was moist and soggy. As we jumped down with armfuls of luggage, we held our breath, hoping that there would not be a ripping sound as the seams of our straight skirts split. We both felt our stiletto heels sinking deeper and deeper into a bed of squishy clay until our shoes were almost embedded. In fact our stiletto heels made us feel impaled, possibly forever!

Just at that embarrassing moment, as we attempted a sideways shuffle to wiggle our way out of the clinging mud, whilst still gripping our hand luggage under our chins, a tall dark male figure made his way along the deserted platform in our direction. He was taking great strides. There was an eerie silence then one sharp whistle blast and our train rumbled off into the darkness. We both shivered. The shadowy figure was dressed in a great big army coat, with its collar pulled right over his ears. The stranger's features were hidden by a dark balaclava. There was not another soul in sight. In the 1960's no one carried pepper spray or a taser, or even a whistle for defence. We both realized that our hockey sticks were stowed in our trunks which had been lifted from the guard's van.

We felt utterly defenceless. Should we kick off our stilettos and sprint to a well- lit area or just stand still and scream!

What a huge relief when through the darkness came a friendly, "Hello young ladies! You must be Lyn and Ruth from Cape Town. Welcome to Mooi River." By now we were under a lamp post and could see the kind face of our new Headmaster who had removed his balaclava. He appeared to be a little more than 6 feet tall, with strawberry blonde hair and we guessed he was probably still in his late 30's. He thought nothing of shouldering all our hand luggage.

He introduced himself as Derek Hudson Reed but told us to feel free to call him by his nickname which was "Huddy." As we walked to his car he apologized for the absence of his wife Marge who was four months pregnant and was struggling with severe morning sickness.

She had experienced a narrow escape just a fortnight before on their journey down from Johannesburg. Marge was driving a second heavily laden car some 100 yards behind Huddy. Their 3 children, Donald (11) Jenny (8) and Colin (3) were taking turns to travel with mom and dad as they moved from St. Stithians College in Ferndale Johannesburg to the resuscitated Treverton Prep. School in Mooi River in the Natal Midlands.

Driving at dusk, after a long hot day, Marge had not seen a poorly lit DETOUR sign propped up on a row of barrels blocking access to the regular route and her car had ploughed headlong into the barrels. Apart from severe dents and scratches on the car, none of the occupants was badly injured, although there was naturally grave concern for the welfare of Marge's unborn baby.

Having collected our trunks from the guard's van, Huddy loaded our luggage and helped us into his car, tactfully suggesting we might feel more comfortable travelling without our hats! We liked our good looking new Boss immediately and realized that he was actually quite shy and unassuming.

We found Huddy to be extremely gracious and considerate in inviting us to have a hot drink before settling into our new accommodation. Marge had thoughtfully laid a tea trolley in the lounge of their flat, setting out beautiful china cups and tasty biscuits before going to bed. She had provided flasks of boiling water and tea and coffee. Huddy was the perfect host, making us feel welcome and completely at home in our new environment. As he poured our tea, he answered the questions we posed about Mooi River and its surroundings. He felt positive about the enrolment of prospective boarders and described the exciting aims he envisaged for his new school. We sensed his genuine passion for education and were soon caught up in the thrill of Huddy's educational vision. His enthusiasm was contagious and Lyn and I felt eager to embrace the exciting challenges awaiting us.

It was soon time to get the lie of the land and view our accommodation, then unpack and settle in before breakfast. The thought of a hot bath after our long journey was appealing and we felt Huddy needed a few more hours of sleep after his disturbed night.

Before parting he very sheepishly apologized for frightening us and explained that he had overslept and had only woken when he heard our train whistling as it rounded the bend from Estcourt and entered the valley below the school. From their school flat, Huddy had seen the long string of carriages with dark compartments and contrasting brightly lit corridors, winding its way towards the station. He only had time to pull on his Army greatcoat over his pyjamas and grab a woollen balaclava and a thick scarf. Huddy admitted he had felt hugely embarrassed when he found us dressed in our Sunday best, with stilettos impaled in the sticky clay beyond the far end of the platform!

16

OUR ADVENTURE BEGINS

*O*ur little tour of the school revealed some fascinating names…

We loved the scattered buildings and outhouses with thatched roofs and almost felt as if we were coming to holiday in a guest house or on a farm rather than work as house mistresses at a boys' boarding school. We found the names of the dormitories enchanting. Lyn and I were to act as surrogate mums to the youngest boys who would be placed in our care in The Chicken Run! None of the little chaps had left home before so what lay ahead was a daunting Adventure for all of us!

En route to our dorm, we passed the Cavern and the Barn. Little Thatch was to serve as a staff room in those early days. The dining room was large and airy and had rows of lockers on one wall and the boys would be allowed to store their tuck boxes there. Alongside the kitchen was a compact little staff flat where we were introduced to the new Caterer, "Mrs J" (Mrs Valerie Joubert) a little widowed lady with a very sweet smile, bright pink cheeks and a neat little grey bun. She came bustling out of the kitchen to welcome us, looking very business-like in her freshly -starched apron embroidered with sprigs of blue berries. We could not help noticing her strong, well-worn hands and arms which bore the marks of many years of strenuous toil as a young widow caring for her family. I shall never forgot Mrs J. describing how she had tried to save money after the difficult war years, by making vests and underpants for her children from tough, durable flour and sugar bags and she assured us that they far outlasted all shop vests and undies!

We were excited to be shown another small thatch building which was to serve as a Games Room for it housed an exercise bicycle, a dart board, a snooker and table tennis table. Lyn and I were delighted when Huddy promised to teach us to play snooker and said that his staff would be allowed to play squash at the Mooi River Country Club.

Lyn and I had been allocated two small bedrooms attached to The Chicken Run where we would initially be responsible for 20 little chaps, aged 8, 9 and 10. The next age group would move into the Cavern and the older boys were to be placed in The Barn. We shivered as we entered our rooms and noticed the concrete floors. Several passengers on our train had warned us that Mooi River was sometimes referred to as "The Icebox of South Africa." We both made a mental note that once our first pay day had dawned, we would head into the village to buy heaters and kettles for our rooms. Our bathroom had bright red floor polish and was right alongside the boys' ablution block. Ours was very basic with a toilet, a washbasin and an enormous rather antique looking bath perched on bandy iron legs. The boys' bathroom had several large old fashioned baths, a row of showers, toilets and a urinal. Later on smaller bright blue plastic baths were purchased and these saved a considerable amount of water. Each little bath contained a moulded built- in seat and these proved popular for lingering in hot soapy water on chilly nights. There was no heating at all in the dorms and we guessed this was to encourage manliness in the little fellows and hardihood for the two new young lady teachers from Cape Town.

I shall never forget our first night in our little rooms attached to the Chicken Run. Lyn and I had come away from Cape Town where we had experienced turbulent political times in the early 60's with marches, protests and serious rioting where government buildings and shops had been stoned, looted and even burnt. I remember a very unsettling phone call from my auntie Pat and uncle Jack Roos who lived in Pinelands. Not far behind their home was an open field, just across from the township of Langa. My aunt phoned to ask if they could load their car with bedding and doss down at our home in Rondebosch, fifteen minutes away, should the rioting get out of hand. As she spoke, my mom could hear gunshots, sirens, whistles and screams in the background. We remained on high alert all night but thankfully they called at 3 am to say that a tense calm had settled over Langa and that the rioters had moved to the Gunners Circle area, which is closer to the industrial area of Epping.

Lyn and I were already in our pyjamas when we heard a frightening hammering on the corrugated iron roof of the Chicken Run. Lyn rushed into my room, the colour drained from her face. We were convinced we were under attack. We knew that Treverton was very close to Bruntville, the nearest township. The clattering sounded exactly like massive rocks or bricks being thrown onto our roof. How long would it be before the corrugated sheets would be ripped apart? Would the rioters then set fire to the newly refurbished Treverton buildings? What could have motivated this terrifying onslaught? Fortunately the little boarders had not yet arrived for the new term or like us, they too would have been petrified.

Just then there was a deafening bang, followed by a sharp crack and we were certain it must be the sound made by an exploding grenade. We were plunged into darkness and our hearts stood still. We had no candles or torches. We looked around for protection. We hastily grabbed our brand new plastic waste paper baskets and pulling them on as protective helmets, we dived under my bed. It was a sturdy hospital- style bed with a firm foam rubber mattress and a metal frame.

We held our breath wondering if rampaging rioters were going to storm into our room at any moment. Thank goodness the little boarders were only due to arrive at the end of the week. Would the Chicken Run still be standing after tonight's attack?

Just then there was a deafening roar of thunder and a blinding flash of lightening. It was as if daylight had illuminated my tiny bedroom. The heavy pounding on the roof intensified and it suddenly struck us that we were experiencing our very first electric storm accompanied by a vicious hail storm. We panicked when we realized that the bed we were hiding under had metal legs so we both slipped off our rubber flip flops and shoved a flip flop under each metal leg hoping that the rubber would provide insulation!

The storm lasted for a full thirty minutes and we both felt in need of comfort so, as soon as we sensed there was a slight lull, we retrieved our flip flops from under the bed legs and sprinted to the Huddies' flat which was close to the chapel and Headmaster's office. It was the first time Lyn and I had ever seen hailstones the size of squashed golf balls.

When the electricity supply had been restored, we discovered that Huddy was a wonderful cook. Sensing that we were both feeling rather shaken, he settled us in front of their blazing log fire and produced his famous cheese and mushroom omelettes and double thick banana milkshakes. When the storm had passed, he gallantly escorted us back to our rooms and left us each with a torch and a candle should there be another power failure.

In the months ahead, Marge and Huddy proved to be some of the most caring and hospitable folk I have ever encountered. Marge kept her tea trolley permanently laid and there was always a welcoming cup of tea or coffee available. I remember how prospective parents, or inquisitive folk passing from Johannesburg or Durban used to pop in to view the new Treverton and on one afternoon Marge served 48 cups of tea or coffee to visitors in their lounge between lunch and supper!

Nearly every winter that I spent at Treverton we experienced snow falls in Mooi River. The boys were in their element and Mr Huddy allowed exciting snowball fights to take place between the two school houses named Judson and Carey. There were of course very strict safety rules in place and the snow fights were only permitted under watchful staff supervision.

During one very wintry weekend there was thick snow piled high along the sides of the highway and the icy surface of the National Road became treacherous. A Johannesburg family en route to Durban suddenly spotted the attractive little Treverton thatched buildings covered in snow and resembling a scene from a European Christmas card. The very cold, hungry family pulled off the road and turned in at Treverton thinking they had come upon a pretty guest farm set in a magical Winter Wonderland! Imagine Marge Huddy's surprise when she found the family settling into her lounge with their shoes kicked off and warming their frozen toes at her fireside! Before she could ask what they thought they were doing marching into her home unannounced, the father of the family said, "Good afternoon Madam, two Ceylon teas and two mugs of hot chocolate please and scones with jam and cream for four!"

You can probably guess what happened. Being the perfect hostess, Marge obliged and graciously provided tea and Milo before explaining that the little family had accidentally turned in at a boys' boarding school and that unfortunately scones and cream was not on the menu that day but Marge happily produced some Chocolate Digestives!

In the week before the new Treverton re-opened, there was still much to do. Lyn and I very quickly felt at home in our brand new environment and were soon caught up in the busy buzz. Volunteer work parties had travelled up from churches in Durban and Westville and enthusiastic youth groups had come to offer their skills. The men were going great guns as they assembled wooden beds, bedside lockers and classroom desks. Lyn and I donned our College Art smocks and helped the ladies paint the assembled items in vibrant shades of red, blue, yellow and turquoise, creating a cheerful and stimulating learning environment and happy, homely dormitories to welcome the 50 boarders we were anticipating.

Actually a miracle occurred... Treverton was one pupil short. Our honorary bursar, Mr Monty Campbell, asked us all to pray that one more boy would enrol in order to make the school financially viable. God is good and we experienced that His timing is always perfect! On the very first night, forty- nine boarders sat down to supper, but before the end of the meal, a Johannesburg father had driven all the way down with his two sons, Michael and Alan, and pleaded with Huddy to include them in the first intake!

Whilst plans were being made for the resuscitation of Treverton a tragedy had occurred. David, the lovely young son of Mrs Gladys and Dr John Jonsson, founder and first Chairman of the school council, was drowned whilst picnicking at a nearby river. It was therefore most appropriate that the Chapel which was being fashioned by a skilful combination of the existing old staff room and an adjoining room be named the David Jonsson Memorial Chapel. Today a greatly enlarged and beautifully modernized chapel forms a focal point in the Prep School.

The Head of the School of Fine Arts at the University of Natal in 1964, Prof J.C.W. Heath, created a magnificent stained glass window, involving a mosaic of more than 1000 perspex segments. It shows a young school boy in a Treverton blazer, with his hands upraised. Above him is an open Bible, and below him can be seen classrooms, a tree of knowledge and the Drakensberg, which forms a majestic backdrop. The window is a striking representation of all that Treverton strives to achieve with its scholars ~ a fine all- round education, based on a solid faith, a love of nature and a deep appreciation of all things beautiful.

At the base of the window is the school motto, "SUPER ASTRA SPERO" Reach beyond the Stars!

Ruth Taylor and Lyn Gowar at our first Founder's Day 1964

STAFF AT END OF 1964

From left to centre
Mr J A Dyer, Mrs H Gordon, Mrs M Griffin, Mrs L Lategan, Mrs S Howard, Mr J F Howard, Mrs L Language
Carpentry   Horseriding   Swimming   Asst Matron   Secretary   Std 4 Master   Matron

From centre to right:
Mr R E Hudson Reed, Rev. J Jonsson, Mrs M Hudson-Reed, Miss L Gowar, Miss R Taylor, Mr E Hills, Mr J E M Campbell, Miss P Taylor
Headmaster   Chairman of   Std 2   Std 1   Trust   Bursar   Afrikaans
                        Council   Teacher   Teacher   Secretary   Teacher

Treverton pupils in 1964

*Bottom: Mr Hudson-Reed and his Treverton staff 1966 - Standing: I. Kern, K. Filby, R.
Burdett, M. Griffin, J. Dyer, V. Joubert - Sitting: R. Taylor, L. Gowar, C. Kreusch, M. and
R.E. Hudson-Reed, I. Andrews, W. and M. Webster.*

17

PEEPING TOMS AND BATHROOM DRAMA

*T*he first batch of founder scholars was very special to us and I was overjoyed to meet some of them fifty years later when I flew to Natal in May 2014 to attend Treverton's Golden Jubilee? What was amazing was that they still recognized me and we now all find ourselves in the Grandparents category and are seriously considering retirement Homes for Seniors!

None of our little boarders placed in The Chicken Run dormitory had ever left home before. Setting off at the tender age of eight was a daunting experience for many. Some little fellows had travelled to Treverton from as far afield as Kenya, Malawi, Zambia and Swaziland so it was not surprising that a number of them suffered from homesickness. Lyn and I realized that we were about to become surrogate moms during term time. Huddy suggested that to start with, we should sleep with our bedroom doors slightly ajar, just in case we were needed in the middle of the night.

We made the hostels look as homely as possible with bright pictures on the walls. The Chicken Run dormitory looked light and cheery with matching bedspreads and the beds and lockers were painted an attractive powder blue and white. We had to teach most of the little boys to tie their shoe laces neatly and to put on their neck ties. To encourage neatness we placed the boys in teams and awarded points and prizes. Bed making became quite an art with corners and tucks being done very neatly as in hospitals and in the Army!

On Saturday mornings Huddy inspected all the dorms and the boys stood to attention like fine young army recruits and each week a different chap got a huge kick out of yelling "A- ttention!" as Huddy approached and then "At ease! "once Huddy had left the dorm after inspecting their beds, lockers and bathrooms.

A big treat at night was to have Huddy visit your dorm to tell riveting ghost stories. Lyn and I would run the bath water towards the end of the Prep. period to save time and to share the hot water fairly. Boys would take turns to shower or bath. We had no electric geysers so great big fires had to be lit and stoked under outside boilers. Sometimes in stormy, windy weather fires were blown out and it was no joke having to wash in ice cold water. On chilly winter nights boys were reluctant to climb out of their steaming baths so we had to introduce time limits and lure them out by awarding points for the first teams to have their lockers tidy and to be in bed ready for a story.

Lyn and I were horrified to find our little boys using the boiler fires to fry flying ants! They were nicely browned and crisped using a teaspoon of margarine to sizzle them in an empty jam tin and were always gobbled up with relish. The invitation was always, "Ah, come on Miss Gowar and Miss Taylor, we'll share our ants with you. They are delicious and taste just like butter and honey." Perhaps that explains why John the Baptist developed an appetite for locusts and honey!

On another occasion, we smelt a delicious barbecue fragrance coming from the boiler behind the Chicken Run dorm. Upon investigation, we discovered that three little Zulu chaps from the local township who were helping as stable hands, were roasting large cane rats on barbed wire skewers and serving their new Treverton pals tasty cane rat kebabs! In return the young Treverton boarders were introducing their Zulu friends to toasted marshmallows for dessert!

Some humorous bathroom incidents are still indelibly etched in my memory. One evening I caught a little peeping Tom prowling round our bathroom area where I knew Lyn was bathing and preparing to go out for the evening. When I pounced and confronted him stooping down and dangerously close to the keyhole, the self-righteous little fellow looked hurt and said, "Oh no, Miss Taylor, I wasn't actually having a proper peep. I'm just testing the crack in case any boys are tempted to peep at you or Miss Gowar having a bath! I was just going to shove some toilet paper in the keyhole to stop anyone from peeping!"

On another occasion there were desperate shrieks from a bathtub where little David was in a sorry state. But not for long...one of his faithful little pals came to his rescue yelling, "Please help! Come quickly Miss Taylor. David poked his Willy up the bath tap and it got scorched and now he says it's stuck! You may have to ask Mr. Huddy to call the fire brigade or a plumber!" Fortunately a splash of cold water and some calamine lotion solved the problem and no external intervention was required that night!

Shortly before Barbara Hudson- Reed was born on 5 June 1964, Marge Huddy had a narrow escape whilst she, Lyn and I were checking the cleanliness of the bathroom area. Whilst doing our rounds late at night, a frantic cry went up that one of the Treverton stallions had kicked down the stable door and four beautiful horses were on the run. Somehow whenever a thick pea-soup mist blanketed the valley, we noticed that the horses displayed rather bizarre behaviour.

In our haste to leave the ablution block and prevent the horses from escaping and running onto the national road in the impenetrable mist, Marge spun round and stepped on a bar of wet Lifebuoy soap which had slipped onto the cement floor in the shower area. Down she went, flat on her back, hurtling at top speed towards the row of urinals. We rushed to pick her up rather gingerly knowing that she was 8 months pregnant! Fortunately she and baby Barbara survived this unexpected, Skid Row experience and suffered no ill effects.

A number of boys owned magnificent horses of their own and the school had bought several too. Horses were fed and stabled free of charge if boys were prepared to share their horses with fellow riders. Riding very soon became an extremely popular sport at Treverton and our highly successful riding instructress, Mrs Judy Veenstra, wife of a local farmer, produced outstanding gymkhanas and musical riding displays. Mr Huddy taught Lyn and me to ride and it was always a joy to be allowed to take boys on out rides into the most beautiful, tranquil Mooi River countryside.

One pupil had a very lucky escape whilst cantering back to school having realized that a fierce electric storm was on the way. Part of the Prep. School stretched across the foot of a koppie which was known to have large deposits of iron ore. As the rider approached close to a lamp post, the feet of his horse passed through a puddle of rain water. There was a deafening crash of thunder and a very bright flash of lightening. Both rider and horse were knocked to the ground and lay motionless for some frightening moments then miraculously both rose slowly and shakily to their feet. Both were momentarily stunned but thankfully survived the terrifying ordeal unscathed.

Round about the same time, a group of boys at the Weston Agricultural College just up the road from Treverton, also experienced a narrow escape.

The chaps were showering after a rugby match when a lightning bolt entered an open bathroom window and several of the boys were badly burnt down the sides of their arms and legs and had to be admitted to Grey's Hospital for treatment.

Corporal punishment had not yet been outlawed in the 1960's and boys developed a healthy respect for Huddy's cane for more serious offences and for my little stick called Toby Taylor. All offences were recorded in a book in Huddy's office and the amazing thing was that no boys ever showed malice or defiance towards us after "getting jacked." In fact, in later years many chaps actually returned to thank us for keeping them on the straight and narrow!

A number of humorous incidents spring to mind.....

When Huddy spanked one disobedient little fellow, the cane made rather a dull thud on his bottom and it turned out that the cunning little boy was wearing eight pairs of underpants! On another occasion a bigger boy had lined his school trousers with several layers of chamois leather before facing the music in Huddy's office! The chamois was normally used for polishing the school bus and he had nicked it out of the cubby hole.

As a reward for good behaviour during Prep and bath time, and to help speed up bed time, I made up an on- going series of adventure stories about The infamous Flat Nose Gang. They lived in a thick forest in Hampshire and could make themselves become invisible, except for their flat noses, which glowed in the dark and could miraculously turn into magnets or suction pads and be used to climb any surface and reach into hidden places which proved inaccessible to most human beings. Each nail-biting episode kept the boys spellbound and when I had forgotten what I had made up in a previous instalment, the boys quickly reminded me of every minute detail.

The female heroine in my crime series was a wealthy, aristocratic widow called Mrs Featherington-Pottinger who lived all alone in a very posh mansion. Her home had been fitted with all manner of ingenious crime combatting gadgets to keep the Flat Nose gang at bay. And just by the simple flick of a button, in times of imminent or perceived danger, the entire house could be made to disappear underground mysteriously and miraculously, away from prying eyes. The brave heroine hired the services of a valiant chauffeur called Percival, to take her on outings or shopping sprees. Her custom built car was quite unique and had been fitted with all manner of ingenious devices to outwit any would- be criminal or hijacker. The Chicken Run boys never forgot Mrs Featherington- Pottinger's name, or the name of her chauffeur or the make of her snazzy vehicle, even when I did!

Mr Huddy had a great cure for homesickness. He gave boys harmless little vitamin tablets with a delicious chocolate coating to swallow and boys instantly felt better!

Lyn and I soon discovered we would never need alarm clocks to wake us. Whether it was from habit or just the excitement of sharing a dorm with twenty boarders, but we found that our little chaps woke at first light. Many of them came from farming backgrounds. We could never enjoy a weekend lie-in because they regarded us as full- time moms who were never off duty. They would knock on our bedroom doors at all hours, requesting old stockings to make tails for their kites, sellotape, string, tissues, nail clippers, scissors and "pills for blocked noses!"

We were reluctant to complain about these little intrusions and inconveniences because we knew that Huddy and his long- suffering Marge, had two Johannesburg brothers of 10 and 12 who insisted on "surprising" them every morning by going into the Huddies kitchen to make tea. The boys would then charge round to the Huddies bedroom window at 6.30am, call out that they had a surprise and would take great delight in passing the tea cups through the window. I should imagine that poor Mrs Huddy must have had to dive under her duvet on a number of occasions when caught by surprise in her nightie!

Both Mr. and Mrs. Huddy were dearly loved and became surrogate parents to boys and staff alike. The door of Huddy's office was always open and anyone who needed to off -load a burden or share an anxiety was made to feel welcome. In my 15 years of knowing Marge and Huddy at Treverton, I never once heard them say that they were too busy to help anyone.

In fact, I recall one hilarious and yet most unfortunate incident which took place in the late 70's.

A retired teacher from Harrismith telephoned Huddy one night to say that if ever Treverton needed a resident Afrikaans teacher, she was available. She loved children and was a fit, able- bodied spinster of 65 who still felt called to teach. There was a terrific electric storm with deafening thunder that night and in between all the rumbles, pops and crackles, Tienie unfortunately got the wrong end of the stick! Huddy had said that IF ever there was a vacancy, he would be very happy to have Tienie visit the school for an interview. I guess it was wishful thinking but all Tienie heard that night back in Harrismith was, "We would be very happy to have you!"

Exactly one week later, Tienie de Beer had vacated her flat in Harrismith and was bound for Mooi River in her gallant little brown Volkswagen Beetle! What she had not mentioned to Huddy on the phone was that she cared for her sprightly little mother of 92 who rejoiced in the name of "Girlie!"

The next thing we knew was that Meridy, our bookkeeper, had bumped into Tienie and Girlie at the garage in the village. She overheard them asking the pump attendant for directions to Treverton so went across and introduced herself. Meridy spoke fluent Afrikaans and welcomed them warmly to Mooi River but was flabbergasted when Tienie introduced herself as Treverton's new Afrikaans teacher! She went on to explain that she would be offering her services as a netball, needlework and ballet teacher! Being a boys only prep school, Meridy struggled to keep a straight face and realized immediately that there had been a dreadful mistake. She also knew that Rev. Hans Botha, the Prep School Afrikaans teacher and his delightful American wife Marian, our school Matron, had given no indication of leaving Treverton in the foreseeable future.

Meridy wisely decided to leave Tienie and Girlie refuelling their little Love Bug and she drove back up the hill to Treverton as fast as she could to warn us that they were on their way. Huddy was at a monthly Rotary meeting so being second-in-charge, I was left to handle a very delicate situation. It was time for lunch and most of the staff complement was already seated. There was no time to warn them of our predicament. Suddenly up the steep hill and chugging round the corner, came Tienie's laden Volkswagen. The staff looked up open-mouthed as we saw there was a heavy old-fashioned bookcase strapped to the roof. The tiny Volksie car was bursting at the seams, packed with items of furniture, clothing, bedding, kitchen utensils, flower pots and two tennis racquets! Tienie came round to help Girlie stagger out of the passenger door from under a pile of sheets and table cloths. She then steadied herself on her Zimmer frame, as she watched Tienie lovingly park their brightly coloured parrot in its cage under a shady tree.

I desperately hoped the staff might think that our visitors were dear old relatives of boys who had popped in for a friendly visit en route to the Coast. But before I could say a word, Tienie had bounced in the door and had enthusiastically introduced herself and her old mom to the staff, giving us a synopsis of her teaching pedigree. Hansie Botha was not amused and looked daggers, announcing in a very emphatic way that to "his knowledge he had no plans to relinquish his teaching post!" The situation was becoming rather volatile so I suggested we all enjoy our lunch and sort out any confusion afterwards.

We dawdled over dessert and coffee because all Girlie wanted to do was to be shown their new accommodation! Whew, was I grateful when the bell rang for afternoon classes and when I saw that Huddy had returned to school and was back in his office. He was brilliant at managing conflicts and had a wonderful way of calmly defusing an explosive situation. After a complimentary couple of nights at Gleneagles hotel which was owned and managed by Treverton, Tienie and Girlie made their way back to Harrismith again. Sadly our Prep boys were denied the opportunity of being taught netball, ballet, needlework and eurythmics by someone of Tienie's calibre who had taught these skills for 45 years!

I'll never forget being woken at 4am in my little room attached to The Chicken Run dormitory. It was in the days of shortie pyjamas and pink foam rubber curlers that resembled marshmallows with rubber bands attached. I was tugged at great speed from my warm bed and led into the darkness of The Chicken Run by two little boys yelling, "Quick Miss Taylor! Please run faster….The Mommy cat has had kittens on Gary Mahon's bed and they are all still in their little plastic bags!" It broke my heart to see a spirited little Rescue 911 squad leaping into action as they pulled paper drinking straws from their tuck boxes and faithfully persevered with mouth to mouth resuscitation for half an hour, all to no avail. All the miniature, hairless kittens were premature babies, no bigger than tiny mice, with no chance of survival.

Before lights out each evening, boys were encouraged to read their Bibles and say their prayers. Boys often shared specific needs openly, like having a sick granny, a new baby in the family, their feelings of homesickness or special requests for a new bike or a pony. We encouraged them to pray aloud using short sentence prayers. There were many times when Lyn and I had to bury our faces and smother our smiles in our hands as the prayers of the eight and nine year old boys were often priceless.

A very regular and faithful prayer was, "Dear Lord Jesus, please bless the staff and all the other animals."

Or "Thank you Jesus for being our good Shepherd. Please turn our moms, dads and grannies into sheep too."

In the 1960's the guerrilla war in the jungles of Vietnam was mentioned frequently in news bulletins on the radio. This fervent little prayer was prayed on several occasions~ "Dear God, Please will you stop all the fighting in Vietnam and tell the baboons (gorillas!) to come out of the forest and become good Christians."

I was touched by this special prayer for my safety after a crime wave in the village. "Dear Lord Jesus, please keep Miss Taylor safe when she leaves our dorm tonight. Please help her not to be struck by lightning, or hit on the head by a big hail stone or tackled by a baddie in the dark as she walks all alone across the hockey field to her flat."

I know the dear Lord heard those heartfelt prayers because I crossed that Treverton hockey field in the dark for 15 years and I am still alive to tell the tale!

In my first week at Treverton I received a wonderful surprise. Quite out of the blue, Ethel, a long lost cousin on my dad's side, and her husband, Eric, arrived at the school with a tuck box full of delicious home- baked goodies. I had no idea they had moved to Mooi River from Creighton and they became a wonderful support to me. In spite of having two young children, Ethel would visit me faithfully bearing delicious treats, just in case our boarding school diet was insufficient! Her speciality was mielie bread, steamed in a jam tin and eaten piping hot with fresh farm butter. Ethel also whisked away my Crimplene jerseys, insisting that she hand wash them in Woolite and dry them on her porch, so that they were returned to me soft and fluffy.

Eric was an expert cheese maker at the local NCD factory which I now understand has been taken over by Clover. Eric arranged for me to take the school boys on tours of the factory and there were sections where they were given delicious nibbles of cheese to sample. We all marvelled at the way shiny strands of copper wire was poked through certain types of cheese to form the bright blue or green veins which run through it, but some boys were more interested in asking the cheese makers the embarrassing question of why some delicious looking cheese smells like dirty socks!

Ethel's mother, Lucille Taylor, was Matron at the Ixopo school hostel and on several occasions we travelled to visit her during the weekends. Ixopo is situated about 86 km from Pietermaritzburg. This trip to see their grandma became quite an adventure for Ethel and Eric's little pigeon pair, Charmaine and Roy. I was fascinated to learn from Lucille that the name Ixopo was derived from the Zulu onomatopoeic word "eXobo" which describes the sound made by the hooves of cattle squelching through mud. If you close your eyes and practise saying IXOPO with a good lateral click, it's not difficult to picture the muddy feet of a team of oxen making slow headway through a drift. With each hoof pulled forcibly from the thick sticky clay, you should be able to hear a very loud "Ixopo!"

It was exciting to hear the town Ixopo being spoken about recently on CNN. Did you hear that the Buddhist Retreat Centre near Ixopo has been recognized as one of the 10 finest meditation centres in the world! It has also been declared a Natural Heritage site being a paradise to bird lovers since it was found to be a breeding site of the very rare blue swallow!

My pupils loved trying to make the African clicks and that was one way I managed to liven up Geography and History lessons. An all-time favourite piece of literature for me was Alan Paton's 'Cry the Beloved Country,' and in his opening lines he writes, "There is a lovely road which runs from Ixopo into the hills. These hills are grass covered, and they are lovely beyond any singing of it."

I used this passage many times in English comprehension or grammar lessons to explain the richness of the English language.

Another tour that the Treverton boys and staff all enjoyed was to the Mooi River Textile factory (Referred to as "Mooitex") which seemed to be staffed largely by Dutch folk. There was a marvellous Factory Shop where we bought beautiful bedroom linen. My favourite articles were their thick, fluffy pastel coloured winter sheets and pillow cases made from brushed cotton. They made wonderful gifts to take home to my Cape Town family and in spite of being washed numerous times, our sheets remained fluffy and lasted for the next twenty years.

I still marvel that Lyn and I survived our very first winter in Mooi River when the temperature dipped to minus 18 degrees! I shall never forget how the water in the tumbler on my bedside pedestal froze solid. Mrs Huddy caused great mirth when she said, "Ruth, just be thankful that you don't have false teeth like I have, or you might be chopping them out of your glass with an ice pick!

Dr Derek Hudson-Reed, Founder Headmaster, Treverton

Prayers in the junior boys' dormitory

Ready to bat for the staff cricket team

Ruth with her standard 3 class

18

JOYS AND SORROWS

One very misty night Treverton's magnificent and much- loved black gelding, Trigger, escaped from the stables, ran across the highway and was very seriously injured by a speeding motorist. I shall never forget hearing one single shot ring out in the night. Huddy had gathered the staff and explained that the only humane way out was for the local veterinary surgeon to shoot Trigger as the horse's injuries were too severe. Tragically, both his powerful, beautifully sculptured front legs had been brutally smashed. There was not a dry eye as we stroked Trigger and looked into his beautiful eyes for one last time.

I had several close encounters with Mooi River reptiles. I heard screams coming from the flatlet in the Koppies residence occupied by our music and choir mistress, Faith Wilson. She had seen a very large cobra slither under her bed. Knowing that cobras can rear up and are able to spit very accurately, often aiming for one's eyes, I went to her aid well-prepared, wearing my gum boots, tracksuit pants, dark glasses and brandishing my trusty hockey stick. I managed to coax the cobra from under Faith's bed and steered it onto the Koppies lawn where it became very aggressive. With so many little boys accommodated in close proximity, I felt it wise to allow one of the brave young Zulu stable hands to kill it.

In the early days of Treverton, I remember how Errol Pietersen was given permission by Huddy to build a snake pit near the tennis courts down Hawthorne Avenue. Who will ever forget the uproar in The Cavern dormitory when Errol's prized collection of snakes escaped from his pillowcase whilst the snake pit was being cleaned. Some of us had to rescue hysterical cleaning staff and laundry maids who had sought refuge on the tops of boys' cupboards and lockers.

Our foundation pupils will remember that at one stage we actually had more pet animals at Treverton than boarders! One of the first Treverton pets was a much-adored pig called Percy who caused havoc when he gate crashed Lyn's 21st birthday tea party in the Little Thatch staff room.

Lyn had provided a marvellous spread which was laid out on low coffee tables. Suddenly Percy, an uninvited guest, burst in unexpectedly and made straight for Lyn's beautifully decorated 21st cake complete with dainty silver bells and delicate iced flowers. Lyn dived swiftly in Percy's direction and held her cake aloft, but Percy, dribbling and snorting, bulldozed his way between her legs! Only an action video would adequately capture the ensuing scene as Lyn, riding Percy bare back and clutching her birthday cake for dear life, was transported through the door, leaving staff members howling with mirth. We all chased Percy round the soccer field until he ran out of steam. Thankfully the birthday girl had managed to jump off his back with her cake still intact.

Imagine the stir caused on the Treverton campus when we woke one morning to hear that Percy had produced a litter of 10 cute little wrinkly pink piglets. Realising this was a serious case of mistaken identity, the little owner of Percy performed an impromptu christening ceremony and we were all introduced to our new friend Percelia!

Steven Kolb from Cape Town was one of the first to introduce us to his gentle pet goat. Many past pupils will also remember the pet Jersey bull calf called Bull's Eye who was amicable to begin with, but later turned vindictive towards certain members of staff. For some reason Bull's Eye targeted Mr John Howard, the Std 4 master, and chased him up a tall oak tree near the stables. I can still hear John croaking fearfully through a parched throat from one of the top branches, "Can bulls climb trees!"

One year there was torrential summer rain in the Natal Midlands and the Mooi River burst its banks in a most spectacular way. The back road leading from Treverton down past the tennis courts and into the village was flooded and remained impassable for days. Down in the village only the tips of the soccer and rugby posts were visible. Mr Huddy gave us permission to take our classes to view the flood damage. The river resembled a beautiful shimmering lake and looked inviting on a hot summer's day. My class pleaded with me to be allowed to have a quick dip to cool off in their "jocks." I tucked up my skirt and waded in with them.

Suddenly Raymond K. screamed a chilling warning.

"Snake! Miss Taylor, snake!" I spun round just in the nick of time, because a very large cobra was writhing its way across the flood waters at lightning speed in my direction! I stood on tiptoe, hanging onto my skirt for dear life and then as the snake came shooting towards me, I lifted my right leg as high as I dared and the cobra shot between my legs. The boys gasped at the speed of the Cobra, then without delay they gallantly grabbed my arms and together we splashed our way to the water's edge in record time.

Lyn and I found the winters in Mooi River particularly challenging. Our rooms were very cold and we had to dash along a draughty passage to reach the bathroom we shared. I shall never forget a second frosty night when the water in the tumbler beside my bed again froze solid. We heard next morning from locals in the village that for the residents of Mooi River it had been their "coldest night in living memory!" We headed straight down to buy simple bar heaters for our bedrooms from Mr Desai's shop which sold absolutely everything and reminded me of Mrs Keyter's General Dealer shop in Pacaltsdorp. We needn't have stocked up with toiletries for six months before coming to Treverton because there was a wonderful little Pharmacy opposite the Post Office managed by a charming couple called Robin and Denise Philp. There was a highly efficient Barclays Bank just up the road and a United Building Society on the opposite side. Knowles was a fine, well-stocked Supermarket and the boys could purchase all their clothing requirements at the Mooi River Outfitters. Mrs Huddy's Mom, Mrs Oosthuisen, affectionately called "Mrs O" was Matron of a school hostel at St. Stithians College, but moved down to Mooi River to be close to the Huddies and to offer practical help wherever possible in their new venture. In her retirement years she became manageress of a delightful little shop, called Femina Fashions, close to the chemist and the bottle store. Before long the mothers of Transvaal and Durban boarders were supporting Femina Fashions which very quickly earned an excellent reputation.

In the midst of all the school adventures and the fun and the laughter, there were very sad times at Treverton too. During a school holiday in his first year as a boarder at Treverton, one of Lyn Gowar's precious little pupils, Mark Torr, aged just 9, was killed in a tragic tractor accident on his parents' farm at Nottingham Road. In just two school terms we had grown to love this affectionate, warm-hearted and very caring little boy from our junior dormitory and Mark's tragic and untimely death left an aching hole in all our hearts.

After two years as house mothers to the little chaps in our care in the Chicken Run dormitory, Lyn and I were overjoyed to be allocated larger and warmer accommodation right behind the Koppies dormitory which was a spacious old house dating back to the Peter Binns era.

We each had a much cosier bedroom and a small adjoining lounge cum study, and best of all, our rooms had wooden floors! A few years later, Meridy Seabrook and her ginger cat, Sandy Seabrook, who disliked men, moved in alongside and we ladies shared the bathroom and toilet. Meridy arrived at Treverton while I was on long leave at the end of 1968. To start with, we were all rather in awe of her because she looked stern and peered at us over her spectacles. She kept her hair very short back and sides and wore men's broad black lace up shoes because she had undergone surgery to all her toes. At first she was very formal and asked us to call her Miss Seabrook!

However, in no time at all she had thawed and we soon discovered that her bark was far worse than her bite. She was a highly efficient book keeper and actually had a very kind heart. After 6 months at Treverton, she gave us permission to call her Meridy. She herself had a powerful soprano voice and successfully trained a delightful little junior choir called The Songsters whom she very proudly drove in the school bus to sing at various Natal churches.

She often rewarded her little Songsters by taking them for an ice cream treat and a swim at one of the Durban beaches before driving them back to Treverton.

I still waken some nights and re-live the 2 am knock on my bedroom door when Huddy had the awful task of coming to tell me that our good friend and much-loved colleague, History teacher, choir master and House Master, Colin Kreusch, had been killed in a road accident, on the N3 highway close to the Lion Park, at exit 65 just 18km outside Pietermaritzburg on 22 April 1971.

Colin was only 28 and had been back in the country just five months having completed his Master's degree in Clinical Psychology in Louisville Kentucky, USA. Upon his return to South Africa he was training the Treverton choir and had prepared very special items for our Founders' Day in May, but instead the choir had the sad task of singing at Colin's very moving memorial service held in his home church, First Baptist in East London.

RUTH STOTT

Something amazing took place not long after Colin's untimely death.His cousin Jeff Fetting and his wife Joy, arrived from East London and proved a wonderful asset to the school. Jeff was a talented sportsman and besides having a teaching qualification, he was a Theology graduate. Joy served as the Treverton nursing sister and Jeff later became the Prep. school Headmaster.Who will ever forget the excitement when the Fettings heard they could hasten to East London to adopt a precious little baby daughter whom they named Nicola.

Just a few years later Nicky welcomed a baby brother, Jonathan, whom we chose to call Jonty when he was little.

I remember the thrill of helping Jeff and Joy decorate the brand new nursery. Our pupils clapped and cheered as they lined the drive way. The trees were festooned with balloons, streamers and banners as Jeff and Joy returned twice from East London with very precious cargo on board!

Just two years before Colin's tragic death, Jessie Anderson, a Cape Town teacher friend and old school pal of mine, and I had the joy of touring the United States with Colin and another well -loved Treverton College member of staff, called Leigh Bradfield. Colin was studying at a Seminary in Louisville Kentucky, not too far from Leigh who was also completing a Master's degree at Columbus University in the state of Ohio. Colin had written to suggest that whilst enjoying long leave, I bring a friend to the USA to spend part of the summer vacation touring with them. Colin and Leigh had each bought a Ford Mustang car when they arrived in America for their two year period of study. They were astounded to discover that for the equivalent of 2 500 South African Rands in US dollars, they could purchase spanking new streamlined sports models. Bearing in mind the favourable exchange rate in 1969, that amount of money in South Africa would only have paid for a very basic Datsun 1200 sedan.

It was very exciting for Jessie and me to take turns driving each of the cars and then to relax and view the scenery as passengers alongside either Leigh or Colin. Just before he left to study in America, Leigh had taught me to drive his little bottle green Volkswagen Beetle. Mooi

River was a perfect place to practise driving skills as there were numerous off the beaten tracks and one of the best open spaces was the polo field when there wasn't a tournament in progress!

I remember how the College boys ragged me on the morning of my driving test. It was a freezing cold morning in June but to make quite sure that the engine survived the night and would perform well for my test, I had very lovingly covered the bonnet of Leigh's Volkswagen with three thick blankets! Now that was a very Blonde thing to do seeing that the engine is where you would expect to find the boot! (trunk of the car)

It was great being on leave in America while our friends Colin and Leigh were starting their summer vacation. We set out on our US adventure in July 1969 starting in Ontario Canada, where Leigh kindly fetched Jessie and me from my aunt and uncle's home in the town of Lindsay in the Kawartha Lakes region. Together we toured down the beautiful eastern seaboard of the USA, through the New England States, down through the southern states described as The Bible Belt, where Colin joined us in his own car. We travelled vast distances on excellent highways, encountering considerate and law abiding road users. We visited the mental institution in Tuscaloosa Alabama where Colin had just completed his semester of practical clinical and counselling practice. We loved the friendliness and warmth of Mississippi, Louisiana and Texas, then we swung west heading through New Mexico, Arizona and ending our tour in Las Vegas, in the state of Nevada. Las Vegas was a real eye opener!

We had a narrow escape way down south when we heard on the car radios that a massive Category 5 hurricane was heading towards the Gulf area of the USA. We had just had a great time staying in an excellent camp site and exploring New Orleans. Colin and Leigh very wisely decided that we should forfeit our stay in that area and head to the west as quickly as possible. The very next day Hurricane Camille (No, not Camilla!) struck with a vengeance causing widespread devastation throughout Mississippi and Louisiana, which resulted in severe flooding in the nearby states of Virginia and West Virginia.

We went icy cold from head to toe when we watched horrific scenes on our motel TV in the days that followed and saw the very same tourist spots which we had visited only hours before Camille's brutal onslaught.

Mountainous waves had swamped the coastal US Highway 90 which we had driven the day before. The massive breakers had flattened the very beach front roadhouse where we had paused to enjoy our lunch time snacks.

Imagine our shock to hear once we were back home in South Africa, that the 1969 Atlantic hurricane season had been the most active season since way back in 1933. Sadly hurricane Camille left 259 men, woman and children dead and carved a path of destruction through countless homes, shops, churches and schools. The rain which followed caused widespread flooding and treacherous mudslides. We heard on the TV that in the Gulf of Mexico the waves had reached 21 metres in height (70 ft) which is close to tsunami proportions.

Marge Hudson –Reed and her daughter Jenny, Treverton's first female pupil!

19

FACE TO FACE WITH THE MOON MEN

On a much happier note, one of the biggest highlights of our summer vacation was being in Canada and America at the time of the first moon landing on 20 July 1969. We pinched ourselves to prove that we were not dreaming! There Jessie and I were, eyes glued to the TV set in my aunt and uncle's home in Lindsay, Ontario. We two visitors from South Africans were actually watching LIVE as the intrepid 38 year old Commander Neil Armstrong safely steered a rather flimsy looking bug- shaped four-legged lunar module, close to an area now known as The Sea of Tranquility. We both gasped aloud as Armstrong boldly announced to the spellbound world, "The eagle has landed!" It was some six hours later, that Armstrong opened the exit hatch, planted the very first human footprint on the rock-strewn lunar crust and triumphantly mouthed his never-to-be-forgotten words "That's one small step for Man, one giant leap for Mankind."

As we watched those heart-stopping moments in full colour on T.V. Jessie and I were enthralled. Time stood still. We kept vigil with the family all night, not wanting to miss one single step of that momentous moon adventure as it unravelled. Back home in South Africa, television had not yet been introduced to our country. It saddened us that our families and friends were missing this ground-breaking Event.

What a momentous day it was in South Africa when our country eventually received limited TV viewing in 1976. Like us, you may recall sitting back in your lounge and watching the test patterns and flickering squiggles on the screen just because TV was still such a novelty!

Neil Armstrong spent a little more than two hours plodding across the surface of the moon with great big strides, collecting samples of lunar soil and testing his ability to move about freely in a cumbersome white spacesuit. We sensed it was not easy for him to commute whilst under the influence of lunar gravity which we understand is one- sixth of that which we experience on our earth! How proud President Nixon and the America nation must have felt seeing Neil Armstrong plant their Star- Spangled Banner on the moon.

And then even more exciting for Colin, Leigh, Jessie and me was the thrill of travelling way down south to Texas, to actually see with our own eyes, the entire Apollo 11 crew, Neil Armstrong, pilot Buzz Aldrin and Michael Collins, 3 larger than life heroes on 16 August 1969 during a ticker tape parade held in their honour in Downtown Houston, Texas.

As we hastened from the parking area towards the seething colourful crowd of Moon Men admirers all hoping to find a good vantage point, the clapping and jubilant cheering became deafening. Hearing our "foreign" accents, and noticing Colin and Leigh wearing short shorts and not American style Bermuda three-quarter shorts, hospitable Americans made way for us and pushed us right to the front. As the astronauts drew closer, travelling in open Mustang sports cars, we realised they had their proud families with them.

They passed by just an arm's length away and our cameras clicked wildly as they actually smiled and waved in our direction. It was an emotional moment for us as we saw their wives and children beaming alongside their very own space Heroes. We realized afresh the extreme tension and anxiety their families must have faced.

There was more excitement ahead. The Parade's Master of Ceremony was none other than Frank Sinatra! The Houston crowd erupted as he sang Fly Me to the Moon! We heard later that as Apollo 11 touched down safely on Tranquility Base, Buzz Aldrin grabbed an audio cassette and played this song. It is not surprising then that this hit sung by "Ol' Blue Eyes" is regarded as the unofficial NASA space song!

Colourful bunting flapped in the gentle breeze. Lamp posts were festooned with balloons and huge posters of the courageous moon men were displayed everywhere. Suddenly windows high up were flung open and down from the tall buildings floated clouds of fake dollars, marked Moon Dollars, each note bearing the faces and signatures of the astronauts. The four of us joined in the bun fight as we eagerly leapt high and scrambled low amongst the frenzied crowd, all attempting to dive through legs in order to grab some of the coveted souvenir bank notes while they were still fluttering to the ground.

We were astonished to learn that upon their return to Earth, and having splashed down in the Pacific Ocean, the moon men had to face some mundane red tape. They actually had to pass through Customs at the Honolulu Airport in Hawaii and declare their moon dust, moon rocks and other intriguing lunar specimens. Furthermore, instead of having spontaneous and joyous reunions with family and friends, Armstrong, Aldrin and Collins were whisked away in special containment suits to be closely monitored in quarantine and in isolation for three weeks, just in case they imported back to Earth any strange moon diseases, germs or lunar bacteria.

What an anti-climax this must have been. Being in the midst of a world-wide Covid pandemic, we can sympathise and identify with the moonmen and their families, having learnt what it means to be in lockdown and to experience the loneliness of self-isolation during quarantine.

Back at Treverton in time for the fourth quarter, I was suddenly in great demand to share our travel adventures. One of the stories the school boys loved to hear, was about a very close eye-ball to eye-ball encounter with a hungry black bear. Our adventure took place in the beautiful Great Smoky Mountain National Park which is one of the largest protected areas in the eastern Unites States where black bears can still live in the wild. We had been warned that bears weighing over 600 pounds had often been seen in the Park. Colin and Leigh preferred to sleep on the reclining seats in their cars while we were touring the USA but Jessie and I slept in a small tent which we zipped closed at night.

We discovered the wonderful KOA campsites (Kampgrounds of America!) which were beautifully appointed and in 1969 we seldom paid more than $10 a night for space to pitch our little tent. The campsites are family owned and run, with the owners choosing to live on site. We found the sites follow strict standards of cleanliness and maintenance and we were hugely impressed by the spotless restrooms (sometimes called Comfort Stations!) where we enjoyed hot showers and hygienic toilets.

On our first night at a very pleasant campsite in the Great Smoky Mountains, Jessie and I were enjoying our hot showers when a friendly American voice drawled from another cubicle, "Hi folks, How ya all doin?" The kind lady who called out in such a welcoming manner was obviously intrigued by our South African accents and promptly welcomed us warmly to the USA and passed a candy bar over the wooden partition in the shower cubicle. We were tickled pink when Americans enjoyed listening to our speech and said, "You guys have such cute British accents!"

On our second night in the Park we had a good old South African braai (barbecue) and deposited our garbage into the very large bin close to our tent. At about 3am I felt Jessie tugging at my sleeping bag. I rolled over and reached for my penlight torch. Jessie's face was pale and her frightened eyes were like saucers and I guessed she must have been having a nightmare. She signalled me to be very quiet and leaned across to whisper "Black bear!"

I was about to unzip our tent flap to investigate when we both heard a chilling sound. A black bear was making very loud chomping noises right outside our little tent! We could picture the bear smacking its lips! I slipped out of my sleeping bag and crawled towards the tent flap, camera in hand.

Jessie slunk back into her sleeping bag and drew it right up to her neck. We both realised how vulnerable we were. We were only separated from the black bear by a flimsy sheet of canvas. Bears have sharp claws and become aggressive when confronted. Upon entering the Park, we had been given a helpful pamphlet entitled The Bear Facts.

What you need to know.

- Bears have a very keen sense of smell, 7 times more powerful than dogs!
- Bears are very inquisitive and intelligent.
- Bears are nervous and can cause serious injury if startled or cornered.
- Bears become bold when hungry. They may be attracted to females menstruating or wearing perfume.
- Bears can climb, run or swim up to 35 mph!
- Stay alert and advertise your presence by rattling a tin of marbles or pebbles.
- If approached by a bear, look him straight in the eye, back away slowly; keep talking to the bear softly so that he knows you are a human and not another bear!
- Curl up in a ball and play possum if the bear catches up with you!
- An effective bear spray is available at outdoor sports and camping retailers. You may use it on the bear as you would use pepper spray.

Jessie and I were beginning to feel helpless. It was 3am. We had no empty tin, no marbles to rattle and no bear spray. Fortunately we had probably showered off the fragrance of our perfume. Jessie suggested I unzip the tent flap just one inch from the top to take a quick peep. Would the bear try and claw his way into our little tent? The black bear was staring straight at me. I quite forgot that I was meant to talk to him very softly so that he would know I was a human and not a rival. Would talking to him in Afrikaans or isiXhosa have told him that I was definitely not from his Clan! Then mercifully he turned his big broad back on our tent and focussed his attention once more on the contents of the garbage can. He seemed happy to have found our chop bones and was tucking in with gusto. Whew, what a relief it was for us when he gave a kind of farewell grunt and plodded off to check our neighbours' bin. Jessie and I dived deep into our sleeping bags and we both played possum until daybreak!

Sunday was Letter Writing day at Treverton. The boys would retire quietly to their classrooms for just one hour before lunch time and were encouraged to send home happy, positive weekly news to assure their families that all was well. The duty teacher for the day would circulate between classrooms checking that letters were neatly written. We "censored" letters purely to check on neatness and to discover whether boys were settling happily or were showing signs of homesickness. Some little fellows wrote "whoppers" in order to get their indulgent moms to 'phone more frequently or to post them bigger tuck boxes! Sometimes it was hard to keep a straight face when letters were checked. One rather pampered little boy of eight wrote, "Mommy, I am sew sad and mizribble without you hear. I have not eatin for one hole weak and Miss Taylor smakked me on my bottim with her little stik called Toby Taylor."

Another wrote, "Mrs Huddy has a dizeeze called pink eye and it is very itchy but she is still alive." Yet another wrote, "Jenny Hudson-Reed has a girl horse called Dawn and she unexpectedly gave birth to a fowl in the middle of the night." Then there was the goody- goody who wrote, "Last night we saw a very funny film in the dining room called Bottoms Up but don't worry, Mommy, it wasn't a rude film."

Little boys often caused embarrassment to innocent visitors. One weekend I had visitors from the UK staying at a local hotel and they were very keen to see Treverton and to meet my friends. They were lovely refined folk, with a double barrel surname and in England would be described as being "Top Drawer" people! I was on duty that weekend and explained to the little chaps in the Koppies dorm that I would like them to be on their best behaviour as I would be showing very important overseas guests round the school. I told them that the visitors had sent their own children to very famous schools in England and would be interested to see how we behave!

It was time for the boys' regular after lunch thirty minute rest period. All the boarders were required to lie down and have a nap or read their library books in silence. I was taking the visitors on a little tour of the dormitories and upon entering Koppies, Mrs Gelbart-Smith spotted a dear little boy cuddled up under a blanket reading a book about steam trains. "Hello my dear," she said in a very friendly voice. "That looks like an absolutely splendid book. You know I too adore steam trains!"

Nine year old Winston from Durban warmed to Doris immediately and in a delightful little voice piped up, "Good afternoon. Are you the very posh lady from England? Miss Taylor told us your son went to a very posh school too!" On another occasion there was an embarrassing moment when some standard eight boys were housed temporarily in the Koppies dormitory. I was crossing the front lawn to access my flat which was situated behind the dormitory. Evening Prep had ended and it was bath and shower time. This was always a happy, relaxed and rather rowdy time. It was a very chilly June evening, but suddenly out through the open front door of Koppies, as if doing an exhilarating ski jump, burst Iain P. on a skate board. He was completely naked having whizzed down the linoleum clad passage at high speed. Iain was unable to brake in time and virtually went into orbit when he saw me.

Very sheepishly he scooped up his skate board and using it in lieu of a fig leaf, fled back into the protective steam of the boys' bathroom.

Films were shown as a special Saturday night treat and there were long intervals when films had to be rewound manually, from reel to reel, on those enormous metal reels. Sometimes the roll of plastic film would snap abruptly and the teacher in charge would have to try and splice the reel or push through the next piece of film. During these intervals, there was always a mad scramble to get to the lockers where tuck boxes were stored. Our vice principal at the time, was Mr Jim Warner, an upright Christian gentleman who was strong on family values and purity of heart and mind. He would sometimes see fit to slip his hand over the lens to censor scenes where there was kissing or cuddling and one would hear disappointed sighs, ah's and groans coming from the older boys.

Mrs Huddy and her elder son, Donald, ran a very popular school tuck shop once a week. An exciting array of treats was displayed in the library and boys purchased great bargains for the 10 cents pocket money permitted each week. Hot favourites were the bull's eyes with a lovely peppermint flavour, black balls previously called by another improper name, jelly beans, gob stoppers, liquorice mice, Caramac and Twix chocolate bars and the ever popular sherbet which sizzled on your tongue as you sucked it through a little straw and pretended you were smoking. Possibly the best value of all for just one cent, was a lovely chewy pink, yellow or white marshmallow fish, coated with a generous dusting of icing sugar. I still haven't worked out why South Africa children insist on saying "marshmellows."

Neil Armstrong with his family in green Mustang at Houston Parade

Excitement as crowds cheer the moon men in ticker tape parade

Apollo space craft displayed at Houston

Black bear outside our tent in the dead of night

20

NEVER A DULL MOMENT

*I*n the first few years our staff complement grew as the Treverton enrolment increased. We were able to spread the load and share hostel duties.

Because most us were single and still in our early 20's, and were far from home, we were drawn together and became a close- knit group, enjoying great times of spirited camaraderie as we enjoyed outings, shared picnics and weekends away. Several romances blossomed and were nurtured at Treverton. Bill Webster married Mary Anderson and Jack Dyer, the handyman married the nursing sister Kath Filby. A favourite destination for off duty weekends was the El Mirador hotel near Winterton in the Drakensberg. This delightful family owned hotel with thatched rondawels was run by Roland and Coral Smith, whose son Herbie went on to become a head boy at Treverton.

El Mirador has changed hands several times and is now known as Champagne Sports Resort. During our weekend getaways there we rode horses, played tennis, attempted lawn bowls and did exhilarating mountain hikes.

An exciting climbing expedition started with a two hour drive to Witsieshoek, which prior to 1994 was in a small homeland, known as a "bantustan." It had the fascinating name of QwaQwa! You need to pronounce the name with a good loud click on the Q. We were fascinated to hear how QwaQwa was named. Because there was so often thick snow on the Drakensberg peaks, the San people living in the area called it QwaQwa meaning "whiter than white!"

The name of its capital was even more intriguing. If you wear dentures, you need to hang onto them while you practise saying this name, PHUTHADITJHABA!

After 1994 this previously self-governed area comprising 655 square km, became re-integrated into South Africa as part of the eastern Free State province.

One July holiday my brother invited our mom and my friend, Margaret, who married my brother 3 years later, and me to join him and a couple of his Stellenbosch friends on an exciting climb in the Drakensberg. Our aim was to reach the summit of the Sentinel peak, to sleep in the cave and to explore the top of the Amphitheatre and be inspired by one of the most breath-taking views in the world. We were keen to see the Tugela Falls, considered the world's second highest waterfall, which plunge a distance of 948 metres into the Tugela valley below. We were promised that we were bound to see a variety of large birds of prey along our 12 km hiking trail. The school boys were keen to catch a glimpse of the Bearded Vulture, also known as the Lammergeier.

We parked our cars at Witsieshoek and began the first part of the initial climb. We followed a clearly defined trail and then slowly wound our way round the rocky outcrop appropriately named "The Witches," then trekked up a series of steep zig zags which eventually brought us close to the foot of the chain ladders. Dave and I were enormously proud of our mom for scaling the precipitous steel ladder which rises to 3000 metres. She opted to spend the night in the cave on the Sentinel summit in honour of her 60th birthday. It was freezing cold and in spite of Dave stoking the fire through the night to warm the cave, five of us battled to drop off to sleep. Mom slept like a log and in the morning we discovered her secret. She had very wisely put her

Icelandic down duvet inside another equally warm sleeping bag which, as a seasoned mountain climber, she kept referring to as her "flea bag!"

And believe it or not, the very next week our spunky mom trekked down the immense Fish River Canyon in the south of Namibia with my brother, David, and a party of his senior pupils from the Paul Roos Gymnasium in Stellenbosch.

The Canyon is estimated to be over 500 million years old and is the largest canyon in Africa. Mom's feet were badly blistered but she managed the 90 km trail in spite of pessimistic folk telling her they had lost their toenails on the steep descent and that you have to shove cotton wool into your ears at night to stop insects and bugs from exploring your auricle and auditory canal!

All those years ago, I never dreamt that 23 years later, on 9 January 2001, in my mid 50's, I would be back at El Mirador, my favourite Drakensberg weekend getaway haven, now called Champagne Sports Resort. I had chosen this idyllic spot to marry Joe Stott, a charming Lancashire widower. Joe had been the principal trombone player in the Central Band of the Royal Air Force until he and his English wife, Jean, and their two younger children immigrated to South Africa in 1975. Joe then joined the CAPAB orchestra (Cape Performing Arts Board) and up until his retirement, he performed with the orchestra in what was then known as the Nico Malan Opera House and later became the Artscape Theatre.

The morning of our wedding in the Drakensberg seemed almost like a fairy tale....

At 11am on a sparking summer morning, Joe and I stood side by side and hands tightly clasped as we made our sacred wedding vows in the picturesque little thatched chapel at El Mirador.

The front of the church has a huge glass window facing the towering mountain range. From inside, everyone has a breathtaking panoramic view of Champagne Castle and Cathkin Peak. Holding the massive glass pane securely in place, is a simple wooden cross. As we gazed in awe at the beauty of the Champagne valley and marvelled at the

Handiwork of our Creator, it seemed so fitting that we had chosen as the opening hymn for our wedding service, the well-loved favourite, How Great Thou Art!

The little chapel was filled to capacity and we were surrounded by 60 close family members and very dear friends who had travelled from Durban, Pietermaritzburg, Cape Town, London and Frankfurt! What a joy it was to have "Huddy," my Treverton headmaster and his wife Marge, to share our wedding day with us. Little did I realise that just two years later, my beloved founder headmaster would succumb to cancer. His widow Marge, who cared for us like a surrogate mother when we arrived at Treverton in 1964 as brand new teachers, has soldiered on bravely into her 89th year and recently moved into a Care Home in Pietermaritzburg.

Many friends said how deeply moved they felt when they saw my beloved old mom, Muriel, aged 84, beaming from ear to ear as she escorted me rather shakily down the aisle to meet my bridegroom. My brother, David, supported mom as we walked, because she had been discharged from the cardiac Intensive Care Unit just the day before to fly from Cape Town to Durban. Mom was overjoyed that we had chosen the 'Berg as our wedding venue and was determined not to miss the occasion in spite of failing health. As a young girl she and her family travelled from their home in Kimberley to spend many July holidays climbing in the Drakensberg where her father, Herbert Liddle, nicknamed Oompie by his climbing pals, has a 2,871 m peak called Mount Oompie named after him. It's close to the towering Sentinel Peak and the treacherous looking Devil's Tooth.

As I gazed in awe through the chapel window at Champagne Castle and the surrounding peaks, my mind strayed and I recalled how our dearly loved headmaster, Mr Huddy, together with some intrepid Treverton boys and hardy male members of staff, had climbed those very same peaks and slept in caves in mid -winter with thick snow piled up at the entrance. They told of their joy and exhilaration at summiting challenging peaks like Sterkhorn (Mount Memory) and seeing milky- coloured frozen rivers and waterfalls with dagger-like stalactites plunging into deep gorges.

Back in the 1960's we young founder Treverton teachers soon learnt to adjust to late nights as we managed the preparation of lessons, marking of books and making apparatus and visual aids to use in the classroom to make our lessons more meaningful. If we were burning the midnight oil, Huddy would be doing his late night rounds checking on security in the dorms. He would tap on our windows and call out in a fatherly way, "Time for bed now!"

Sometimes Elijah, the faithful old Zulu Night Watchman, would be on his beat and would suddenly press his nose against our window panes and startle us by shining his laser- like torch into our bedrooms to check that all was well.

The Treverton boys had no idea of the fun and games that their spunky young teachers were having on their off duty nights once the boarders were snugly tucked up. I remember how we piled into Bill Webster's little blüe Volkswagen Beetle one Friday night and spent an exciting time racing each other at the Go Kart circuit at the Blue Lagoon in Durban North and then enjoying late night double thick malted chocolate milkshakes at The Tropicale drive-thru restaurant next to Albert Park. If I close my eyes, I can still picture the great big fat plastic straws we were given. We had to suck extra hard but were well rewarded. I shall never forget the glorious, rich, malted chocolatey taste and the extra creamy texture of those double thick treats from that very popular roadhouse. Plastic straws had only just been invented in the 1960's so were a novelty to us but sadly those fat straws would not have pleased the world's environmentalists for they were definitely not re-cyclable!

Isn't it sad that Drive-In movie theatres have disappeared! When I was teaching Afrikaans at Treverton I would take a bus load of boys to the Estcourt Drive-In whenever hilarious films were on circuit. Some of the favourite bilingual movies of that era were Lord Oom Piet, Dirkie, Kruger Miljoene and Fratse in die Vloot! The much- admired South African movie stars I remember from the 1960's era were Jamie Uys, Bob Courtney, Jan Bruyns, Madeleine Usher, Juliet Prowse, Gert van den Bergh and the hilarious Al Debbo.

Lyn and I were able to pursue our love for hockey in our free weekends. She joined the Mooi River Country Club where ladies and men played mixed hockey and very often a braaivleis (barbecue) and a friendly social would follow the match. Lyn made friends with some delightful Mooi River residents, many of whom farmed close to Treverton.

Mary Webster, the music teacher and I joined a Pietermaritzburg ladies' hockey club called Rippington. We shared transport and travelled to mid- week practices and Saturday afternoon league matches.

I kept my burgundy hockey skirt and socks for years as a practice outfit for coaching hockey, just to remind me of those happy Rippington times.

Huddy encouraged his staff to start Clubs and Societies and to introduce the boys to hobbies and absorbing pastimes. I shall never forget the thrill of seeing a packed chapel of little boys, bubbling over with enthusiasm, all bathed and showered and warmly clad in pyjamas and gowns one Thursday night. It was the inaugural meeting of the J.C.A. or Junior Christian Association. We aimed to present the Christian message to the boys in a dynamic, down- to -earth way, giving them practical hints on handling life as young people living in a challenging world. Scripture quizzes took the form of Prick- A - Balloon or Pick a Box shows. The prep. school boys sang their favourite hymns and choruses lustily, with Lyn or Mary providing rousing piano accompaniment.

Another of my clubs was the Pioneering Club where together we learnt how to erect a tent, prepare for wet weather when camping, make camp stew, brew coffee in a Billy can, prepare an outdoor fire and bake stokbrood. (bread on a stick) I also taught the boys practical first aid and other useful methods of surviving outdoors. I think we might have done very well as a Treverton team participating in the ever popular TV show Survivor South Africa, but filmed mid- winter in Mooi River, rather than in tropical Malaysia!

Huddy taught his young staff members to play squash and we were able to use the courts belonging to the Mooi River Country Club and several of the male members of staff tried their hand at golf.

A favourite pastime that provided great excitement during weekends was rapid shooting down the Mooi River. The local farmers kindly supplied us with old tractor tubes which if punctured, Huddy helped the boys to patch. It was advisable to wear old shirts and pants for this venture as the strong currents swirled you over rocks and submerged logs at considerable speed. Tests were done regularly and we were assured that our section of the Mooi River was free of bilharzia, which we knew was a problem in other areas of Natal. During the summer rainy season there were exciting whirlpools, deep potholes and scoured out cauldrons to negotiate and staff members were always present to supervise. To be allowed to rapid shoot, boys had to first prove that they were able swimmers because they were promised thrills and spills galore.

A memorable Float-arama was organized one hot summer's afternoon when boys challenged staff members to build rafts and race them downstream.

Who will ever forget our indefatigable school secretary, Miss Rita Burdett, proudly launching her raft with the Treverton flag waving merrily on a tall mast. Her happy, yapping family of corgis had been hoisted safely aboard and were tottering around her in excitement, with their pink tongues wagging enthusiastically. Rita's raft was a masterpiece, made with 4 tractor tubes spliced together and covered with a neat platform of bamboo poles. All went well to start with and Rita and her gallant little team of corgis was well in the lead until a surging current swirled her off course. Sadly she and her valiant corgi supporters suddenly found themselves marooned on an island in the middle of the swollen river.

At this point Mr Huddy swished past Rita on his brightly decorated tractor tube and he crossed the finishing line just ahead of a cluster of bedraggled looking but jubilant Prep school mariners.

Soon after Rita's raft ran aground and her sad elimination from the Float- arama, she became a real hero in the eyes of all the school boys. It was because of an unfortunate mishap which occurred in chapel one morning. Each staff member took a turn to lead devotions on a different day of the week. We tried to make our talks as practical and dynamic as possible, giving boys sound Godly principles for daily living. Many of us chose to use visual aids and some even dressed up to illustrate vital points. Rita was a spinster in her 60's but was great at attracting the boys' attention and winning their confidence by sharing stories of her own school days in England. She told the boys how she had played cricket for Cheltenham Ladies' College.

This impressed them no end and their attention was riveted as she demonstrated how she had been a spin bowler in the first team. Just at that dramatic moment, as she brought the cricket ball down fast over her right shoulder, the zip in her tweed skirt let her down badly and all was revealed! There stood Rita, without a petticoat and in all her glory, clad in sensible pink flannel bloomers. Being a true gentleman, Mr Huddy, who was seated up front, covered his eyes and looked away. The boys were convulsed and we staff members didn't know where to look. But Rita's reaction was incredible. As she retrieved her skirt from the chapel floor and yanked it up over her ample hips, she very sportingly said, "All right chaps, let's all have a good laugh! It serves me right for not wearing a petticoat! Perhaps someone can go and find me a good strong safety pin and then I'll finish what I was saying."

I seem to remember that it was Kath Filby, our school nursing sister from Cape Town, who obliged and hastened to Rita's rescue. That was one chapel talk no one will ever forget! The message? Keep your eyes on the goal!

We staff members were a pretty healthy bunch and from time to time we received challenges to play against the boys' sports teams. The matches were played in a light-hearted spirit and I still have a vivid memory of our school secretary Rita, once again, game for anything, volunteering to play hockey "goalie" and being armed with a garden rake and a broom to help her sweep the ball away from the goal posts. In a rugby match against the Under 13 Treverton team I played wing but the little boys were too gentlemanly to tackle me and I managed to burst through their ranks and scored my first ever try close to the corner flag!

To reward good behaviour, Lyn and I sometimes allowed the boys in The Chicken Run to have midnight feasts. It was freezing cold in winter so some little chaps donned thick woollen balaclava caps and climbed into their sleeping bags while they tucked into their sardines and condensed milk. The boys were always fascinated when I told them the name Balaclava came from the use of this clever headdress at the Battle of Balaclava during the Crimean War when unique protective caps were sent over from Britain in 1854 to help keep the heads and faces of the embattled troops warm.

Strangely enough members of the Russian feminist protest Punk Rock band called Pussy Riot choose to wear balaclavas to hide their identities!

The mention of balaclavas tied in beautifully with our History lessons about Florence Nightingale who took a team of 38 volunteer nurses to care for the British soldiers fighting in the Crimean War. Tragically it was whilst visiting soldiers at Balaclava, that The Lady with the Lamp developed a dreadful bacterial infection that became chronic, caused no doubt by the unsanitary conditions she encountered. Over the years her strength was sapped and she never fully recovered and it is quite amazing after all she had endured, that she actually lived till 90!

Lyn and I both celebrated our 21st birthdays at Treverton. Lyn treated us to a superb dinner at Rawdons Hotel, situated in a lush and serene setting in Nottingham Road, in the heart of the Natal Midlands. The thatched buildings, rolling lawns and beautifully laid out gardens gave us a sense of being in a charming little village in England with a timeless country atmosphere. Just the kind of tranquil English country setting you might enjoy if like us, you love watching Midsomer Murders or the Vicar of Dibley!

With my birthday being close to the beginning of the school year, I was able to celebrate it whilst still on holiday in Cape Town. My parents organized a braai (barbecue) for family and friends at the beautiful home of our widow friend, Marcelle Kolb, in Rondebosch. She lovingly opened her heart and her home and thirty of us enjoyed her warm and caring hospitality as we appreciated her attractive garden and swimming pool. Shortly afterwards Marcelle made the decision to send her son Steven to Treverton. He loved animals and made a fine contribution in helping to increase the boys' pet population!

When my actual 21st birthday arrived on 6 February I wasn't expecting any special celebration but had the surprise of my life. When I walked into the staffroom at morning tea break I found parked in the centre of the room, an enormous box with my name and address on it. Everyone had gathered round to admire the beautiful wrapping paper and the massive bright pink satin bow. Suddenly the box started to wobble and sway sideways. There was a deathly hush.... then the lid popped open and out jumped my spunky mom, looking a little flushed in the face due to a shortage of oxygen!

Having shared her plans with the Huddies, my mom had planned a surprise train journey all the way to Mooi River on the Orange Express. And like Lyn and me, she too had arrived at the unearthly hour of 4:12 am that morning. Huddy had very kindly met her, but not in his Army great coat this time!

Mom had been smuggled into the Huddies flat where she enjoyed the warmth of their hospitality for a week-long visit. She was soon caught up in the happy Treverton family atmosphere and saw for herself exactly why Lyn and I loved every moment of our boarding school adventure.

We teachers enjoyed great companionship in the evenings. Once a week we had Staff Fellowship in the Huddies lounge where we shared practical Bible studies and enjoyed each other's company over a cup of tea or coffee. On cold nights there was a roaring log fire in the grate. A regular hearth -side attender or gate-crasher, at all staff meetings was Rover, the headmaster's pet bull mastiff. Unfortunately he embarrassed the Huddies no end by his after-dinner snores and grunts and worst of all, his gaseous emissions! It was at these regular fellowship evenings that we could relax and unload the burdens of the day and seek advice from our fellow colleagues. It was here that we experienced the power of prayer as we saw difficult boys responding to discipline or learning how unique and precious they are to their Creator.

I shall never forget the fun we teachers enjoyed one night when we had a biblical Fancy Dress! We each had to select a Bible verse, dress up accordingly and our colleagues had to figure out which text was being portrayed. Some clever costumes really stumped us. Mrs Huddy came in wearing a pretty dress and had added a dainty floral apron. She carried an oval china platter with one single lonely- looking meatball, known in South Africa as a "frikkadel," which was plonked in the centre. We were all flummoxed.

Imagine the mirth when Marge revealed that the Bible verse she had chosen was,

"Behold I shew you a mystery!"

— (King James Version. 1 Corinthians 15:51)

One never does quite know what goes into producing a meat ball or a mince patty!

No one could guess my verse either. I had borrowed the football outfit of one of the U13 boys, complete with his rather large studded boots. I padded my tummy and posterior and stuffed tennis balls into my sleeves and the back of my socks, creating very impressive biceps and calf muscles.

(I love the proper name given to those calf muscles. They are known as the gastrocnemius muscles yet have nothing to do with anything gastronomical.) My text came from the Old Testament. Deuteronomy 32: 15 where we read "Jeshurun waxed fat and kicked!" I discovered that "waxed fat" simply means he put on weight and became very bloated!

Dressed as Jeshurun I think I looked the part of a pretty solid Kwazulu Natal Sharks rugby prop!

It was exciting being part of a faith mission where our salaries were well below those of government school teachers. There were times when we were paid a little late, yet somehow we knew that because Treverton was involved in God's work in the lives of young people, He would always remain faithful to His labourers. I was overjoyed when I received my very first pay cheque. I'll never forget it was for the princely sum of R87! My bubble was burst when having donned my brand new Treverton staff blazer, I jauntily set off to cash my cheque at the local bank. A rather surly teller looked up and muttered, "Mmm, that's a lot of money for a little girl like you." I guess I did look young and unsophisticated for 19 and I remember feeling annoyed when elderly folk asked me what class I was in at school.

Later on when I was acting Head for Mr Huddy who was Mayor of Mooi River and Rotary Chairman, a prospective parent from Johannesburg popped in unexpectedly to view the school. He knocked on the Headmaster's door and seeing me seated at the desk he called out, "Hello girlie, is your daddy not in today?"

It was quite amazing how far my R87 salary stretched in those days. I was even able to save some of it because we received free accommodation in exchange for being house mistresses to the junior boys. In the Easter holidays in 1965 Lyn and I sailed home to Cape

Town from Durban on the Edinburgh Castle and paid little more than a train ticket would have cost us. It was one of the Union Castle mail ships, easily recognisable by its lavender coloured hull, and striking black and red funnels.

When my brother David and I were children, a favourite holiday outing would be a visit to the Cape Town docks on a Thursday afternoon to wave goodbye to the Union Castle Mail ship which always set sail for Southampton at 4pm. At exactly the same time, a sister ship would be leaving Southampton to sail south to Cape Town. The ship's band would play and the on- board passengers would yell down their goodbye's to those thronging the quayside.

Rolls of brightly coloured paper streamers would be flung down from above and we would hold on for dear life trying to keep the connection with those on board for as long as possible. It was a poignant moment when the fragile bond was finally severed. Then as busy little tugboats heaved and grunted as they edged the liner away from the packed quay, the ship gave one last melancholy blast. We watched with heavy hearts as our tattered streamers drifted down into the cold sea and our loved ones sailed on towards the Breakwater.....into Table Bay and then finally across the Atlantic Ocean to faraway Southampton.

Lyn and I shared a cosy two berth cabin on the Edinburgh Castle and enjoyed every moment of our coastal cruise from Durban to Cape Town. We hadn't bargained for such gigantic rollers as we travelled down the east coast towards East London. No wonder it's called the "Wild Coast!" We enjoyed the deck sports and table tennis, which was tricky because the ball would bounce in one direction, then a huge swell would rock the boat and the ping pong ball would shoot off in another direction.

After an absence of three months, it was exciting to see our family members smiling up at us with eager happy faces as they waved to us from the quayside. Sailing into a serene Table Bay at dawn on a beautiful autumn morning in April, with Table Mountain as a stunning mauve backdrop, must surely be one of the most breathtaking and moving experiences one could ever experience!

It was great enjoying the Easter holiday back at home with our families and when the Cape Town teachers returned to school, Lyn and I still had 10 days of holiday left. This bonus came because Treverton notched up extra hours by holding classes on Saturday mornings. This enabled boys who had to travel much further afield to Kenya, Malawi, Zambia or Zimbabwe to enjoy quality time with their parents.

In 1970 I was able to pay cash for my very first little car. For R600 I bought a second hand Morris 1100 from the deceased estate of a dear old lady. She had spent a number of years living in England and upon her return, had decided to ship her precious car back home with her. I felt so blessed to have acquired her beautifully pampered little dove grey gem, with a low mileage and boasting genuine red leather seats which still had a deliciously new smell.

I filled the petrol tank for R2 and it seemed to last me for weeks. It served me well for 6 years and took me safely to and from Cape Town several times, until I splashed out and bought a brand new 1976 avocado green Datsun 120Y costing R1 800 from Eddy Veenstra at Umvoti Motors in Estcourt.

In 1970 I clearly remember paying 8c for a litre of petrol but then we enjoyed other bargains too. Do you remember buying 4 pieces of bubble gum for 1c and a box of matches cost you 1c. You could buy a decent loaf of bread for 25c in 1970 and a kilogram of A grade lamb would set you back 70 cents!

Those really were the 'good old days!'

Ruth in soccer gear at staff fancy dress parade

21

WAS IT A COW OR A BULL?

*L*ooking back in time now, I guess some of the pranks we young teachers played on the older members of staff were highly irresponsible or considered a little too impulsive or reckless, but thankfully we were forgiven because we had youth and innocence on our side. There were memorable close shaves too when we were almost caught red handed.

Sadly, one of our matrons, Dorothy, actually resigned because what she saw in the tree on a very dark night was just "the last straw" after a hard day's work. One of our pranksters hung a very tall, life-like body in the tree outside her flat at the Koppies dormitory. In 1978 Treverton admitted girls for the very first time and upon returning from evening prep, they would have encountered a very realistic "body." It was a very large fat body, made by stuffing clothes into black garbage bags and the body was then clad in a man's navy raincoat. The unknown stranger wore a large pair of black gum boots (Wellingtons) and in a rather ingenious way, a torch had been put inside the face, making his eye sockets glow in the dark. A thin strand of fishing line was tied to the right boot and the prankster wiggled the string and yanked it up and down from behind a nearby bush. The effect was rather too realistic in the dark especially when it looked as if the body was literally about to turn up its toes! Unfortunately Matron Dorothy, having rather a gentle disposition, was the first person who encountered the body and she almost fainted.

What none of us had realised, was that Matron Dorothy had undergone heart valve surgery. Immediately her poor, startled heart started pounding vigorously, with the valves clicking so frantically that it sounded to us like a bevy of ladies going flat out as they competed in a knitting contest.

Another rather nasty prank which backfired somewhat happened when Faith, our fun-loving and spirited music and choir mistress, and later on our librarian, placed a very realistic male in Miss Seabrook's bed. Meridy had a heart of gold and was our down-to-earth and rather straight-laced book keeper who looked austere because she cut her hair very short and always wore "sensible" black lace- up shoes because of a foot problem. She often joked and said that men were her least favourite specimens on the planet! Furthermore her much- loved ginger cat called Sandy Seabrook was wary of men and would growl and raise his hackles if a man so much as crossed the threshold of his mistress' domain at Koppies.

Faith was artistic and highly creative and her efforts to create a grown male figure to slip into Meridy's bed proved far too realistic! She dressed the male image in borrowed striped pyjamas and a red beanie with an unkempt and decidedly bushy wig framing the chunky masculine features. Meridy's blankets were tucked under his chin but his left very hairy arm rested across his chest. In his right hand he clutched a walking stick as if ready to defend himself. What made him appear very life -like was that a half-eaten apple was resting on his chest and a crumpled cigarette packet was on her bedside table. Meridy always said she could not tolerate cigarette smoke! Here was a strange man in HER bed, with his greasy hair on HER pillow and smoking cigarettes in HER room! To make matters worse, he had taken a great big bite of HER Granny Smith apple!

Faith hid behind the cupboard and waited… Supper would be over by now. It was quite dark already so Meridy would have to lean over the bed to fumble for the switch on her bedside lamp. Everything went according to schedule. As Meridy bent forward to reach the switch, Faith tugged at the string attached to the walking stick. Another string made the man's foot twitch under the bedclothes. The stick crashed to the ground and Meridy ran screaming out of her room, straight up to the Headmaster's house on the koppie yelling, "Man in my bed, strange man in my bed!"

Unfortunately even Huddy's special little chocolate coated vitamin pills would not have helped to cheer her. Not even one of his famous banana milkshakes or mouth- watering cheese and mushroom omelettes would have saved the day. Meridy never saw the funny side of this story even though the staff pulled her leg at breakfast and said, "Well Meridy, at long last you had a man in your bed!"

Another rather unfortunate and risqué prank was played on our school secretary Rita. She was spunky for her age, did wood carving, loved gardening, bred Corgis for dog shows, iced cakes and had a great sense of humour as we discovered when she lost her skirt whilst taking a chapel service.

During a bitterly cold spell one Mooi River winter, when temperatures dropped below freezing, Rita was telling us at breakfast time, that to simplify matters on a frosty night, she would resort to using a potty rather than stagger along the outside verandah in the dead of night to use our shared bathroom. We all thought that a potty sounded like a great idea for use on icy winter nights. Fortunately we knew just where to purchase them too. We had spotted a really good line- up of potties made from plastic, porcelain and enamel. Brrrrr! There were all shapes and sizes at Mr Desai's hardware store, close to the shoe maker's shop where we had already discovered that Winston and his old dad did excellent repairs.

That evening a little band of pranksters headed for Rita's flat while she was finishing her supper. Her large china potty (chamber pot) was hauled out from under her bed and "doctored" in two ways! A healthy dose of effervescent Eno's fruit salt was sprinkled liberally in the potty and a strong, stretchy piece of elastic was attached to the handle on one side and then fastened to the nearest leg of the bed. The elastic would cause the potty to spring back and retreat rather hastily under the bed each time Rita tried to put it firmly in place.

As you can well imagine, the results of this prank proved disastrous. Rita told us next morning that she feared she had developed a serious kidney disorder. Whilst we were tucking into our scrambled egg and toast she went to great lengths to describe exactly what had happened at 3am with much frothing, foaming and bubbling. We simply had to own up to our misdemeanor because it was impossible to stifle our laughter. Rita was so grateful to hear that there was nothing wrong with her kidneys and she forgave the pranksters unreservedly. Don't you just love the other names given to chamber potties! A Po, a Jordan, a Jerry, a Guzunder, (It goes under!) and best of all, a Thunder Pot!

At about midnight, on a freezing night in June, with a pea-soup fog blanketing Mooi River, Lyn and I were both still awake, marking exam papers when we heard car tyres screeching and a very loud, sickening thud….Then complete silence.

We knew instinctively that a vehicle travelling at great speed had attempted to brake or swerve and had then slammed into something very large and very heavy. We immediately thought of our Treverton horses and prayed that none had escaped. We both hauled on our tracksuits and grabbed torches and raced towards the national road which in the 1960's passed just below the Koppies dorms and several of the staff houses.

A dreadful accident had taken place. By now the Huddies too had heard the loud screech and heart-stopping thud and had driven down at high speed from their new home on the koppie. (small hill.) Their original flat had been turned into a sick bay and they had moved into a new house built on the hill just above the stables and the Koppies dormitory and sports field. It was nothing short of a miracle that there had been no human fatalities. A Volkswagen Beetle packed with six Army boys had been travelling from the Tempe base in Bloemfontein to Durban for a long weekend when it slammed into a stray cow or bull crossing the national highway. The scene that greeted us was horrific. The poor animal had been killed outright and was a heartbreaking sight. The little Volkswagen "Love Bug," was a mangled wreck and its roof and bonnet resembled a fragile sardine tin that some giant of a man had stamped on. Two young men had been rocketed through the windscreen. Both had broken noses and cracked ribs. Their fellow passengers were all a sorry sight.

Because no one would be manning the telephone exchange at midnight, Huddy leapt into his car and raced straight to the police station. He knew they would respond immediately. Mooi River had none of its own ambulances and the nearest hospital was in Estcourt. Mrs Huddy and I agreed to transport the three seriously injured chaps straight to hospital. Dr Mc Call was our school doctor and he arranged for those whose injuries were less severe to be accommodated in the nearby Gleneagles Hotel.

There had been great excitement in the Village in June 1966, when we heard that Gleneagles, the lovely old hotel, full of character and happy memories, was to be auctioned. It was proposed that the Treverton Trust should purchase the hotel. It could perhaps solve the problem of providing accommodation for the standard 8, 9, and 10 boys and could be used for parents travelling from afar to visit their children. A debenture scheme was established and interested folk bought shares for R100 each. Imagine the hype on the day of the Auction held in Pietermaritzburg, when the Gleneagles Hotel was knocked down to Treverton for a figure of R27 000 which included all the furniture and effects as well as a dedicated staff Team!

In the very first month, the hotel made a profit of R500 and soon there were 26 permanent residents, which meant that the hotel was always 80% full.

Gleneagles was efficiently managed by Mrs Huddy's mother, Mrs Oosthuisen, who was affectionately known as 'Mrs O.' She joined her Mooi River family having moved from Johannesburg, where she had been the matron at St. Stithians College. In a flash on the night of the accident, she converted a hotel bedroom into a comfortable hospital ward for the wounded army lads and she kept the accident victims comfortable until help arrived from Durban the next day.

What amazed us when the police finally arrived on the accident scene were the intriguing questions they asked. We felt they were wasting precious time. The injured young men needed urgent medical attention and were in a state of shock. The police were determined to establish who or what had caused the accident. We had rushed from warm bedrooms and the night air was chilly. Our teeth chattered as they fired questions at us and scribbled copious notes on their well - thumbed note pads.

"Who was the guilty party?" They barked. "Was the car speeding? Which of you has a valid driver's licence? Did the animal cross the road in front of the car or did the car not see the animal? Was the animal a cow or a bull? A male or a female creature? What was the approximate speed at which the said beast was moving? Then the police directed questions at us. Did you hear the screech of brakes before or after you heard the thud? What were you two ladies doing at the precise moment of impact? Was the cow or bull stationary at the moment of impact or what was the estimated speed of the animal after the impact? Which one of you here present is the owner of the deceased animal? "

We could not seem to get the police to accept that at midnight on a freezing cold night in mid- winter there had been no spectators or witnesses! We guessed that the poor unfortunate animal had probably strayed from a neighbouring farm. No one here present was in fact the owner of the deceased! Furthermore not one of us had ever encountered a female bull or seen any bovine creature fitted with a speedometer! All we wanted to do was to get urgent medical attention for the army lads and for us to be able to jump into warm beds.

The injured young men were a sorry sight as they shivered at the roadside, huddled under a khaki army blanket and trying to understand why all these irrelevant questions had to be answered while they were bleeding. We heaved a sigh of relief when the police had concluded their cross- questioning. We finally dropped into bed at 4am, grateful that there had been no fatalities and thankful that we had been able to offer support and comfort.

The three young soldiers who were taken to Gleneagles by Dr. Mc Call were fetched by Durban family members the very next day. The three chaps whom Marge and I transported to the Estcourt Provincial hospital were only kept there for a few days in spite of two having broken their noses, while their army pal suffered several cracked ribs. I must admit our thoughts were very much with the local farmer whose cow or bull had so tragically lost its life on the highway that night.

As mentioned near the beginning of this chapter, 1978 was a very exciting year because it saw the arrival of girls at Treverton. As it happened this was also my 15th and final year on the staff.

We teachers were enormously grateful that the Governing Body recognized the importance of in-service training and the need to further our studies for the benefit of improving our teaching skills. I shall never forget being sent by Treverton to Johannesburg in 1970 to attend a course in Remedial Education run by Dr Sonia Mackanick, one of the fore-runners in South Africa in the field of helping children with Learning Disabilities. Sonia was a highly qualified medical doctor, author and educational psychologist. Her innovative pioneering efforts to help children hampered by dyslexia, attention deficit and hyperactivity disorders, provided wonderful help and huge emotional support to numerous children, as well as to their often perplexed and anxious parents. Having attended Dr Mackanick's course on remedial education held at Japari, the special school she started in 1966, I came away from Johannesburg motivated, enthused and yearning to be able to help more effectively our own Treverton pupils who were struggling to read, spell, write neatly or concentrate in class. It was thanks to the inspiration of Dr Machanick that I applied to study further in this field at the University of Cape Town two years later.

The junior boys moved from the Koppies dormitory across the road to Warner House where they were cared for by Miss Seabrook, our very efficient book keeper, who had made a good recovery from the shock of finding a strange man in her bed and was slowly getting round to thinking about forgiving the prankster involved!

The first batch of Treverton girls moved into the Koppies dormitory in January 1978 and I became their housemistress. It was quite a challenge keeping the peace as the girls ranged in age from 9 to 13 and their interests were so varied. They all vied for my attention. Some were concerned with plaiting their doll's hair when it was time for lights out, another wanted me to darn the hole in her teddy's jersey, while the bigger girls quarrelled over cupboard space, fought for softer mattresses or tried to get away with wearing mascara and a touch of eye shadow.

We noticed that since the arrival of the girls, our boys were becoming more particular about their grooming. Some even asked to have their hair cut and remembered to tuck in their shirt tails and pull up their socks.

One night when I was supervising the girls' bath time, I heard whispers and giggles coming from high up in a tree strategically situated outside the Koppies ablution block. I was quite certain I could hear muffled boys' voices! I shot out into the garden and bellowed in my fiercest tone, "Come down immediately!" Two 12 year old Peeping Toms leapt down on the side of the tree furthest from me and darted into the night, sprinting across the hockey field, hoping to reach the safety of their dormitory, The Barn, under cover of darkness. What the boys didn't realize was that I was still in my hockey track suit and trainers and I sprinted after them as fast as I could. Back in the 1970's I was without a titanium left knee! Once under the lamp post closest to their dorm, I was able to recognize their faces and marched them straight to the Headmaster's office. I focused my attention on the little blonde chap whom I suspected to be the instigator. He had a tendency to stutter whenever he felt nervous. Looking him straight in the eye I barked, "Yes, Alan, what do you have to say for yourself!" (His response floored me completely)

Without turning a hair, he stuttered, "Mmmmiss Ttttaylor, I didddn't knnnow you cccould run so fffffast!

How could I possibly ask Mr Huddy to give him a whack after an answer like that!

There was great excitement and hilarity one morning when Whisky, the friendly Shetland pony, climbed three steps and came to visit our class, putting his head, shoulders and front legs right inside our classroom. Finding nothing exciting like a carrot or an apple, and not having a head for Maths, Whisky gave our class a farewell little neigh, shook his mane, then retreated backwards without stumbling and plodded back to the stables.

Then there was the time in my Std. 6 English poetry lesson when I asked all the pupils to close their eyes, relax and float off.......

I did my best to create a beautiful peaceful atmosphere. I started to read William Wordsworth's much- loved poem:

> *"I wandered lonely as a cloud*
> *That floats on high o'er vales and hills, When all at once….."*

The atmosphere was shattered.

Suddenly there was a throaty squawk and a great flapping of wings and a flurry of feathers. The mother hen had produced a beautiful free-range egg in our waste paper basket!

I clearly remember another occasion when the atmosphere was disturbed.

I was helping the Huddies entertain a well-heeled family who had driven down from Johannesburg with a view to sending their two sons to Treverton. They had brought the boys' grandparents with them to enter into the spirit of their grandsons' exciting new boarding school venture. The family enjoyed an extensive tour of the school and the newly-acquired 70 acres of prime land generously given to Treverton by the Mooi River Municipality. There was an exciting plan in the pipe line to build a high school, so that our Prep. boys could remain with us until matric. After their tour the visiting family was invited to relax and enjoy afternoon tea in the Huddies' lounge before returning to the local hotel for the night.

Several staff members had been invited to be present at tea time to make the newcomers feel welcome and to answer any questions the boys might raise. The Huddies' cute little daughter, Barbara, born in the first six months of Treverton's existence, was aged 3 or 4 at the time and was with us in the lounge.

Mrs Huddy asked her to offer the plate of biscuits to the seated guests. The Johannesburg grandma was enchanted by Huddy and Marge's little curly- haired blonde daughter who looked exactly like one of the adorable little characters in Mabel Lucie Attwell's illustrations. The granny gave Barbara a hug as she thanked her for bringing her a biscuit. Upon returning to her mom, the cheerful little helper jumped up on her lap and asked in a very audible little whisper, "Mummy, why has that granny got a tickly moustache if she's a girl?"

Somehow these hilarious or hugely embarrassing incidents remain with one forever.

Many boys and staff who were at Treverton in 1965/ 66 will remember the outstanding chapel talks given by Mr Bill Webster, who later entered the ministry and served at St.Andrew's Church in Benoni and then in Mowbray Presbyterian Church in Cape Town. Can we ever forget the morning he dressed as an elderly spinster called Miss Violet Godfrey, a volunteer doing noble charitable work for The Society for the Blind. Bill's feminine attire, his make-up and his vibrato soprano voice was so authentic that he had his entire congregation flummoxed! He even fooled everyone in the chapel by saying that his fingertips were so sensitive that he could read his Braille Bible through his gloves!

The point of his message was "Be yourself, don't pretend to be on the outside what you are not on the inside, because the Lord looks on the heart!" Only Bill's wife, Mary, Marge Huddy and I were part of the conspiracy because we had applied Miss Godfrey's make up and helped Bill acquire a wig, a pretty head scarf and suitable clothing. He looked great in Marge's floral skirt and Rita's sensible brown sandals.

Once Miss Godfrey had arrived at the chapel, we let Mr Huddy into the secret too, because it was only right that our Headmaster should welcome the guest speaker.

Huddy assigned two prefects to open the car door and escort Miss Godfrey into the chapel. Wearing dark glasses, "she" then tapped her way up the aisle with a cane smuggled from Huddy's office and doctored with white paint.

She smiled warmly and patted a few boys affectionately on their heads, uttering pleasantries as she felt her way to the lectern.

Miss Godfrey then requested that the boys sing her favourite hymn before she delivered a marvellous address. But quite incredibly, after speaking off the cuff for 15 minutes with such fervent zeal and passion, about her volunteer work in the service of The Cape Town Society for the Blind, not one of the boys had realised that the guest speaker was a fake! It was Mr Webster in drag!

Bill didn't know how to end his talk because everyone was spellbound and had warmed towards Miss Godfrey and the great work she was doing for fellow blind folk through the auspices of her Society.

But now time was up, so Bill jumped from behind the lectern, yanked off the wig and floral head scarf and beamed at the boys. Their mouths dropped open and they exploded with mirth. They could not believe they had been fooled for 15 minutes. Like Rita's message, on the morning she found herself stripped of her tweed skirt, Bill Webster's was another excellent chapel talk no one will ever forget. Be genuine. Just be yourself!

Bill's performance as Miss Godfrey was such a hit that we decided to have some fun and test his authenticity further afield. His wife and two of us planned an outing to take our blind friend for a surprise jaunt. She had undergone a name change and was no longer Miss Godfrey. She was our Auntie Violet or Vi for short! We were treating her to dinner at the Gleneagles Hotel, now run as a Treverton venture and managed by Mrs Huddy's mom. Our night out turned into a hilarious experience.

Bill's wife, Mary, acted as Auntie Violet's chauffeur and carer and led "her" gently towards our reserved table. Mary cut up her food and steered it onto her fork and wiped her chin when it became messy! Most of the folk at dinner were permanent residents who boarded at Gleneagles on a monthly basis. There were two or three business folk using the hotel as an overnight stop en route to Johannesburg or Durban. Several of the single gentlemen present showed a great interest in Violet as we sat sipping coffee in the lounge. We sensed that one or two wanted to pursue a friendship with her!

In fact it was the local Postmaster who couldn't take his eyes off Violet. The manageress told us afterwards how he had whispered to her, "That lady has a beautiful face, but my word she does have a very long back!"

The situation was becoming a little tricky to manage so we decided that our dear old Auntie Vi needed to be taken home to have an early night. To save face, we bundled her and her white cane into the car and beat a hasty retreat up the hill and back to Treverton.

22

ANGELS WITH GUMBOOTS AND BUCKETS!

*A*s Treverton teachers, we were enormously grateful that the Governing Body recognized the importance of in-service training. As mentioned earlier, I shall never forget being sent to Johannesburg to attend an inspiring in- service course in Remedial Education run by Dr Mackanick, a leading pioneer in Remedial Education in South Africa. It was her course which motivated and enthused me and made me apply to the University of Cape Town to study for a Diploma in Clinical Remedial Education in 1972.

It was exciting and stimulating being back in a learning environment at the age of 29. I was able to stay in our family home in Rondebosch for that year and played league hockey for the Green and Sea Point Ladies' Club.

I thoroughly enjoyed the Clinical side of the course, where we studied Neurology and were shown at the Red Cross Children's Hospital how an irregular EEG could indicate a problem area in the brain and often helped experts understand why some children find it more difficult to sit still and concentrate, or to learn to read, write or do Maths. Besides our daily lectures on campus, we attended lectures and therapy sessions at the University of Cape Town Child Guidance Clinic in Rosebank and at the Bellville School Clinic and did regular teaching practice with individual pupils at the Vista Nova School in Rondebosch.

Upon my return to Treverton I was able to turn a spare little thatched building near the tennis courts into a colourful fully functional, hands-on Remedial Clinic with all the apparatus I required for improving the pupils' visual skills, gross and fine motor co-ordination and balance. My UCT Training also qualified me to do scholastic assessments and IQ tests so I was able to diagnose learning problems from an early age. It is essential to do early assessment to determine a child's strengths and weaknesses so that programmes and activities can be designed to meet the needs of each pupil. I remember the joy when John F. aged 12, learnt to read properly for the first time in his life and amazingly enough, his stutter almost disappeared! It was rewarding and heart-warming to see how pupils with a low sense of self - esteem because of their learning disabilities, responded to individual tuition and many of their emotional problems like nail biting, aggression, inattention, hyperactivity, poor appetite, bed wetting and even insomnia disappeared.

By 1969 Treverton had grown from 81 scholars in standards one to four (in 1964) to 186 pupils in standards two to nine in 1969. In 1966 the Board of Governors had committed themselves to the establishment of a high school which would be known as Treverton College. Initially it was felt that the std. 6 boys should remain on the Prep side of the school to provide more maturity as prefects and house captains in their respective leadership rôles. The high school architect was to be Mr Pat Gibson and it was an exciting day when we were invited to view his drawings of the Master Plan for the high school. But what was even more exciting, was when at the beginning of 1971, the first four classrooms and cloakrooms over the hill on the new College site were brought into use.

In my 15 years at Treverton I had the remarkable privilege of teaching a variety of subjects at every single level from standard one right through to our very first matriculation class in 1970. A very close bond developed between us and before I knew it, the young lads who arrived at age 8 or 9 were now fine young men launching out into the world to embark on meaningful careers.

Being asked to teach in the College as well as in the Prep. school encouraged me to study further and to complete a Natal Teacher's Senior Diploma. I was able to enrol as a part- time external student and studied through the Natal Teachers' Training College and the University of Natal and was able to qualify within two years. There were now two distinct schools with two separate headmasters. Mr Huddy remained headmaster at the Prep. School and Mr John Robertson was appointed Headmaster of Treverton College. My teaching schedule became more of a challenge to juggle. I taught on the Prep side of the koppie until morning tea break, then jumped into my little Morris, drove across the hill to the College, grabbed a cup of tea in their staffroom, taught 3 or 4 lessons in the new College classrooms, before returning to the Prep side for lunch and the afternoon lessons.

Speaking of my trusty little 1966 Morris 1100, reminds me of a frightening adventure I had one Sunday evening. My friend, Avril, from Cape Town had just completed her nursing training and was taking a little break while visiting a relative in Pietermaritzburg. Avril was very keen to see Treverton so spent a weekend with me. She met all my staff friends and entered into the excitement of rapid shooting down the Mooi River. The time came to drive her back to 'Maritzburg and Christa Odendaal, our lovely Afrikaans teacher from Harrismith, offered to keep me company on the journey.

We set off shortly before dusk and just about 10 kilometres outside Mooi River we encountered what looked like a hi-jacking in progress. A smartly dressed Indian gentleman resembling a travelling salesman appeared to have been robbed. Five burly attackers had dragged him onto his back at the roadside and were kicking and punching him repeatedly. His suitcases and merchandise was scattered all over the highway. Not having our hockey sticks (or pepper spray!) in the car with us, we girls felt utterly defenceless and dared not rush to his defence. However, we figured that if we drew up alongside his assailants and hooted frantically we might attract the attention of fellow road users to the unfortunate man's plight. The new National Road had not yet been completed and the old road to Pietermaritzburg and Durban was delightfully scenic with many twists and turns.

At this time of day the highway appeared to be deserted making us feel even more vulnerable. I pressed hard on the hooter and Avril and Christa bellowed through the windows for all they were worth. We passed as close to the attackers as we dared then reversed at high speed towards them, hooting and gesticulating wildly hoping they might scatter and disband. The injured man lay motionless and we feared he might be left for dead. There was not another vehicle in sight. So we took off as fast as we could, realising that we had to head into a town this side of 'Maritzburg to seek emergency police and medical help. I could picture where I had previously noticed a police station situated in Howick, so pressed my foot flat on the accelerator. We still had about 35 kilometres to cover. Darkness was fast closing in on us.

Imagine our panic when glancing into the rear view mirror, I saw that the five attackers had leapt into the old putty coloured Opel parked at the roadside and were pursuing us.

There were only three of us and five of them. We realised they had abandoned their poor beaten up victim lying sprawled in a lifeless state at the roadside. Christa was sitting behind me and became terrified.

She started to pray aloud in Afrikaans in wavering tones and told us she was too frightened to peep out.

She pulled her jersey (jumper) right over her head. Avril told me to keep my eyes glued to the road and to drive flat out while she promised to keep her eyes fixed on the Opel which was in hot pursuit.

Within moments the occupants had drawn up alongside us, waving their fists and glaring menacingly. Then they shot past us at high speed. We heaved sighs of relief assuming they were making a hasty getaway, but instead they ducked in, right in front of us causing me to swerve violently and then apply the brakes dangerously. For the next twenty minutes it was a frightening cat and mouse game. I stared solidly at the road, gripping the steering wheel until my knuckles ached as my intrepid little Morris negotiated the many winding twists and turns. We three females were participating in a deadly chase.

At times the Opel and its occupants would sweep ahead of us, attempting to block our approach and we would have to negotiate a narrow gap. It seemed like a miracle when we finally saw the road sign alerting us to take the next left exit for Howick. The Opel was just ahead of us and slightly out of view round the next bend. Seizing the moment, we ducked left and sped into the welcoming little town of Howick where we fell into the arms of the policemen on duty in the charge office. They leapt into action and immediately telephoned Mooi River to organize assistance for the unfortunate roadside victim and promised to set up roadblocks to be on the lookout for the occupants of the beige Opel.

There was no sign of the car or its occupants on our return journey to Mooi River at 9pm. However, about 10 days later Sergeant van Coller telephoned me at Treverton to thank us for the part we played in the arrest of five dangerous criminals and for helping to save the life of the hijacked salesman!

Sadly our dear friend Christa passed away some 30 years later after a courageous battle with liver cancer. She had been happily married to a Clanwilliam farmer. When her children were older she returned to teaching. We were shocked to hear that her husband had suffered a heart attack and died at a relatively early age.

My very brave, level- headed friend and navigator, Avril, is now a fit seventy year old widow, with three grown daughters. She has used her nursing skills as a regular Care Giver in the UK. Whenever we see each other, we re-kindle that 1970's memory and we feel weak-kneed at the thought of that very close encounter! News just in is that Avril is hoping to retire from her U.K. nursing duties and settle in Cape Town.

Another frightening highway drama featured our lovely friend, Win Robertson, who was the wife of the Treverton College Headmaster. John and Win Roberson were very caring, warm- hearted folk noted for their generous hospitality and compassionate hearts. On her way back from the village one morning having fetched the College mail at the Mooi River post office, Win spotted a forlorn looking female hitch hiker standing at the roadside with a suitcase at her side. It was a very chilly day, with an icy wind blowing straight off the foothills of Giant's Castle which had been dusted with a good sprinkling of snow. Win wound down the passenger window and shouted to the hitch hiker that she was welcome to have a ride out of the village and up the hill to where she would be more visible close to the Treverton entrance. The shivering hitch hiker clambered aboard placing her suitcase rather gingerly on the back seat.

As they drove off up the hill and out of town, an uneasy feeling suddenly gripped Win. As she glanced sideways to question her passenger she became suspicious that the "she" was actually a "he" in wolf's clothing! As the hitch hiker turned sideways, Win spotted stubble peeping out from beneath the head scarf and realised that the jawline and rather gruff voice was that of a man. She told us how she prayed for wisdom in a very dangerous situation and had a strong conviction that the thought that suddenly popped into her mind was divinely inspired.

Shortly before Win Robertson's chilling experience, we had heard how our Treverton staff colleague, music maestro and good friend Robin Radue, had been overpowered in his own car having offered a lift into

Pietermaritzburg to two smartly dressed, Bible-bearing hitch hikers near Howick. He was hit over the head by the passenger sitting behind him and was rolled down a steep embankment in an unconscious state. The hijackers then drove off in Robin's car, leaving him to spend the night in a donga. (a ravine caused by soil erosion) Miraculously Robin survived the horrific ordeal and was able to crawl back up onto the highway next morning. In a bruised and badly battered state, he bravely flagged down a passing motorist who rushed Robin straight to hospital for urgent medical attention.

So with Robin's alarming experience still fresh in her mind, and whilst engaging her passenger in further friendly conversation, Win lowered her window slightly, allowing her silk scarf to flutter out. She pulled over smartly and apologised for braking so suddenly, explaining that she had lost a treasured scarf. Then she asked the hitch hiker if "she" would mind retrieving it. As he clambered out of the car, Win performed a swift U turn and headed straight back to the village. She drove post haste to the police station where she breathlessly related her story and asked them to investigate the suitcase on the back seat in her car. There was a screech of tyres and Win heard a police van speeding off to offer a lift to the hitch hiker, last seen wearing a long olive green skirt, a floral headscarf and tan sandals which revealed rather hairy ankles!

Imagine Win's shock and horror to be told that the suitcase she had been transporting on her back seat was found to contain several explosive devices and a number of firearms! The hitch hiker had panicked, changed direction and was arrested as he headed back into the town. He was easily spotted because he realised the game was up.

He had yanked up his skirt and was taking very large unfeminine strides. His head scarf had slipped round his neck revealing a very distinct male countenance and a rather pronounced Adam's apple! But his hairy bowlegs were the biggest give-away! Win was a gentle unassuming lady but earned Heroine Status that day for remaining cool, calm and collected in an extremely dangerous situation. It was her quick-witted and decisive reaction which led to the arrest of a criminal linked to acts of terrorism in Northern Natal.

My last Carol Service at Treverton proved to be an unforgettable experience. It was decided to host it on the last evening of the fourth term because many parents would have arrived to spend a night at a local hotel or time-share establishment so as to attend the final Assembly on break up day with their sons and daughters.

Using the very popular idea of a family Drive-In cinema, Huddy had decided that parents and friends would be encouraged to bring picnic hampers and park their cars in neat rows on the cricket field facing the recently refurbished Sports Pavilion. Visitors could remain in their cars or enjoy their suppers seated on picnic rugs alongside. We almost felt transported to the fields of Bethlehem as we looked across to the gentle rolling hills and farmlands. It was a beautiful calm starry night. Strains of familiar and well- loved Christmas favourites floated across the cricket field. Some school families lit candles as darkness fell and here and there torches flickered.

Part of the pavilion had been transformed into an authentic stable setting with bales of fresh hay. There was a rugged wooden manger and realistic cardboard cut outs of cows, sheep and an amiable donkey or two. Joseph held his lantern aloft and glanced tenderly towards Mary as she bent low over the crib and tucked baby Jesus' little feet under the straw. The country air was crisp and pure. We could smell the freshly mown grass on the cricket pitch. Overhead the stars twinkled in a velvet sky. The atmosphere was magical.

Just as the radiant Bethlehem star, cleverly suspended on a cable between two tall Norfolk pines, travelled slowly above the Nativity scene and the Treverton choir sang out melodiously, Hark the Herald Angels Sing......... onto the peaceful Holy scene rumbled the faithful Mooi River Sewage Truck, which our founder pupils had christened The Honey Sucker! Instead of the Heavenly Host appearing, out jumped 3 sturdy Zulu gentleman, not wearing glistening wings and shining apparel but sombre grey overalls and gum boots! Instead of bearing gifts of frankincense, gold and myrrh, they clanked in with empty buckets. And then, instead of sharing glad tidings of joy but chatting at the tops of their voices and most amiably, the 3 valiant Zulu men carted out the soiled toilet buckets. They waved enthusiastically and gave a thumbs- up sign to the 3 wise men as they passed between the bucket bearers to present their gifts to baby Jesus. Joseph clung to his lantern and looked somewhat startled when he received an unexpected High Five from the lead bucket bearer.

The Bethlehem Star beamed down on all six men and the choir continued to sing as if nothing was amiss........

"Pleased, as man, with men to dwell, Jesus our Emmanuel! "

I know Charles Wesley would have been proud of them!

At the end of 1978, after spending 15 unforgettable, joyous and fulfilling years at Treverton, I decided that the time was approaching for me to return to my home town, Cape Town, to be closer to my widowed mom and my brother. However, a wonderful opportunity arose for a year's study in Johannesburg at the Rosebank Bible College. My best friend, Margaret, who later became my sister- in-law, much to our family's delight, had been on a tour of the Holy Land with me in the Easter holidays of 1978. It was a very special experience for me because my mom and several other close friends were also in our tour group and the Rev. André Erasmus proved to be an outstanding leader.

It was wonderful to be walking where Jesus had walked and to visit the places which He and His friends and disciples had frequented. A guided tour of the Holy Land certainly makes the Bible come alive, so the timing was perfect to consider spending the following year at a Bible College. Margaret and I were both accepted and went as roommates to Rosebank for a year and became 'Vaalies' (A nickname in those days for folk living in the Transvaal)

We made some wonderful new friends there, many of whom still serve as missionaries, nurses or teachers in far- flung lands. That year was a life- changing experience for all of as we were taught, nurtured and sometimes even disciplined, by the much-loved Monty Sholund, our College Principal, and by Reg Codrington, his right hand man. What a privilege to have lecturers of the calibre of Ralph Christensen, Lizann Vercuiel, Ernie Hack, Rev.Terry Rae and others like the inimitable Dr Rex Mathie and Rev Colin Bishop who taught us on a part -time basis.

I shall never regret taking that year of unpaid leave to study at the Bible College where I enjoyed a wonderful leadership opportunity when elected Chairperson of the College SSLC. ~ The Student Staff Liaison Committee. Together with the staff, our committee maintained discipline on Campus, helped make vital policy decisions and fulfilled a pastoral and counselling ministry among the students.

After serving for 15 years at Treverton, 1979 served as a refreshing "Gap Year" and yet it proved to be a "Stretching" experience for me with disciplined hard work, involving the submission of two challenging assignments per week and 12 hours of final exams. Having graduated, a number of my Bible College friends headed off to far flung mission fields. However, I have always known that my Calling was to reach and teach young people, so back into the classroom I went one year later.

I accepted a challenging new teaching post as Deputy Headmistress and grade 7 (standard 5) class mistress at Rustenburg Girls' Junior School in Cape Town in January 1980. It was wonderful to be back at my old junior school, exactly 24 years after I left to enter high school at age 12!

Back in the Mother City, after an absence of 16 years, I formed lovely new friendships on the teaching staff and taught some of the most delightful, hardworking and gifted pupils I have ever had the privilege of teaching. One of my greatest joys was being entrusted to train the prefects in their leadership rôles and when my 1980 class reached Matric in 1984 two of my team of dedicated grade 7 prefects, Lindy Smith and Chantal Muller, became Head Girl and Deputy Head Girl at Rustenburg Girls' High School. That was a proud moment indeed. I am now finding that I bump into former pupils wherever I go and am introduced to their children who often openly express amazement that their mom or dad's teacher is still alive!

When I think back to January 1964 when I climbed down from the Orange Express wearing my pale pink suit, hat with satin bow and my stiletto heels and began my teaching career, I treasure the 15 years I spent at Treverton and thank God for a Headmaster like Derek

Hudson– Reed, our much loved Mr "Huddy." He taught by precept and example. Under his guidance I learnt to respect the uniqueness and preciousness of every single pupil I taught.

Huddy put the interests of others first and taught us the importance of first winning the respect and trust of our pupils, before earning the right to teach them. We learnt to present lessons in an innovative way and to make each lesson relevant and meaningful. South Africans are natural story tellers and the boys and girls I meet years later, tell me they still remember the real life stories with touches of humour, which were interwoven into their lessons.

23

AMOROUS ARABS, CAMELS AND NUDISTS!

*C*onfucius said, "Wherever you go, go with all your heart." I went with my heart and without doubt, some of my greatest adventures took place whilst travelling and many of my loveliest friends were made whilst visiting other countries.

Back in the good old days when teachers were granted a term's paid leave every five years, I was able to travel extensively and had the privilege of visiting the Lebanon, Israel, the UK, Europe, the United States and Canada. My mom and dad had been avid travellers too and had formed lasting friendships across several continents. Whenever their warm- hearted friends heard that my brother or I was planning a foreign trip, we were invited to visit them and received generous and caring hospitality. We shall be eternally grateful to the countless overseas friends who met aeroplanes, coaches and trains at unearthly hours of the day or night to welcome us with open arms and to share their lovely homes and beautiful towns and cities with us. You learn so much about other countries when you meet their citizens, stay in their homes, shop where they shop, eat the food they love and ride alongside the locals on their buses, taxis, trains, tuk-tuks, sky trains and rickshaws!

On my very first overseas trip in the December of 1968, I remember delightful Jewish friends called Mr and Mrs Kay who were loyal Westerford parents when our dad was Headmaster. They eventually moved to Israel and very kindly offered to meet my travelling companion and long-time friend Jessie Anderson and me at the Ben Gurion Airport in Tel Aviv. Mr Kay either had a clothing factory there or had a friend who owned one and Mrs Kay took us there to buy warm coats at factory price for our winter in Europe.

The fleecy jackets were reversible and water repellent and helped us to survive even in the Ice Palace up the Jungfraujoch and in heavy snow in Innsbruck.

Israel was a great place to start our travels. It is a fascinating country, so rich in history. This little country is scarcely more than 150 miles in length and 90 miles in breadth. Jerusalem is about 41 km from Ben Gurion Airport. Jessie and I found excellent affordable accommodation at the Christ Church Guest House just inside the Jaffa Gate and within the Old City. The Staff there was composed of a multilingual team of volunteers from all over the world. We were overjoyed when we suddenly heard a cleaning lady call out in Afrikaans to a fellow helper in Jerusalem!

The guest house is in a secure compound close to the Christ Church which was founded in 1849 and is believed to be the oldest Protestant church in the Middle East. Travellers are offered a variety of rooms set around a shady Garden Courtyard. Our rooms were spotless and uncluttered and we even had our own small bathroom.

The Guest House has a unique situation within the Christian Quarter of the Old City and adjacent to the Armenian Quarter. You discover a tranquil safe haven the moment you slip through the gates of the guest house. You are suddenly separated from the hustle and bustle of the busy narrow little streets of the Old City with so many interesting sights, sounds and smells.

If you ever have the joy of visiting the Old City, be sure to sample the tantalising almond halva and their Turkish Delight. Like us, you will probably find the hot, freshly baked flat bread irresistible.

Being blonde in certain parts of Israel proved challenging at times. A word of warning! Only use registered tour guides. Quite often you will encounter volunteer, self- appointed guides who prove very persistent (rather like some of our self- appointed Cape Town car guards!) Out of sheer desperation, and just to see them on their way after much nagging and begging, you may even relent, feeling sorry for them and allow them to give you a quick tour. But ladies beware! Some of the guides offer "Extras" which you were not expecting! Keep well away from dark corners and avoid underground tombs and tunnels!

One such "guide" who had obviously bought or made an authentic looking bronze TOUR GUIDE badge, insisted on showing us the underground tunnel leading to a dark cave under the Church of the Holy Nativity in Bethlehem. It was right here we were told, that Saint Jerome spent 30 years translating the Scriptures from Hebrew and Greek into Latin. He was born in the North East of Italy in Dalmatia but was sent by the Pope to the Holy Land in about AD 386 to tackle this mammoth and very daunting assignment.

"This holy cave," said the self-appointed guide excitedly, having led us down into two dank adjacent subterranean caves, "was where St. Jerome, revered in the Roman Catholic Church, and fondly remembered as The Doctor of the Church, dedicated his life to the Word of God."

"Now close your eyes tightly," he continued…. "and just picture the devout monk, bending low over his scripts and hard at work…"

It was already so dark and murky underground that we could barely see the outline of our Arab guide, let alone picture the monk hard at work! Just then I felt, not the monk or St Jerome, but an over- amorous guide grab me in the pitch dark. I jumped back as he tried to run his hands up my leg.

He then had the audacity to continue telling us, quite ironically and in a very pious voice, as if nothing was amiss, that the most noble Jerome's finished work was called the Vulgate from which we get the word "Vulgar," because the common people would now be able to read the Bible in their own language.

At this point we abandoned our tour and fled into the fresh air and the bright sunshine, leaving our bogus tour guide to slink off without receiving a tip.

Be cautious too about accepting very tempting little cups of Turkish coffee served by shop keepers who disappear behind silk curtains to prepare the promised brew. You actually need to see what is going into your coffee and to make quite sure that no favours are expected from you in exchange for a thimble-size cup of coffee served with a few almonds or green figs. You will discover that sugar is added to your cup before you receive it and it is often so sweet and sickly that it will make your hair stand on end! Coffee is often served without milk or with very little milk and there will be enough caffeine in it to keep you revving all night long!

Another rather dodgy tourist attraction is to accept a camel ride with a camel herder who says that his brother or uncle will accompany you for safely, in case the camel breaks into a canter and you might fall off! Rather accept a donkey ride because you know there won't be room on a donkey's back for a brother or an uncle, or insist on being strapped securely onto the camel's back. I guarantee you will feel a lot more secure venturing forth alone or else travelling in tandem with a close friend. But if you must undertake a camel derby, don't attempt it bare back or side-saddle (like the Queen,) and never stand behind a camel. I am not sure whether it is nervousness or just a genuine camel tendency, but they have a habit of back-firing very loudly when you least expect it. I assure you the gaseous emission they produce is far, far worse than being stuck behind a diesel bus in a traffic jam in Bangkok or Beijing. It's also not a good idea to stand in front of a camel. You may think the camel is just being friendly and grinning at you, but when a camel opens its mouth very wide and you stare straight at those very big yellow teeth, step back and hold your breath. Camels suffer from severe halitosis.

On two more recent trips to Jerusalem I noticed that there always seemed to be an Arab gentleman hiring out his very docile donkey on the Mount of Olives. Bear in mind that some shrewd owners of camels and donkeys will demand payment even if you only want to stand beside or pat their beast for a photograph or pretend you have just jumped off its back!

Something else to avoid, especially if you are blonde, is to travel alone in an unregistered taxi. Your hotel staff will advise you which ones are kosher!

Some taxis in Tel Aviv and Jerusalem are notorious for extending their route and then over- charging you. Don't fall for the driver who says, "Sorry, I forgot to switch on my meter while I was handling your luggage."

Never stand in front of your accommodation waiting to hail a taxi. If you are outside a hotel, it implies that you are wealthy! Walk a few blocks away and then while looking footsore and weary, wave at a taxi and the driver will welcome you aboard. You will be delighted to discover that you paid far less than your friends who boarded outside their B&B or hotel. If you want to look like a local, stick your arm out and point down at the curb at a 45 degree angle. Climb in and check that your driver has switched on his meter. (moneh) I noticed that most taxis were Mercedes Benz cars but I also saw a shared type of taxi called a Sherut, which was a cross between a taxi and a small bus or a larger car with three rows of passenger seats. Sharing a vehicle is nearly always a more economical option.

We found the guest house the perfect base for a five night stay as most of the significant historical and biblical spots you would not want to miss, are within walking distance. The guest house arranged day tours for us with a walking or a driving tour guide called Michael who took us further afield.

We so enjoyed staying at Christ Church guest house with its friendly vibe and hard-working staff who could not do enough to help, that I chose to return there with my widowed Cape Town friend, Pat, twenty four years later. Since then, I have heard that there is a marvellous coffee shop in the courtyard which serves the best coffee and cheese cake for miles around.

Being able to picture where biblical events took place and to grasp more clearly the culture of those times, gives one a far better understanding of Scripture. For me the Bible came alive when I walked in the footsteps of Jesus. We rubbed shoulders in the Old City with the very kind of people He would have been drawn to, as He sensed their needs. We were fascinated by the same sights Jesus' eyes would have seen. We visited many of the places where Jesus performed miracles, where He healed people, where He rallied His followers and where He was crucified and then miraculously rose again!

Ruth reading her local Tatler in the Dead Sea

24

FLOATING WHERE HEROD FLOATED!

*I*t was an unforgettable experience to discover that no matter what you weigh, you suddenly become unsinkable because the Dead Sea is 9.6 times saltier than the ocean. That is why no fish or plant can survive in the Dead Sea.

I sat back as if in a comfy armchair and bobbed about in the Dead Sea reading a completely dry newspaper. That photo caused some mirth when it made its way into the school magazine. I was reading our local Tattler in Israel.

I suddenly remembered being told by a tour guide that in certain parts, the Dead Sea is almost 300m deep and that at 430.5 metres below sea level, I was now wallowing about at the lowest point on earth! Soon after, it was somewhat mind blowing to be whisked off in a cable car that same afternoon to the heights of Masada to enjoy a mountain top experience.

But before that unforgettable experience, we were invited to take a mud bath in a resort believed to be one of the world's first health spas. Our guide informed us that a swim in the Dead Sea followed by a mud bath would be beneficial for all our ailments, including acne, boils, cellulite, dandruff, muscle aches, psoriasis and even stress! The reason for its health benefits is that the Dead Sea contains up to eight times more minerals than most sea water.

If like me, you prefer to keep your swimsuit on when you bathe or sun tan, and if you have never been to Cape Town's famous nudist beach at Sandy Bay, you may find a nasty shock awaits you. The rude awakening comes soon after a very arid stretch, where archaeologists believe the infamous cities of Sodom and Gomorrah once stood. (Where a dear little white-haired lady on our bus called out to the guide, "Are you going to point out the sacred spot where Lot's wife was turned into a salt cellar!") Your tour bus or taxi suddenly comes upon an attractive oasis Spa with a glass dome and a sign saying Nudist Friendly. It's a popular Dead Sea Spa with cool fresh water pools and soothing hot springs and mineral baths. It was just a few kilometres away from the spot where the Dead Sea scrolls were discovered in clay jars by a young Bedouin shepherd, his cousin and a shepherd pal in a series of caves at Q'mran.

It was at this Spa, that we conservative South Africans all wore our swim suits or shorts for the sake of modesty, as we sipped our refreshments or relaxed in the water bubbling from the hot springs. Suddenly our attention was diverted to a steaming pool alongside the restaurant. There we saw men and women of all creeds and colours, in all shapes and sizes, prancing about unashamedly in their birthday suits, showing off their assets, and in some cases, their liabilities! Some of the spa visitors should really have kept their assets under wrap. Many of the male bathers with steaming bodies resembled walruses covered in thick black mud but judging by the blissful expressions on most faces, those wallowing were revelling in every joyous moment of the experience.

Our guide told us this spot is believed to be one of the oldest health spa's in the world and is now being flooded with Russian tourists. I guess since they no longer feel politically repressed, their new -found sense of freedom gives them this desire to relax and just let it all hang out!

Our guide believes this spa is probably situated where Herod the Great enjoyed coming to wallow in the hot springs or cover himself in the healing black mud, if he knew of its miraculous healing powers.

With your Bible in your hand as you walk where Jesus walked, you can see in a most remarkable way how biblical prophecy is being fulfilled. Best of all, you can venture into the future with a bolder sense of trust and a firmer faith knowing that there is hope and a bright future for the Promised Land and all its people. It is so good to know that my faith is rooted and grounded in events that occurred in real places and upon my belief in a real Person who walked and talked, who conquered death and who loves and cares about every unique individual on this planet.

When asked what I remember most, and what stirred me deeply having visited Israel on three separate occasions, three memories are indelibly etched in my mind and my soul.

I shall never be the same after my visit to the Yad Vashem Holocaust History Museum in Jerusalem. The museum occupies over 4 200 square metres and presents the horrifying story of the Holocaust (or Shoah) from a Jewish perspective, describing the intense suffering of the victims at the hands of Hitler and his Nazi Wehrmacht. (Military) Viewers pass exhibits in shocked silence and disbelief. Sometimes the silence is broken by gasps and uncontrollable sobbing. One is gripped by the grim reality that the Holocaust was no Myth. It actually happened and affected millions of innocent people, young and old. There you see original artefacts, letters, diaries, photographs, and personal possessions right before your eyes. All these bear testimony to this heinous period in our world's history. There was not a dry eye at the end of our tour as we had listened to heart breaking recordings made by survivors. I shall never forget the sight of a pair of pigtails belonging to a beautiful little girl whose mom had cut them off and tucked them away in a bag hoping to save them. Tragically both mom and daughter were killed. I found the Children's Memorial deeply disturbing. One walks past hundreds of reflected candles, and as you hear names being continuously read out, you are reminded that every single burning candle is there as a heart- breaking reminder of a precious young life that was cruelly snuffed out.

Before departing, we were taught why Jewish people prefer to use the word "Shoah" rather than "Holocaust." Apparently the word "Holocaust entered the English language as a word coming from Greek and used to describe a sacrifice or burnt offering such as we read of in the Old Testament where Abraham was actually willing to sacrifice his only son in obedience to God.

The Jews therefore felt it was totally wrong to imply that the murder of the Jews was a sacrifice acceptable to God. In fact, many felt it was blasphemous, so you may quite often hear it being referred to as the Shoah. Some parents even teach their children to avoid referring to the Holocaust.

Many fellow travellers I meet, quite often seem fearful about planning a trip to Israel for security reasons and because of unrest and political tensions on the West Bank. However, on my three visits to the Holy Land I have been most impressed by the security one encounters when flying with El Al Airlines and by the competence of their skilled pilots. You have to try and separate the politics from the reality of daily life on the ground for the average Israeli citizen. I have found Israelis to be courageous and resilient.

They appear to have learnt to live boldly and as normally and as positively as possible. You will see the locals all around you, pottering and haggling in markets, chatting in the supermarket or sipping coffee on pavement cafés with their friends and loved ones. Of course there is always the fear that there could be a terrorist attack anywhere and at any time, but hasn't this become a risk one faces the world over after recent attacks in London, Paris, Nice, Madrid, Manchester, Brussels, Berlin and even in Stockholm and Toronto, previously considered very safe havens for tourists.

Israel as a country is extremely security conscious and I don't think I have felt safer in any other airport I have ever passed through than in Ben Gurion.

There are armed guards wherever you look and your luggage will be scrutinized to make sure that it's completely safe. I bought several little salt and pepper sets in Bethlehem to take home as gifts. They were beautifully carved from olive wood and looked innocuous, yet when my luggage was opened and searched the souvenirs were tapped, peered into and scanned with a special instrument checking for dangerous contents.

There is excellent unobtrusive security provided at all the tourist sights. If there was any real threat of unrest or terrorist activity you would be warned in advance to avoid that area. Do not let fear stop you from a life- changing experience by visiting the Land of the Book and walking in the steps of Jesus and His friends.

A visit to Tiberius and the Sea of Galilee is a definite spiritual highlight never to be missed. Grab the opportunity to sail on a wooden boat, a replica of the kind of fishing boat which Jesus and His fishermen friends used regularly.

You will even have the thrill of being able to cast a net over the side of the boat and will be reminded of the disciple Peter's utter amazement, when under the direction of Jesus he netted a catch of 153 very large fishes after a whole night of fruitless labour. The waves may suddenly become boisterous as often happens, when without warning, the wind funnels through steep valleys surrounding the lake. The tranquil surface is whipped into fierce waves and you will have a very clear picture of how alarming it must have been when the disciples' little fishing vessel was swamped by monstrous waves. Yet there was their friend Jesus, sleeping peacefully in the stern just waiting for them to trust Him. What comfort and confidence the memory of this event brings to folk feeling swamped by life's problems, to realise that Jesus is with them in every stormy situation and at just the right moment, He will intervene on their behalf. As we pass through life's stormy waters, we often need to pause and hear Him speak those very same words, "Why are you so afraid? Peace be still! "

One of the most beautiful scenic spots to visit in the Holy Land is undoubtedly the site believed by many Christians to be the burial and resurrection place of the Lord Jesus Christ. The rock-hewn tomb in the form of a cave was unearthed in 1867 and from this tranquil garden, which is outside the city walls, one looks across at the rugged hill many believe is Golgotha, known as the Place of the Skull, just 97 metres away, where Jesus was crucified with two criminals, one on either side of him. One can distinctly make out caves and indentations which resemble eye sockets and a definite nasal cavity. The Golgotha site is considered by many believers to be an alternative to the one inside the Church of the Holy Sepulchre.

It was there that a sacred moment was marred as we waited for over an hour in a long, jostling queue suffused in a haze of sickly sweet incense. Upon entering this site, we found it lacked the natural unspoilt authenticity of the Garden Tomb because it had become a glitzy and ornate tourist trap.

We were soon pounced upon by self -appointed "Pilgrims" requesting that we buy their sacred candles, make wishes, say prayers and place coins at the supposed burial site, whereas in the Garden of the Tomb, we were enfolded in an incredible sense of peace and joy. Like me, you too will surely be filled with tremendous hope and optimism when you step inside the far more authentic looking, roughly hewn empty garden tomb and read the inspiring words of the angel on guard, carved in a wooden plaque,

HE IS NOT HERE - FOR HE IS RISEN!

25

OUR OWN CAVE ADVENTURE IN
THAILAND

*I*t is ironic that as I have been reflecting on my own memories of the Q'mran caves near the Dead Sea where we learnt of the incredible discovery of 7 very precious biblical scrolls found hidden in clay jars and rescued by a young Bedouin shepherd, so one of the biggest ever cave rescue missions has been underway. This rescue was taking place up in the north of Thailand, very close to the Myanmar border. This mammoth operation involved up to 1 000 volunteers and captivated the world's attention and attracted the focus of global media. Many of us sat glued to our T.V sets for the duration of the heart- stopping Thai rescue operation which lasted almost three weeks.

Twelve very precious young soccer players, ranging in age from 11 to 16 and their devout 25 year old Buddhist assistant coach, were rescued and brought out into the daylight after what must have been a terrifying ordeal.

It all started on 23 June 2018 as innocent fun after a hot tiring soccer practice. A number of the young team members from the Ma Poo Academy or The Wild Boars Football Team had explored the caves on previous occasions and were mindful of all the dangers. The outing was designed to encourage team building and was also a form of initiation. As part of their fitness training, the boys had to cycle for 45 minutes, straight after their soccer practice in their home town of Mae Sai, to reach the notorious Tham Luang cave complex. It is believed to be Thailand's longest cave network, with an intricate series of twisting tunnels and bends, some only 15 to 18 cm wide, and with slippery rocks and jagged limestone cliffs where sections suddenly drop away into treacherous bottomless chasms of Stygian darkness.

The boys were in high spirits. The head coach also wanted to test his young assistant, Ekkapol Chantawong's leadership ability and see whether he was able to manage the young soccer team on his own. They left their bikes and soccer boots near the cave entrance, and barefooted they ran the 2, 5 km length of the cave tunnel, proudly scrawled their names on the back wall as proof of their courage, then turned back hoping to scramble out into the warmth and daylight again.

The large warning sign at the mouth of the caves should possibly have curbed their curiosity and dampened their boyish enthusiasm. It warned would-be explorers in no uncertain terms of the possibility of very rapid and highly dangerous flooding during the monsoon season but the boys and their coach had scanned the sky and decided that rain was not imminent. They felt fit and were well -prepared so in they went, expecting to emerge within an hour.

But suddenly the heavens opened. They had not bargained for a torrential monsoon downpour that flooded the entrance tunnel with metres of muddy water and made the young fellows crawl further and further back into the darkness in a desperate and treacherous search for a little island of dry land on which to perch. The raging flood waters completely cut off their escape route to home, parents, school and friends. The cave was dank and cold and became so dark they could not see their own fingers held up before their eyes. Some boys had torches but their coach wisely suggested they ration the light and extend the battery life.

At 7 pm the head coach of The Wild Boars soccer team, Nopparat Kathawong (I just love the Thai names!) knew that something was terribly amiss when he started receiving frantic telephone calls from the boys' desperate parents.

When interviewed on TV the wide- eyed and grief stricken head coach told how his body went completely cold when he heard that the boys were still missing long after dark.

His and the desperate pleas of the boys' parents, triggered an international rescue operation which seemed to jerk the entire world into action. The Thai government was outstanding in co-ordinating a well-oiled and incredibly efficient and logistically sound rescue and relief mission, which at the same time was passionate and heart - warming. It became a marathon race against time to save the team as oxygen levels dwindled and monsoon rains pounded the Chiang Rai district. The world realised that any remnants of the boys' little picnic snacks would long since have been gobbled up and their water bottles would have been drained soon after their hot thirsty bike ride to the cave.

The tragedy united the nations of the world. People of every faith and creed prayed earnestly for a miraculous rescue and God intervened and answered in an incredible way.

After being trapped in complete darkness with no food and only surviving by licking drops of water seeping from the rain drenched rocks, the boys and their stout-hearted young coach, Ekkapol, were first spotted by two highly- trained and very experienced British divers at 10.30 pm local time on the ninth day. Thanks to fantastic high tech Israeli communication devices resembling walkie talkies, a direct line was established whereby those trapped deep in the cave network where cell phone reception was impossible, could actually be in contact with their rescuers and their families and friends over 4km away. Will we ever forget the first words of those divers spoken to the bedraggled little band of wide- eyed boys huddled on the slippery ledge, "How many of you are there?" The only one who could speak English responded immediately, "Thirteen," and the triumphant cry of the diver resounded throughout the cave, "Brilliant!" The entire team was still alive after what must have been a formidable and chilling ordeal.

The world watched and waited in rapt suspense and marvelled at the boys' resilience, fortitude and discipline. Their humble coach proved to be a selfless and inspiring young leader, who sacrificed his own food rations to build the boys' strength. He kept their spirits high and we are told that his training as a young Buddhist monk helped him teach his team to meditate, stay calm and to keep a bright spirit of optimism alive. By the 18th day the last group of boys and their young coach had been safely brought out of the cave.

Tragically one of Thailand's own ex- Navy seal divers, Saman Kunan, from Roi Et and aged only 38, one of the first volunteers to hasten to the rescue, lost his own life sacrificially while delivering oxygen tanks to enable those trapped in the cave to survive. Saman was a highly respected diver who loved adventurous sport and was a talented triathlon athlete. It is suspected that this heroic young man suffocated when he himself ran out of oxygen having placed air tanks all along the 4 km route to the trapped boys. Upon reflecting on her husband's death, Saman's lovely young wife, Waleeporn, spoke these thought provoking words when interviewed by the BBC, "My husband always used to say, We never knew when we would die. We can't control that, so we need to cherish every day."

The entire world was riveted to TV screens, laptops, tablets and cell phones, hardly daring to breathe, eat or sleep, not wanting to miss a moment of one of the most momentous modern day miracles. Every nation and tribe watched with bated breath as the young boys were gently bundled up and sedated by an Australian anaesthetist. Supported by two of the world's best divers, each boy was then steered to safely through an intricate maze– like network of treacherous tunnels. What profound relief and joy was felt when in batches of four, the boys were all rescued alive. After a period of quarantine and isolation in hospital to assess their medical conditions, they were joyously re-united with their families and friends.

What a tale they have to share with their teachers and school mates! It was hard to hold back tears when seeing Akarat Wonsukchan's tears of relief and gratitude as he said he could not wait to hug his 14 year old son and tell him how happy he felt.

Two days later, I sang along with Adul Sam-on, the 14 year old Christian member of the soccer team who beamed broadly as he was welcomed back to his family's local Baptist Church with a bucket of Kentucky Fried Chicken, warm embraces and songs of praise. He was the only member of the Wild Boars soccer team who speaks English. Adul was the one who responded when the British divers first came upon the mud- caked stranded group and asked how many survivors there were. It was heart-warming to see this brave young fellow kneel before the church congregation and demonstrate how every single day, he had knelt in the cave and asked God to spare their lives. What a powerful witness this young man is going to be as he shares the news of his faithful God who intervenes in the affairs of our lives and who hears and answers prayers beyond our wildest imagination!

Joe and I are passionate about Thailand. We first visited the Land of Smiles in 2003 and loved everything about the country. The happy, warm-hearted Thai people really do smile all the time and seem to exude warmth and joy. They make you feel so welcome on their shores. Joe learnt to sing their National Anthem which has a lovely rousing tune. The Thai people we bump into, who are either working here or visiting South Africa, swell with pride and joy every time they hear their anthem. When they hear a "farang" (foreigner) strike up, they become quite emotional and get tears in their eyes because they immediately sense that we too love their country.

You won't be surprised then when I tell you we recently returned after our tenth visit to Thailand! So you will understand why we became engrossed in every detail of the cave rescue. We stayed in Thailand for a whole month this time and caught up with many of the delightful friends we have made over the years.

The spine chilling drama in the flooded Thai cave kept me up late at night as I followed fresh developments and breaking news from heart-stopping radio bulletins and TV news updates. We also received SMS messages at all hours of the day from our friends in Thailand who knew how much our thoughts and prayers were with the trapped soccer team.

What made it all so real to us was that a few years ago on one of our Thai holidays Joe and I actually dared to undertake a cave adventure. "Sheer Madness!" some wise old friends said!

Joe and I were by far the oldest couple on the full day excursion and I am sure some of the youngsters wondered how an old chap in his 80's with heart stents and a wife in her 70's with a bionic knee would manage to scramble up and down the metal rungs of the ladder on the tour boat! And then be required to hop in and out of a bobbing rubber canoe many times during the day. We got some very strange looks to start with but I think we surprised them!

Joe is a huge fan of Roger Moore and he loves seeing heart-stopping James Bond movies. Arriving in Phuket, we had been reminded that many exciting films have been produced in Thailand, one of which was a favourite of Joes' called The Man with the Golden Gun which was filmed in 1974.The breathtakingly beautiful setting was Phang Nga Bay which is part of the glorious turquoise Andaman Sea. The Bay is 400 square miles and lies between the east coast of Phuket and the mainland of south Thailand. The Bay falls within the Ao Phang Nga National Park and we had heard it was a protected pristine area, home to numerous fascinating land and sea creatures as well as lush tropical plant life.

Joe had decided that the James Bond and Phang Nga tour should definitely feature on our bucket list and preferably before he reached the age of 90! I think he may have tried to picture himself hanging onto a walker or a Zimmer frame and trying to manoeuvre himself in and out of a kayak if he waited until he had celebrated a few more birthdays! So without further delay we asked the lovely Thai ladies at the front desk in our hotel to book us on an Adventure Tour.

Joe recalled how James Bond was sent to Thailand in search of the Solex Agitator, a device which could harness the sun's power. Of special interest would be our visit to the now famous James Bond Island and other fascinating tropical islands in the bay. We both felt certain that the highlight of the day would be our cave adventure where we would follow in the steps, or should I say, paddle along the exact kayak route which the heroic Roger Moore, had taken in the rôle of M16 Agent Bond! Like Joe's screen hero, we too would explore the deep, dark inner recesses of a network of caves and take in all the sights and sounds which had filled James Bond with awe and wonder!

The tour company fetched us from our hotel very early in the morning and transported us to our double decker motor boat moored at the Laem Sai Pier. Thirty of us climbed aboard and found it to be comfortable and clean with a functional kitchen below deck level as well as having toilet facilities. It took us about 90 minutes to reach Phang Nga Bay. Tea, coffee, fruit juice and bottled water was available throughout the tour. Joe and I have always found that February or March are favourable months to be in Thailand. The peak holiday season has ended and tourist prices begin to drop. On two occasions we visited in April to experience the joy and excitement of the Thai New Year known as Songkran but we found it extremely hot and humid, being the beginning of the rainy season.

The scenery on all sides of our motor boat was spectacular. Cell phones and cameras were clicking and videos were buzzing and whirring all around us. The soaring limestone cliffs and crags often rose 300 meters into the sky. There were amazing rock formations. With a bit of imagination, you could clearly make out majestic stallions leaping skywards and crocodiles with wide open mouths and vicious jagged teeth. Our guide was attentive to our needs and was highly informative throughout the day. He mentioned that there were about 48 islands dotted about. Some have centres which have collapsed over centuries due to erosion and volcanic action. Exquisite secret lakes and lagoons have formed inside these centres, with some only accessible by canoe or kayak via very narrow twisting tunnels.

It was a relief to hear our guide say that motor boats and speed boats are not allowed to enter the caves. Imagine a high speed collision in the pitch dark!

All fear was momentarily dispelled as we drank in the sheer beauty of Phang Nga Bay with its towering limestone cliffs, monumental tusk-like pillars and giant fangs which soar artistically into the azure sky.

The sea was calm and alluring. It was deep turquoise or jade, depending on how the bright shafts of sunlight filtered through the rocky chasms and fissures. In parts the sea was less appealing. Where there were menacing overhanging ledges, the sea suddenly became a dark, oily olive green.

We sailed past the Viking Caves and found them to be rich in history. The impressive caves have become home to thousands of birds called Swifts. We were astounded to hear that these birds form nests using their own saliva! What amazed us even more, is that the Chinese risk life and limb climbing up treacherous ledges to retrieve these nests which they turn into birds' nest soup! Believe it or not, it is regarded as a very tasty treat in China. Joe and I sampled some when we were in

Singapore but we both found it rather watery and salty. Furthermore, the little chunks of birds' nests and pieces of flimsy foliage could easily have been mistaken for floating noodles! We both felt it wasn't worth risking a broken neck climbing up cave ledges and decided a tin of mushroom soup or hearty beef would be preferable!

There are two Phi Phi islands ~ Koh Phi Phi Leh and Koh Phi Phi Don. "Koh" means "island" and Phi Phi is pronounced Pee-Pee. The islands are part of a group between the large island of Phuket and the west Strait of Malacca. Phi Phi Don, a favourite destination of ours, is the largest and most populated island of the group and has some beautiful hotels and self -catering bungalows. Phi Phi Ley is where the very popular movie, The Beach, was filmed and the island has a number of uninhabited and unspoilt little sandy beaches.

The motor boat dropped anchor close to Bat Cave. It was almost time to clamber down into our rubber kayak. Every two canoeists would be accompanied by an expert Thai paddler who knew the layout of each cave and understood the intricacies of the winding dark tunnels and very narrow gaps through which a kayak could only just squeezes. The leader of our tour group drew three members of our party aside and very tactfully told them that they were a little too large to manage the entire route. I held my breath and pulled in my tummy. Several others said they suffered from claustrophobia and asked to stay on the motor boat rather than risk entering the dark recesses of the cave as they feared they might suffer panic attacks.

Joe and I suddenly remembered all we had heard and read about the hazards of undertaking cave exploits. Birds, bats and rats often carry harmful microbes including rabies! Some obscure fungal infections can afflict intrepid explorers with a ghastly Marburg virus. We might encounter venomous snakes, killer bees and spiders in these pitch dark tropical caves! We had been warned that we would find some caves to be decidedly smelly. We knew we would be shown thousands of bats all hanging upside down and resembling tiny rumpled academic gowns or bedraggled black rain coats. We knew that bat droppings often contain pathogenic fungi.

Someone with a medical background back at our hotel had frightened us by saying, "Beware of Leptospira and Melioidosis!" The names of these ghastly afflictions are somewhat intimidating, aren't they! They could be the names of two Vampires or two Land Grabbers invading our planet from Outer Space! One could possibly contract Leptospira and Melioidosis if you trudge through infected mud, clay or dirty water in a cave or in a swampy rice paddy.

How wise that the young members of the Wild Boars soccer team were immediately given antibiotics upon arrival at the Prachanukroh Hospital in Chiang Rai after their miraculous cave rescue to prevent any of these diseases from taking hold in the boys' weakened state.

The dreaded Melioidosis can cause severe headaches, disorientation, pneumonia, chest pains and even lung nodules. The guerrilla fighters, trudging through mud and clay and sloshing through sodden rice paddies called this disease the Vietnam Time bomb and in their language it could be translated to mean The Distemper of Asses! Many soldiers contracted another nasty disease called Leptospira caused by corkscrew- shaped bacteria lurking in the urine of rodents. If the urine finds its way into water or soil and comes into contact with your eyes, mouth or nose, or penetrates your skin, one might become feverish and experience severe headaches, myalgia, skin rashes or eye problems. Some unfortunate victims have even developed meningitis, kidney failure or hearing loss.

It was too late to turn back now. Joe and I had both managed to climb gingerly down the metal rungs of the ladder from the swaying boat and we plonked down in our inflatable rubber kayak without falling backwards into the Andaman Sea. Surely the Thai government would not permit tour companies to take unwitting tourists into dangerous caves where all these deadly dangers could be waiting to strike! Let's banish these dreaded fears and enjoy the cave adventure!

Somsak, our experienced Thai paddler, was rearing to go....we clung onto the sides and off we glided, straight towards the caves.... His knowledge of English was limited and he could not pronounce his r's but he was cheerful and encouraging. "You not flightened?" he asked.

"A little bit", I said trying to muster some courage. "No ploblem " he replied. " I velly good in dark caves. Papa and Mama no be flightened. Somsak plomise to not lost you in dark tunnels."

I took a deep breath, remembering my Arab guide in Bethlehem who also said he was very good in dark caves and then misbehaved underneath the Church of the Nativity! That's where he was supposed to be an upright gentleman showing me where Saint Jerome translated the Vulgate!

Our canoe glided effortlessly into the first cave. Somsak called it Ice Cream cave because of the fascinating rock formations which looked like melted ice cream dripping down the walls. The beauty of the first cave surpassed all expectations. Apart from the gentle swish of the paddles and the rhythmic drip drip-drip from the roof of the cave just above us, we were enfolded by darkness and silence. The atmosphere was magical and soothing to the soul. Our paddler explained that we had entered a "Hong" which in Thai means an open space like a large room inside a cave. Some writers have described hongs as being like secret sanctuaries. A wonderful sense of peace came over us as we glided through the Hong and out into the dazzling sunshine on the other side.

Next we paddled into Bat Cave. Here we felt more apprehensive. It was pitch dark and very smelly. We could not see our hands in front of our noses. We lay flat on our backs in our kayak as our paddler flashed his torch upwards.

There were literally thousands of bats hanging upside down between jagged looking stalactites. All the bats seemed to be fast asleep with their wings folded as if clad in creased gowns but Somsak's bright flashlight disturbed them and some made faint whimpering or squeaking sounds. Rising up from the floor of the caves were tapered stalagmites stretching upwards in menacing poses.

The air was pungent with the smell of bat guano. We were all relieved when Somsak paddled out of the blackness and took us through a sunlit mangrove forest. We learnt that mangroves are surprisingly resilient to saline water and thrive if the temperature remains above 19 deg C.

We almost expected to see Tarzan swinging from a bough in the mangrove forest as our canoe wound its way through the massive inter-meshed root system, but instead we were greeted by an egret and some secretive macaque monkeys. A graceful sea eagle soared overhead.

We then swished our way silently though Diamond Cave where the walls and roof appeared to be encrusted with a myriad glistening diamond chips. Then followed some chilling moments....the spring tide was coming in a little earlier and a little faster than expected. Somsak told us to pull in our tummies and make ourselves as flat as possible because we were about to negotiate a very narrow tunnel. It was 80 metres long and would take us to a beautiful secret lagoon. Suddenly our canoe had slipped into pitch darkness again.

Somsak was grabbing at the roof of the cave to pull us along. There was no room for the paddles. We tried to help him but the ceiling was covered in slimy barnacles which tore at our palms. This became a frightening and claustrophobic experience...suddenly there was a very loud hissing noise. We both froze.

Joe shouted, "Puncture, puncture!" We could feel that our canoe was losing air very quickly and sinking lower and lower into the inky water. But the intrepid Somsak quickly re-assured us saying, "No fear Mama and Pappa. It's only me, Somsak. I pull stopper. Let air out. Make kayak smaller or we may not get out safe. High tide is coming fast to catch us in the cave! "

So we forgot about the barnacles and tugged for all we were worth to help Somsak get us out of the cave before the tide trapped us. There was no way back and no dry ledge to clamber onto and no British or Thai Navy seals to rescue us! By the time we saw daylight our noses were almost scraping the barnacles!

As we emerged from our cave adventure, we noticed that our motor boat had dropped anchor nearby and was rocking gently on the rising tide. It was a relief to hear that we would be served a Thai buffet lunch back on the deck. Our legs were like jelly by the time Somsak had hauled us from the rather deflated and dejected looking kayak and helped us up the rungs of the ladder and safely back on board.

Lunch was a delicious Thai buffet with fresh seafood, appetising barbecued meat, and fragrant chicken curry, kebabs and satays and a variety of vegetables, salads and fresh fruit. The fragrance of lemon grass, coconut, crushed chillies, coriander and grated ginger tickled our taste buds.

Smiling Thai hospitality and Thai culinary skill is hard to beat!

After lunch we were taken to a beautiful little beach on Lawa Island where we were given bamboo mats to enjoy a tranquil siesta under the shady palms. One could have a quiet read while there was also time to snorkel or swim in the crystal clear water. In spite of some hair raising moments in the dark, Joe and I both agreed it was an excursion not to be missed. However, after our own heart-stopping moments in the stygian darkness, it has made us realise just how frightened the young Thai soccer team must have felt being trapped for 18 days and what an incredible miracle their rescue was.

26

I LOVE THAILAND!

We have come to love and respect the Thai people for many reasons. Joe owes his life to two fantastic doctors, Jakkawan Wongiwat and Arora Varin who inserted two heart stents for him when, on the third day of our holiday in 2012, he was suddenly admitted for emergency surgery to the Bangkok International Hospital in Phuket. The name is a little misleading but it's the sister hospital to the larger Bangkok hospital. What amazing medical care and compassionate attention Joe received there from an exemplary Team of dedicated cardiac surgeons, doctors and nurses in a pristine hospital environment.

An intensive cardiac and neurological check-up following Joe's 'funny turn,' in a delightful restaurant called The Two Chefs at Kata Beach on the night of my birthday, revealed that Joe's droopy left eye and skew mouth was indicative of having suffered what is often referred to as a T.I.A. or Transient ischaemic attack, caused by temporary blocking of an artery to the brain by a small clot. Despite appearing normal again within ten minutes after I had popped a soluble Disprin tablet under his tongue, I realised Joe needed to be admitted to hospital urgently to distinguish the T.I.A symptoms from an actual stroke.

Fortunately we were still on the mainland of Phuket for ten days. It could have been a very tricky situation had we needed to be airlifted at great expense by a helicopter from Phi Phi Island in the middle of the night!

The senior lady in charge of bookings and room reservations at The Boathouse Hotel in Phuket is an amazing Thai lady called Jarinee Thongmool who has worked there for the past 30 years. We met this charming and highly competent lady in 2004 when we first discovered this intimate boutique hotel right on Kata Beach. Since then we have returned regularly and have formed many lovely friendships there. The Boathouse Team has created for us a warm and nurturing Home from Home atmosphere. So much so that Jarinee arranged private transport to rush Joe straight to the hospital and when he was admitted, the hotel management sent him magnificent floral arrangements and a number of their staff even made the journey through heavy traffic to come and visit him.

Upon admission to hospital, an impressive battery of tests followed, including an MRI and an echo-cardiogram, following which two cardiac specialists recommended that Joe urgently have two heart stents inserted. It was his first experience of acupuncture to help control the pain together with a light local anaesthetic. Joe says he floated through the procedure called a coronary angioplasty and found it fascinating to be sufficiently alert to watch what was happening on a large monitor ahead of him. He marvelled at the skill and dedication of the Indian and the Thai cardiac surgeon as they worked side by side. A small tube called a sheath was inserted into an artery in the groin. The sheath they explained, would help to keep the artery open while they guided a long, flexible plastic tube called a catheter into the opening of Joe's left coronary artery. The next stage was intricate.

Joe held his breath as Dr Varin explained that a thin flexible wire would be passed down the inside of the catheter, taking with it a very tiny sausage- shaped balloon which would be inflated for probably not more than 20 − 30 seconds at a time to help clear any fatty deposits causing blockages along the route. Quite miraculously there were two stents made of metal mesh, positioned in the little balloon and they were skilfully deposited in the artery once the balloon was deflated and removed. Coloured dye had been injected into the arteries and the doctors used live X ray pictures to help identify any blocked arteries.

The surgeons advised us that Joe would be kept in the Intensive Care Unit for two nights before being transferred to a private ward.

You can well imagine that having an traumatic experience like this in a foreign country right at the start of our holiday, and being thousands of kilometres from family and loved ones, in an unfamiliar hospital with very few people around us able to speak English, was a very frightening experience. The surgeons had taken us aside and explained that there were certain risks involved, and more so for patients who were over 80. They said they would give us five minutes to consult the family and make our decision regarding surgery. However, Thailand is five hours ahead of South Africa and we figured it was still far too early back home. We did not want to cause alarm by telephoning at an unearthly hour. We realised that it was actually essential to have the operation performed without further delay. Joe said he felt quietly confident and was completely at peace. Before he entered the operating theatre, we prayed that God would grant the surgeons wisdom and skill as they performed this emergency procedure on Joe in his 84th year.

We were most grateful for the international medical insurance benefits offered by Joe's medical aid and his operation and hospital stay was covered in full. We are amazed at how many folk set off on overseas holidays without any thought of taking out travel insurance, not realising that a mishap like breaking a leg in a skiing accident or falling off a scooter in a foreign country, could run into thousands of rands, pounds or dollars in hospital bills.

We had rushed to the hospital at 6.30am on the morning after the T.I.A. and were both unprepared for an extended stay. Joe was soon kitted out in a fresh hospital gown. Because the temperature was 30 deg. C, I was wearing light-weight cotton pants, a short-sleeved blouse and open sandals. I was provided with a comb and a toothbrush which was very helpful. The hospital functions with a skeleton staff on night duty, so I was expected to stay for the entire week. This proved quite a challenge! I had to doss down on a couch in the ward to help with simple tasks and to listen out for the bleeping of the various heart machines. Joe was called Papa by the Thai nurses and was cared for in a most loving and attentive way. There was much mirth and frivolity as he was showered by a giggling bevy of three Thai ladies who insisted on lathering him from top to toe with a great big soapy sponge attached to a long stick!

Our hotel was way down south on the island of Phuket, almost an hour's drive away in a taxi and much longer in a crowded bus. When I suggested I take a taxi to our hotel to pack a little suitcase of clothes and toiletries, the medical staff insisted I remain with Joe. What was originally expected to be no more than a 5 to 7 day stay in the hospital, turned into an eventful ten day period because of a setback caused by the anti-coagulants. (blood thinners)

Remembering the Afrikaans saying " 'n Boer maak 'n plan," (A farmer makes a plan!) and being used to re-cycling in Cape Town, I quickly formulated a plan to re-cycle my outfit! There was a handy little 7 Eleven café in the alley behind the hospital. I made a wonderful discovery there. They sold basic make-up, roll- on deodorant (with the enticing name Blue Moon!) and best of all, packets of disposable panties! I spotted a bargain! A whole fortnight's supply. They come in pretty pastel colours and have dainty Thai flowers printed on them. The size was a problem! I settled for Xtra Large because Thai ladies are diminutive. The panties were made from rice paper and had an intriguing warning printed on the wrapper, "Not advisable for the Consumption of Humans!"

A solemn word of cautious at this point! Do not wear disposable panties to the beach if you think you may have to sit on damp sand. Not only will you have a bare posterior when you stand up to leave, but the vibrant dye used in the panties, may cause you to leave the beach with a delightful little posy of orchids, jasmine or frangipani printed on your nether regions for a good few weeks. Perhaps the name Fannypani would be more appropriate!

Instead of a blanket at night, the Thai nurses provided me with a white cotton cover resembling a very large beach towel, so after my shower each night, I would wash one item of clothing. The air conditioning was very effective so it drip-dried overnight and in this way I managed to recycle my garments and keep clean. I really did miss not having a nightie and because of the heat and humidity outside, the air conditioner was set at a decidedly cool temperature.

Sadly the café behind the hospital did not sell hair rollers and of course my hot brush was back at our hotel, but fortunately in a little side street not far from the hospital, I spotted a welcoming sign on a window …

"Kitty's Hair Parlor… come as you are. Leave Beautiful."

I sincerely hoped that the sweet gentle little Thai Kitty could provide me with a quick shampoo and blow dry. The only problem was Kitty couldn't speak a word of English and didn't seem to know what a blow dry was although I tried to demonstrate using her dryer and a brush. Kitty knew three English words "I make beautiful" and insisted that I should have my hair set in her tight little pink rollers. I dreaded what my recent perm would look like if small rollers were used. I have discovered since living in a Retirement Village, that some old ladies seem to think they are getting better value for their money if they ask for a tight perm. They then choose to use small rollers so that that their hairdo stays intact for a fortnight!

What I was really looking for, was a natural- looking style which was suitable for going snorkelling or doing aquarobics in the waves once back at Kata Beach.

I battled to keep a straight face when Kitty had finished. She fetched a hand mirror and proudly showed me the transformation she had performed.

Should I laugh or cry! Once again I was very thankful that it was highly unlikely that I was going to encounter any of my past pupils or colleagues back at our hotel. Kitty had very gently removed all the rollers then instead of combing out her handiwork, she had patted all the little rolls into place in neat straight rows and sprayed enough hairspray over them and my entire scalp, to prevent a bullet from piercing my skull!

I knew Joe would be startled by my new look, so for fear of setting his heart machines a-buzzing and a-bleeping, I quickly shot into the ladies' cloakroom to try and comb some normality into my hairstyle so that I would be recognisable to my husband. At least my hair felt fresh and clean again and Kitty's Coiffure was well worth the bargain price of less than fifty rand in our currency!

Somehow I never seem to travel anywhere in the world without experiencing some humorous incidents. This impressive Phuket hospital with its highly skilled Team of medical experts is renowned for its Aesthetics Department.

All through the year, but particularly during the favourable summer months when the weather is at its best in Thailand and at its coldest in Europe, overseas tourists flock there for all manner of beauty treatments and transformations. I marvelled to see the numbers of tourists leaving the hospital to head back to Europe after successful surgery for tummy tucks, breast augmentations, (boob jobs) rhinoplasty, (nose jobs) brow lifts, liposuction, chin shaving and gender re-assignment!

Advertisements in our Cape Town newspapers recently encouraged us to rush to Computicket to grab the last few tickets available at The Artscape Theatre to see one of the biggest Stars to have come out of Rupaul's Drag Race, the inimitable Bianca Del Rio, whose real name is Roy Haylock. Seeing this advert for the forthcoming attraction, reminds me of what happened to me in Phuket.

While Joe was in ICU for the first two days, after the insertion of his heart stents, I was sitting minding my own business and quietly munching a ham and cheese croissant in the hospital restaurant. Suddenly out from the Aesthetics Department strode a real amazon of a person....She was 6ft 2 inch tall with chiselled Nordic features and flowing bottle blonde hair. She glanced around her, as if checking out the landscape, removed her diamanté encrusted sun glasses and quite boldly approached my table and proceeded to try and "chat me up!" I felt intimidated seeing she looked twice my height and had very impressive biceps. I looked down at the Bangkok Post I was reading and showed a great interest in my half eaten croissant!

I pretended to be so foreign that I didn't understand her broken English, German, Swedish or pigeon Thai! When she received no response, she pulled out a chair at my table and sidled in alongside me and cuddled up close. The next moment her hair was draped across my arm. Then in a husky foreign voice she said, "You speak English?" I pulled my chair sideways, desperately needing some breathing space. I was still trying to figure out whether my admirer was a male becoming a She or a She becoming a He because I knew they perform sex change miracles at this hospital! She was beautifully tanned and had shapely waxed legs, yet her stride and mannerisms were manly. She appeared to have had implants resembling tennis balls inserted in her calves. Her profile too struck me as being definitely male. I could see that he/she was wearing a blonde wig which had shifted slightly off centre. I tried staring ahead and acting dumb but she snuggled closer and stroked my hand!

I felt embarrassed and was grateful that I was munching a croissant in Phuket and not tucking into a Spur burger back home in Pinelands. I could imagine my grade 7 past pupils staring and whispering to their parents, "Just check that blonde dolly trying to chat up our Miss Taylor!"

At this point I wondered how I could make a quick getaway without being hurtful or offensive. I thought of responding in Afrikaans but realised she/ he might understand if he/she could speak German or Dutch. I settled for isiXhosa and thought of all the Xhosa words I had ever learnt and strung them together in one long torrent making sure that my clicks were loud and forceful.

Do remember this trick if ever you are trapped in a similar predicament!

It works wonders! My admirer was completely caught off guard and was totally bewildered. She let go of my hand, nearly jumped out of her size 14 gold sandals and disappeared towards the lifts. Whew, that was another close encounter of the amorous kind and this time I wasn't even underground in a dark cave with an Arab guide.

Kata Beach, Phuket, from our hotel at sunset

Our delightful Thai friends in Phuket

27

FLEEING A TSUNAMI WITH BROEKIES, BRA AND BIBLE!

$\mathcal{O}$ ne of our favourite holiday resorts is the Holiday Inn on Laem Tong beach on Phi Phi Island which can be reached by speedboat or ferry from Krabi or from the harbour at Phuket. Since we first discovered this tranquil Thai gem in 2003, we have enjoyed seven blissful stays in beach front bungalows looking across the powdery white beach sand to the emerald Andaman Sea. Just ahead and slightly to your left, one's attention is drawn to two uneven little dollops which appear to have been dumped in the bay like scones dropped on a baking sheet. These are actually fascinating little islands called Bamboo and Mosquito. (Thankfully not for an abundance of "mozzies" on the island, but rather for its shape as you view it from Phi Phi Island.)

The Holiday Inn is situated on the quieter and more secluded side of the island. It has three swimming pools and its own private beach with comfy deck chairs and loungers. What pleased us greatly about this beach was the fact that it offers plenty of shade and has inviting looking hammocks strung between the overhanging trees just waiting for you to clamber in for a quiet read or a gentle snooze. But best of all, the Holiday Inn has its own house reef teeming with exquisite marine life. You do not need to book a snorkelling trip and hire equipment. The hotel loans you snorkelling gear and you can launch straight off the beach and head for the reef. The sea temperature is nearly always 27 or 28 degrees Celcius and before you know it, you will have spent two or three hours wallowing close to the reef and marvelling at the Wonders of Creation.

On her first snorkelling experience out on the reef, we suddenly noticed that a family member on her first visit to Phi Phi had burst into tears. Fearing she had been stung by a blue bottle or had stepped on a sea urchin, we gently enquired what the problem was. She shook the sea water out of her goggles, blinked back her tears and sobbed, "No, nothing is the matter…it's just all so beautiful!" And it was indeed!

Having been enraptured by the sheer beauty of Phi Phi island and the surrounding islands and blessed by the warm hospitality and generous spirit shown by the ever cheerful and smiling Thai staff at the Holiday Inn where nothing is ever too much trouble, you can imagine how stunned Joe and I were to hear news of the 2004 Boxing Day tsunami. It came as an enormous shock to hear that up to 230 000 people throughout S.E. Asia and in 14 countries had lost their lives. We had departed from Phi Island only 8 months before it struck and the numbing news that thousands of local Thai folk and visiting tourists on Phi Phi Island had died or been swept out to sea never to be seen again, left us reeling.

We learnt that the epicentre of the powerful Indian Ocean earthquake was just off the west coast of Sumatra, Indonesia and had a magnitude of 9,1! It had been caused by shifting layers of rock, which my Geography pupils will remember, are called tectonic plates, found deep, deep under the sea. As the plates moved and shook violently and often snapped, many layers of rock were rigorously and haphazardly displaced. Shock waves were sent to the once tranquil seabed which lifted and roared as if in agony. This undersea energy generated massive waves which surged ferociously towards the land. We were told that some waves reached 30 metres high and thundered onto the land at terrifying speeds of 500 miles per hour. It was no wonder then, that we saw terrifying scenes on the TV News of trucks, boats and even train carriages (as happened in Siri Lanka) cruelly tossed about like the little plastic toys our grandchildren throw about in their bath tubs!

In March 2004, Joe and I had made friends with the delightful Australian Hotel General Manager Michal Zitek and his Kiwi fianceé Clare and their Holiday Inn Staff Team and were extremely distressed to think that any of these wonderful new friends might have lost their lives. We made up our minds to return to the island three months after the tsunami to see for ourselves exactly what had happened and to offer our moral support and comfort.

The ferry from Phuket dropped us at the Tonsai Bay pier. From there we were to be taken in a long tail boat to the Holiday Inn on the NE side of the island. We simply could not believe the scenes of utter devastation which met our eyes. We stepped out onto a wasteland. It reminded me of watching Neil Armstrong step down from the Apollo 11 craft and step out on the barren surface of the moon. It was a chilling experience to cross the narrow sandy neck of land separating Ton Sai Bay from Loh Dalum Bay where once lush tropical gardens with vibrant flowers and shrubs had lined the beach and where proud tall palms had waved a warm welcome to Paradise. It is ironic that the name Loh Dalum or Dalam means 'idyllic' or 'exotic' in Thai.

This was all surreal. Two monstrous waves had struck on both sides of the narrow sand spit. Survivors told us harrowing stories of how in the face of a towering wave bearing down on them from one side, they had charged to the opposite side, only to be hammered by another three-storey wall of water which hurled them about as if in a vicious washing machine. The cruel waves felled everything in their wake.

Many victims died when they were struck by massive chunks of concrete, roof rafters, swirling furniture, room safes and air conditioning units. The once pristine beach with its blinding white sand like talcum powder had been churned up and was strewn with rubble and piles of splintered wood, thatch and tree trunks which had snapped like tooth picks. A few palm trees still stood proud but had been stripped of their shady fronds and looked sad and gaunt. Someone had tied a yellow ribbon round a lone trunk. Pinned on the remnants of splintered beach bungalows and shattered walls, were desperate posters. The heart rending words screamed at us...

'MISSING.PLEASE HELP ME FIND....My wife, my child, my brother, our darling baby, my precious grandmother.'

There were happy, smiling holiday photographs attached to the posters and it was impossible to hold back our tears.

The beautiful 5 star Phi Phi Princess Resort and PP Charlie Beach Resort had been completely wiped out. The central shopping hub on the island with all its quaint little shops, dive centres and restaurants had been flattened and resembled crushed match boxes. One of the volunteers helping with cleaning operations told how one of the swimming pools had been used as a mass mortuary while Thai officials waited for relatives to claim the bodies of their loved ones. It was heart-breaking to see huge mounds of items which had been salvaged from deep under the sand. There was clothing, linen, curtains, broken chairs, smashed cameras, diving equipment, beds, souvenirs and once treasured hotel equipment.

Our long tail boat had just pulled in at a make shift jetty so we lugged our suitcases across the scoured beachfront, now flat, colourless and featureless. I tugged gently on a brightly coloured corner of material peeping from the sand and pulled out an exquisite sarong with multi coloured tropical fish and birds. A few paces further my foot struck something sharp protruding from a barren patch of soil and I realised it was the heel of a dainty high heeled evening sandal. Joe and I trudged on in silence....

We both knew exactly what the other was thinking. Had the wearer of that colourful beach sarong and the young lady who wore the pretty gold sandals made it out safely, or were they numbered among the hundreds still missing?

It was a relief to jump down into the warm turquoise water as our long tail boat chugged right up to the beach in front of the Holiday Inn on the north east side of the island. We were grateful to find that the hotel and bungalows appeared unscathed. We thanked God when we heard that no lives had been lost there on Boxing Day. Because the hotel was on the eastern side of Koh Phi Phi, the devastating effect of the two massive waves had been greatly reduced. Much smaller breakers had smacked into the beach bar, damaging chairs and tables, filling the swimming pool with sand and silt and damaging the little thatched massage hut on the beach front. But miraculously the bungalows, the little boutique shop, the reception area and the dining room had escaped the full fury of the tsunami.

As our feet touched the warm sand on the beach, we spotted the smiling face of Michal, the good-natured hands-on General Manager. He welcomed us cordially as returning post tsunami guests. It was a humbling experience to have him wash the sand off our feet with a cleverly designed Thai ladle made from a coconut shell attached to a long stick. We were overjoyed to hear Michal affirm that none of his staff or guests had lost their lives as a result of the tsunami.

We were delighted to find that we had been allocated a beachfront bungalow just a few paces away from the shimmering white sand and the gently lapping azure waves which lulled us to sleep each night. Everything was as perfect as it was on our previous two visits. We recognised many of the ever smiling Thai staff ~ Kuhn Ann, Poo, June, Kai, Ay, Toomi, Jean, Pom, Pan…. who had all cared for us so wonderfully calling us mama and papa and teaching us useful Thai phrases.

Many of the staff members shared heartbreaking stories of close friends and family members who had died in the tsunami or who were still missing at Phang Nga, Krabi, Phuket or Khao Lak. The Thai nation has enormous respect for their Monarchy and many of our Thai friends told us how shocked they were that their king, the late HM King Bhumibol Adulyade, had lost his own grandson, Bhumi Jensen, who was among those killed in Khao Lak. Many told how they had lost close friends who earned a living as fishermen or as sea gypsies and had been washed out to sea. Some were still missing 3 months later. Joe and I were deeply moved by their pain and heartache and this has drawn us very close to the people of Thailand who have worked incredibly hard to rebuild their lives and their nation. They attempted to calm our fears by telling us that not far from our bungalow we would find a sign post directing us to a clearly defined Evacuation Route and promised us that there was now a very effective warning system in place. We would hear loud sirens wailing and would know immediately that a tsunami warning had been issued by the Governor of Phuket.

With this comforting reassurance in our minds, we settled blissfully into our comfortable beach bungalow and spent five care free days relaxing in our pool recliners, reading, swinging in the hammocks, snorkelling for hours on the house reef, eating Häagen-Dazs ice cream and having meaningful chats with our Thai friends.

Five days into our stay, we were joined by three travel-worn relatives of Joe's who had arrived by ferry from Phuket having visited Lao, the River Kwai and Bangkok. They had come to Phi Phi on our recommendation to enjoy a few tranquil days after the hectic buzz and stifling heat of Bangkok. They too are avid nature lovers and outdoor folk and couldn't wait to snorkel. Like us, they were soon overwhelmed by the beauty and tranquility of the island and marvelled at the Wonders of the Deep.

It was a joy being able to share with Cape Town family members all that we have come to love about Phi Phi Island. They were awe struck by the beauty of the flaming tropical sunsets and explosive sunrises which turn the sea into magenta satin. They too were spellbound as they dived deep into the underwater paradise and flippered their way gently through the waving fronds of sea grass and shoals of multi coloured fishes. Through their snorkelling masks they drank in the unsurpassed beauty and fragility of the coral reef with its myriad array of fascinating shapes and vibrant colours.

After snorkelling on the house reef for two hours we floated to the shore to relax in hammocks as we watched the crimson sun begin to slip into the Andaman Sea. Then it was time to shower and freshen up and head for the outdoor deck at the Tai Rom Prao Restaurant to enjoy an al fresco candle-light dinner under the stars. This was Penny's first al fresco experience and she took great delight in the experience. We introduced the new arrivals to delicious fresh sea bass caught that very morning, seasoned with ginger, lemon grass and chilli, wrapped in banana leaves and steamed to perfection over hot coals by the chef from the Cha Bah beachfront restaurant.

We enjoyed our happy, relaxed little family reunion in the moonlight. We could hear the gentle rhythmic swish of the waves and the soft Thai music being played in the background. This gentle, soothing ambience was such a welcome contrast for our family members who had spent the previous night in the heat and the frenetic hype of Bangkok, the Thai capital that stays awake all night.

After a delicious meal, we took a moonlight stroll along the beach before heading into our respective beachfront bungalows to enjoy a good night's rest.

It was 12.45 am when we were rudely awoken by the telephone ringing shrilly close to Joe's pillow. Who on earth would want to contact us at this unearthly hour? Thailand is five hours ahead of South Africa. Could it be bad news from family in England or South Africa?

I fumbled blindly for the lamp switch. Joe was wide awake now and was sitting bolt upright in bed. His sleepy eyes were suddenly saucer-sized. Was this all part of a hideous nightmare caused by what we had experienced upon arrival at Tonsai Bay a few days ago? I froze as I realised that the chilling phone call was from Michal, the General Manager when I heard Joe exclaim, "On no, Michal….Not another tsunami….8,9 magnitude! We'll get out as fast as we can! "

Joe dived into a pair of shorts and grabbed a T-shirt as he headed for the wall safe in the cupboard yelling, "Move it! Tsunami on the way … 8,9 this time.

Same place. Banda Aceh Indonesia."

I could see him delving for his British passport and our air tickets as he gasped, "Michal wants us all up on high ground in the top TV lounge and Sports Room within three minutes!" This was no nightmare and our bungalow was closest to the beach, a mere five metres from the lapping waves. With the horror and utter devastation of the Boxing Day tsunami still so fresh in my mind, I imagined what could happen if we couldn't make it out on time.

RUTH STOTT

Joe continued to fiddle and scratch for his valuable documents. The minutes were ticking by. By now the light in the safe had gone off. He had to punch in his code again and his fingers weren't working fast enough. "Fetch me my specs!" he bellowed. "Ruth, you stand at the door," he yelled, "and scream when you see the waves start to recede!"

This was sheer madness. We had been told that tsunami waves move faster than an express train. I was on the waiting list for a knee replacement and knew that I couldn't even outrun a donkey cart! In the event of the Sports Centre not being sufficiently elevated even though it stood high above our bungalows on its sturdy wooden stilts, we would be summoned by the Manager to the Sunset Terrace and tennis court area. No waves could possibly reach us there. This evacuation route was far steeper and led to the summit of what we in South Africa would call a "Koppie" or small hill. We would all be safe if we made it to the summit in time. We would be 80 meters above sea level and well beyond the grasp of the fiercest tsunami wave.

But how could I leave Joe fiddling in the safe to die alone? We're in this together I thought, but I grew impatient and yelled, "Leave everything... five minutes has passed......Just Run! All those worldly goods can be replaced!" At a time such as this, one is faced with establishing one's priorities. I knew immediately what I would like to have with me if we were stranded on the koppie until rescuers reached us. Quick as a flash I grabbed a pair of broekies (A light- hearted South African word for panties) a bra and my trusty old Bible! After all a bra is a girl's most cherished means of support and my Bible has proved a wonderful comfort and encouragement through many difficult times! Panties would drip dry in ten minutes in the glorious Thai sunshine, so what more could I possibly need! After all, if we were airlifted from the koppie we were sure to be given drinking water, soap and toothbrushes!

After what seemed an eternity, Joe triumphantly held up his British passport and together we headed for the evacuation route, through the silent gardens and up the steep wooden board walk. Thankfully the sea had not started to recede yet. We seemed to be the last guests to leave our bungalow. We were impressed to see the very caring hotel staff

218

sprinting from bungalow to bungalow to ensure that everyone was awake and had heeded the Manager's emergency call.

As I trotted up the board walk I heard Joe shout, "Hey, you've lost something!" For a moment the tension was eased as I swung round to see him twirling my lace panties on his forefinger. In my mad dash to higher ground, my "spares" had slipped from under my arm and fortunately Joe rescued them from adorning the hibiscus bush in our neighbours' garden!

Huffing and puffing we were very grateful to join the Holiday Inn staff and all the other hotel guests who were being calmed and briefed (no pun intended!) by Michal, the competent, hands-on General Manager. Our family members were hugely relieved when we finally joined them as they were beginning to fear for our safety. We were wonderfully cared for by Michal and his dedicated staff Team who had ensured that not one life had been lost at the Holiday Inn on Boxing Day 2004. It was quite uncanny.

This was Easter time and the date was 26 March. It was three months to the day since the tsunami struck the island!

We were made comfortable on mattresses and handed tea, coffee, bottled water and fresh sandwiches. The evacuation drill had been impressive and we felt secure.

The 80 meter Sunset Terrace would be a wonderfully safe haven if the tsunami struck. No one slept a wink. Instead we watched tsunami alerts all night long, on a large TV screen. The Thai government officials told everyone to leave the coastal areas immediately. The police and army were patrolling the streets with loudspeakers to ensure that everyone heeded the warning. We saw folk on the mainland loading their scooters and motorbikes with clothing and household goods and speeding to high ground. Many had barely recovered from the Boxing Day devastation and were now grabbing their meagre possessions and having to flee their makeshift shelters.

Many young children and older folk were sobbing as memories of 26 December were still raw. The Governor of Phuket provided updates until dawn. New friendships were formed as we sat huddled on our mattresses, chatting quietly and sipping coffee but with eyes riveted to the TV screen. Throughout the night Michal and his staff remained calm, re-assuring and attentive to our needs.

Spontaneous and jubilant applause broke out just after 5.30 am when the Governor of Phuket announced that the threat of a tsunami had been averted. The General Manager gave us the option of returning to our bungalows or remaining on high ground until daybreak just to be quite sure that all was well.

No one moved....

Then there was more good news. Breakfast would be served until noon

giving us time to catch up on a few hours' sleep. That evening all the hotel guests were invited to a complimentary barbecue up on the Sunset Terrace. After the efficient and caring way in which Michal and the Holiday Inn Team handled that emergency situation, Joe and I returned to the idyllic island resort for six more uneventful and blissful holiday visits.

This was the start of a wonderful friendship which has already spanned 14 years. Michal and Clare were married on the beach at The Holiday Inn on 7 July 2007 and moved on from Phi Phi Island to manage hotels in Singapore, Bangkok and Vietnam. Now they are back in Phuket Thailand and shared breakfast with us at Kata Beach just a few months ago. We have had the joy of staying at three of the beautiful hotels Michal has managed and it has been our joy to see their delightful children, Emma and Timothy, grow from tiny babies into very special young people.

Our hospitable Thailand friends, the Zitek Family in Phuket

28

OUR TENTH VISIT TO THE LAND OF SMILES

*T*hailand is an amazing holiday destination, with breathtaking scenery and dramatic contrasts and it is where South Africans are still able to get good value for our Rands. It is a country with towering mountains, lush jungles, ancient ruins, inspiring Temples, shimmering white beaches, limestone cliffs, coconut palms, islands and sparking emerald sea. Never forget the world- renowned Thai cuisine!

On our very first visit to Thailand we met up with our lovely South African friends, Dave and Sandy, who were living and working in the village of Hang Dong, about 15 km south of Chiangmai. As we sat under the stars, enjoying supper on the banks of the River Ping (literally meaning Iron Bridge) Dave and Sandy, who have both learnt to speak Thai, shared invaluable tips about Thai customs, etiquette, traditions and their cuisine. We had our first experience of learning to share a variety of main courses and were delighted to be introduced to a Thai Steam Boat. It's a type of communal hot pot placed in the centre of the table and kept warm over glowing coals. Diners cook their own shrimps, prawns, slivers of beef or chicken, dipped into a spicy soup -like sauce containing fresh vegetables.

It makes for very companionable dining and we grew to love this method of cooking.

Thailand offers plenty for those who enjoy history or music and who seek culture. Those who enjoy night life, fine dining, shopping or excitement will not be disappointed. Lovers of the sea will rejoice in the diving and snorkelling opportunities. Unforgettable experiences for us were our Chiangmai elephant trek deep into the Chiangmai jungle, parasailing at Karon Beach and floating high above Pu Island to celebrate Joe's 80th birthday, a 48 km speedboat ride from Phi Phi Island back to Phuket, our exciting canoe trip into the James Bond caves, bamboo rafting on the Mae Wang river near Chiangmai, a buffalo ride and a visit to a rubber plantation in Phuket and numerous snorkelling excursions in beautiful little bays round Phi Phi Island and on the hotel reef at the Holiday Inn.

The national animal of Thailand is the elephant, revered for its incredible strength, longevity, durability and faithfulness in service. We learnt on our tour to the elephant training centre that elephants start working from the tender age of 10 and only retire at age 60!

Current estimates show that in 2020 Thailand has a population close to 70 million, with more than 93% of Thais following Buddhism, the majority basing their core beliefs around Theravada Buddhism which is based upon the teachings of Gautama Buddha. The calm, happy smiling Thai people have taught us so much ever since we first visited their beautiful country in 2003. When they greet you, they lower their heads, bend forward slightly as a sign of respect and place their palms together in a gesture known as a Wai. We have found Thai nationals to be warm-hearted, loving and gentle people who appreciate nature and love beautiful things like mountains and valleys, the sea, animals, trees and plants and young children. They are extremely hospitable and many of their hotels rank as some of the finest in the world.

At several Thai hotels we were even offered a Pillow Menu upon arrival and the choice was vast! There were 10 pillows on the menu at The Pan Pacific Hotel in Bangkok! Non – Allergenic, Duck- Down, Ultra Soft Micro Fibre, Firm Ball Fibre, Latex, Neck Support,

Contour, Contour Massage, Cervicalopaedic or even a Natural Buckwheat Pillow!

One couldn't help but have sweet dreams in a hotel which pampers you like that!

Upon returning to Thailand one receives a most wonderful heart - warming welcome back. You find your hotel bed beautifully decorated with freshly picked flowers and artistic swans, elephants or sea creatures created by cleverly twisting the hotel towels. Even the bathrooms and toilets are lovingly decorated with hibiscus or orchid blooms.

The Thais place an emphasis on wisdom and understanding and have a deep respect for the elderly. They greatly revere the Monarchy and tourists have landed in jail for showing disrespect or for making improper jokes about those in authority. We learnt that it is very rude to point at anyone. Even when sitting on the floor a Thai will not point his or her toes in anyone's direction so as to avoid sending evil in that direction.

Sometimes a Thai person will choose not to open a gift from you in your presence for fear that his or her face may reflect disappointment or distaste! One needs to understand this custom as the recipient may appear ungrateful upon receiving your gift, particularly if the recipient suddenly disappears with it, without further comment!

Thais prefer not to purchase wedding gifts for fear of duplication. Instead they often pop money into the envelope bearing the wedding invitation and return it, leaving the bridal couple to choose what they really need. This sounds like a very sensible and practical arrangement because who really needs 4 kettles, 3 egg beaters and 6 pop up toasters!

We were shown how when indicating how tall a child is, a Thai parent will show the height with the palm of his hand pointing upwards rather than downwards as we tend to do. Their reasoning being that people should never be put down and demeaned, but rather uplifted and appreciated for their intrinsic worth. Thai people seldom become irate or show their frustration.

They try and avoid conflict situations by keeping calm and speaking in soft tones. We were amazed to see this in action when our taxi was involved in a road accident. Our driver remained calm and forgiving even though the driver of the other vehicle was clearly at fault. It goes against the grain for Thai folk to moan and complain. They always seem to make a plan and have a lovely saying which you will often hear a Thai person repeating, "Mai Pen rai, Mai pen rai" which could almost be translated as " No problem! Not to worry! "

Some of the Thai customs are fascinating. The left hand is considered the dirty hand and is used when visiting the toilet so it is important to remember to always use your right hand when taking a gift from someone, when passing an article or when greeting someone.

Most Thais believe in Reincarnation and try their utmost to live good upright lives so as to be returned in a future life as something of beauty like a swan or a peacock. Superstition often plays an important rôle and some of the Thais we met told of parents they knew who had given their babies demeaning names to trick the evil spirits, like frog, ant, flea, snake, toad, slug or Fatty! Many Thai folk who work in hotels give themselves very easy English names so as to simplify things for foreign tourists. At one hotel we were intrigued to find seven staff members with the names Pee, Pu, Pim, Pom, Poo, Pan and Pong!

Many Thais wear certain colours on specific days. Their late King was born on a Monday and many believe that yellow is a fitting colour for a Monday but others choose to dress in blue on Fridays in honour of their Queen's birthday.

Education is very important to Thai people and they may sometimes strike you as being very inquisitive when they want to know all about your schooling, the size of your house, the number and names of your children, the cost of your coat, shoes, your air ticket etc. When eating with Thai folk at a local restaurant you might find yourself footing the bill if you come across as being the most well- heeled and best educated person present.

Thai folk are very hospitable and good manners are important to them and are considered a sign of good breeding. We were impressed when younger folk and school pupils gave up their seats for us older folk on trains and buses. That used to happen in South Africa a long time ago! Thai people leave their shoes on the doorstep or in the passage when they enter a home and step over the threshold upon entering a house, to avoid misfortune. They very seldom eat alone. In fact some consider it anti -social to eat on one's own. A lovely practice when eating in a restaurant is that each person in the group orders a separate dish off the menu, then everyone samples a little of each. Big bowls of noodles and rice are delivered to the table so there is always ample food to be shared. Thais eat using a spoon in the right hand and a fork in the left for guiding the food onto the spoon. You will need to request a knife or chopsticks if preferred. It is polite to wait for your host to seat the guests and you will soon discover that there is a certain type of pecking order to be taken into consideration. We noticed that one should try and leave a little food in the bowls so that your host does not think you arrived hungry and went away still feeling ravenous! It is considered very rude to lick your fingers as that means you really are desperate! Never take the last portion of anything on offer and only have seconds when the host offers you another helping.

Thai people have an excellent work ethos. They do not expect tips and never hang around waiting for a tip as is sometimes the case in our country! When you do tip them they show incredible humility and gratitude.

One of our biggest challenges was coping with the traditional Thai long drop squatting toilets. You will be relieved (unintentional pun!) to find conventional Western style toilets in the hotels! In some of the malls in big cities you are requested to deposit your used toilet paper in a separate receptacle to avoid blocking their sewage system. The squatting position poses an additional challenge if you suffer from arthritis or have bionic hip and knee joints! Being very conscious of personal hygiene, another

fascinating feature in Thai toilets is a compact little hose pipe attached to the wall closest to the toilet cistern. The aim being is that you aim too, and use the nifty little trigger on the hose to squirt yourself thoroughly clean after a visit to the toilet.

On one of our first visits we were delighted to discover in our hotel what must surely be the Rolls Royce version of Asian toilets. It had a fascinating name too. It was called a Dobidos and we were informed that these toilets are imported from South Korea. In South Africa we have seen similar products described as Zen toilets. We had never imagined that such a toilet could almost provide you with a Spa outing! The Dobidos surpasses your wildest dreams! It not only has a heated seat, but it provides the following multi functions:

It washes, blow dries and deodorises and furthermore some even have an enema feature! The advertiser's desire is to "Inspire bathroom dignity and to bring health and happiness to your home." The pamphlet adds…"The Dobidos has cutting edge technology, ergonomic design and is fitted with temperature control and self-cleaning nozzles."

The last time Joe and I felt so pampered was when we visited Disney World Florida in 2001. In our hotel bathroom we discovered a posh toilet with a heated seat. When you sat down it played a happy little tune called "Whistle While You Work" and the toilet paper had cross word puzzles on each sheet!

There is just so much to see and to do in Thailand and it's an all-year destination.

All over Thailand you will find brightly coloured little Buddhist shrines called phi houses or spirit houses where devotees place gifts of fruit, bread, rice, flowers etc.to appease the spirits which they believe inhabit the little houses. Incense is burnt regularly to get rid of bad energy. We were told that at the end of each day, the food and fresh fruit and vegetables is distributed to the poor but liquids are normally poured away.

Monks are very important in Thailand and are greatly revered. They are nearly always easy to spot because of their orange robes and shaven heads. Monks are called upon to bless everything you treasure, like your new home, your dog, your cat or your car. Thai people never hand anything straight to a monk or touch his head. Instead they place their gift at the monk's feet.

Buddhist funerals are very different from ours. They are regarded as important events because a funeral represents Rebirth and the Transition from one existence to another. Crying is frowned upon as it is thought to upset the spirits. Mourners usually wear a mixture of black and white. Some of the loved ones write good thoughts to the deceased person and pop the note into their mouth. Sometimes gifts are piled on top of the coffin or money is slipped into envelopes for the grieving family. A funeral may be spread over a period of two years. Bodies are often washed with scented water. Mourners step forward and pour water over the right hand of the corpse as they make a blessing or ask for forgiveness. A beautiful lotus blossom is often placed in the hands of the corpse and some funeral guests have been known to pop a coin into the mouth of the dead person wishing them prosperity. In some circles a white string is attached from the ankle of a nearby monk to the corpse to help transmit holiness.

Only close family members normally stay for a cremation. Coconut juice is often poured over the corpse and it is quite usual for rockets and firecrackers to be lit. Monks officiate at the cremation and collect the ashes the next day. The urns holding the ashes are often kept in the Temple for 50 to 100 days.

Urns are sometimes floated down rivers on homemade rafts and the ashes are wrapped in white cloth and sprinkled overboard. Family photos and other cherished articles and heirlooms may accompany the deceased on their little rafts. Pretty floral petals are tossed into the stream and loved ones are afforded a serene and beautiful send-off. Thai people avoid having cremations on Fridays because the Thai word for Friday sounds very similar to their word for 'happiness.' At funerals Thai people avoid wearing black, green and blue together.

An exciting time to visit Thailand is in mid-April although April is the hottest month of the year. It's when the Thai nation celebrates their New Year which is called Songkran and takes place over 3 days, but virtually the entire Nation shuts down for a week of jubilant festivities and water blessings. It is an extremely joyous time for the country and one which has great spiritual significance for this Buddhist nation. The idea is to wash away the "dirt" or baggage of the past year and to go into the new year refreshed and clean and to bless as many others as possible by showering them with cleansing water blessings too.

We found it hilarious on our very first April visit to see elderly grannies and grandpas rushing about dousing each other with jets of water squirted from massive 2 litre water pistols with fascinating names like Supa Soaka, Who Dunnit and best of all, Drench-a- Wench! Others grabbed buckets, hose pipes, watering cans, household jugs, milk bottles or any receptacle that could hold water. Many shops had positioned water cannons on the pavement outside and anyone who passed within range got drenched with torrents of water.

With the weather being so hot and humid in April, it actually comes as a huge relief to be blessed from top to toe by a refreshing shower of cold water. I just wished I had been able to warn those granting us the water blessings that I had travelled to Thailand with a brand new perm!

Most Thais choose to return to their hometowns to celebrate Songkran with their families and loved ones. Many show their love and gratitude to their parents by taking home gifts of food, fruit or flowers. As a sign of respect the younger Thai folk are expected to ask older people for permission before chasing them with water pistols or drenching them from head to toe. We noticed some Thais with white chalk smeared on their faces. They explained that when it gets washed off, they feel as if they have turned over a new leaf and are able to enter a brand new year with a clean slate. Many devout Buddhist devotees queued up to bless the Buddha and washed his body with fragrant water but told us it was irreverent to wet his head.

Later in the year, if you happen to visit Thailand in November, you will be deeply moved as you watch Thai people participating in what is known as Loy Krathong which falls in the twelfth lunar month and is held in the evening.

It's held at the end of the Monsoon rainy season. They make the most beautiful little miniature handcrafted rafts from bamboo sticks, coconut shells, baked bread, banana or lotus leaves then decorate them exquisitely with flowers, incense sticks and little candles.

In a way Loy Krathong is similar to our Harvest Festivals where we give thanks to God for supplying good rain and express our joy for having full barns, overflowing granaries and store houses. In gratitude we then share some of the bounty with less fortunate citizens.

By November, the main rice harvest season has drawn to a close in Thailand. The Thai people are now full of gratitude and desire to thank the Water Goddess in a meaningful way. Many believe this is also a good time to "float away any baggage" that might be dispelling their joy and usefulness. So at Loy Krathong Thais are encouraged to surrender any anger, malice or nasty grudges they may have been harbouring.

They may write little notes or messages admitting their failures. Some will even include a piece of fingernail or a few wisps of their hair as a symbol of their willingness to release part of them that is making them feel unhappy. They then gather beside beautiful lakes, canals, rivers or at sheltered beaches and release their little rafts called Krathongs in the full moon light.

It is a most beautiful and deeply moving sight to watch processions of miniature glowing rafts making their way across the moonlit water. TheThai people believe that if the candle on your Krathong stays alight until it drifts out of sight, you can look forward to a new year brimming with health and prosperity.

What a challenge and inspiration this annual celebration is, even to foreign tourists and those not of the Buddhist faith. So often we remember the past and hold onto deep grudges, resentment, bitterness, anger or malice. We know how this saps our joy and peace and negatively affects our health.

Let's learn from our Thai friends.......Forgive, release and move on!

Special friends Khun Jarinee and Thai hotel staff

29

SUPPER AT BUCKINGHAM PALACE AND LONDON EXPLOITS

t was wonderful being able to afford to travel in the 60's and 70's when at one stage a British Pound cost R1 and you could purchase $1 for about 87c! As a house mistress living in a small room in the boarding house at Treverton Preparatory School for 15 years, where I received free board and lodging in exchange for hostel duties, I managed to save enough to enjoy 3 months of furlough after every 5 years of service. Once I returned to Cape Town to teach in a State school from 1980, we were fortunate enough to receive birthday bonuses once a year. This took the form of a double cheque in our birthday month and helped to pay for an air ticket.

Unfortunately the 1960's were troubled times in South Africa because of the Nationalist Party's policy of Apartheid and Bantu Homelands. South Africa at one time was regarded as an outcast and treated with contempt and ignominy. When our beloved Madiba (Nelson Mandela) became our first democratically elected President in 1994, you may recall him saying that his heart's longing was that South Africa would no longer be in the unsavoury position of being regarded as "The polecat of the World!"

As citizens of South Africa in the Apartheid Era, as it is often referred to, severe restrictions were placed on us. We can all name Freedom Fighters and Stalwarts whose lives were made so intolerable that they were forced to leave loved ones behind and live in exile in foreign countries. I had a taste of what it was like to be downgraded to junk status the first time I left South Africa in December 1968 to enjoy a furlough lasting 9 months and for which I had worked and saved very hard.

My good friend and travelling companion, Jessie and I found an excellent travel agent who booked multiple flights for us using London as our base. A Swiss 8 day Rail Pass, available only to non-residents of Switzerland, proved a wonderful way of providing unlimited travelling throughout Switzerland on the Swiss Travel System network of trains, buses, boats and trams and offered a 50% reduction on most mountain railways and cable cars.

But first a nasty shock awaited me ......

Upon landing at Heathrow Airport in London to assume a temporary teaching post at a boys' preparatory school in Horsham Sussex, a sullen immigration official snatched my green South African passport and pounded down an official stamp stating emphatically NO SKILLED LABOUR.

Now what?

Fortunately Jessie and I had been offered accommodation with a very dear family friend who had a lovely home in Bickley, Kent. Miss Gwen Martin - Harvey had her 60th birthday while we were staying with her and we celebrated it by having a picnic in the bluebell woods. To start with Jessie and I were rather in awe of this tall spinster with a long neck and a very straight back. She rolled her grey hair into a neat little sausage in the nape of her neck and kept it in place with hair pins and an almost invisible hair net. We were relieved when she gave us permission to call her Auntie Gwen because Miss Martin-Harvey was quite a mouth full. We were amazed to discover that her only brother was called Martin Martin- Harvey and her older sister was called Doris

Gelbart- Smith. Her younger sister, Wendy was the only one who had a single barrel surname. Auntie Gwen spoke beauuuuuu-tifully, which was not surprising because she had just retired from being a lecturer in Speech and Drama which involved elocution, at a College in London. She was still single because she had dutifully cared for her parents until they died in their mid-nineties. Gwen was meticulous and her house was spotless.

She rang a little gong at the foot of the staircase on the dot of 8am each morning and Jessie and I were expected to be seated at the breakfast table one minute later. She told us that South Africans have "frightful accents" because we "talk through our teeth and do not open our mouths to enunciate properly!" She corrected us frequently saying, "Now Jessie and Ruth dear, dooooo please open those lips and say after me, "Chair, where, here, there!"

We learnt some fascinating new British phrases too. When Gwen was referring to classy or posh people she would describe them as being "top drawer folk." Her favourite way of expressing delight or satisfaction was to say "How splendid," or "how absolutely topping!" or "Oh I say dearie, isn't that glorious!" When something was amusing, she would often say, "What a hoot!" and if she was startled or amazed she would say, "How extraordinary!" Or "Well I never!" Whenever she was exhausted she was "Jiggered" or "knackered", whereas we were just pooped or zonked!

We often battled to keep straight faces because our South African vocabulary was so different. She strode in from the garden one afternoon declaring that she had "never seen so many beautiful tits in her life and all on one afternoon!" No one had ever told us that a Blue Tit is a beautiful little English bird. (the feathered variety!) Then one morning after breakfast she rushed out telling us that she was going to go all round the garden doing little jobs! As South Africans another naughty thought had entered our minds!

Being a "top drawer" person herself Auntie Gwen used the services of a housekeeper in her late 50's whom she referred to as "My Mrs Mop" who was a white lady with bright pink hair. She had a strong Cockney accent and called herself "Mrs Glize- brook." Mrs Glazebrook was also an excellent cook and would prepare several meals for us during the week. Gwen only used genuine silver cutlery, Royal Doulton China and crisp starched napkins in silver serviette rings. Having eaten in the school dining room at Treverton for five years, this felt like being a guest at Buckingham Palace.

And believe it or not, some years later, my best friend Margaret (who is now my sister-in-Law) and I soon became invited guests at Buckingham Palace!

I often have to pinch myself to make quite sure that we actually entered those hallowed Royal precincts! During supper one night, on another delightful visit to the U.K. our dear friend "Auntie" Gwen introduced us to a South African friend of hers who was working in London. Kitty Bluett once worked as a secretary at the Teachers' Training College in Grahamstown.

When it closed down, she decided to spend time travelling, then just for fun Kitty responded to an advertisement for a position on the staff at Buckingham Palace. Much to her delight she was accepted as a household maid! She was extremely happy working there and was a great admirer of the Queen and the Queen Mother. Kitty was overjoyed that she was allowed to invite friends to supper in the staff quarters. But best of all, if the immediate members of the Royal Family were not occupying the Royal Box at the Festival Hall or Royal Albert Hall, staff members were allowed to sit there with their friends. Margaret and I were tickled pink when on two occasions concert goers peeped at us through their opera glasses and when it was time for interval, we were approached in the Royal Box, curtsied to and asked very politely to sign their programmes! And we did, just for fun!

Security precautions at Buckingham Palace were impressive but we found the guards extremely courteous and efficient. Kitty would meet us at the gates to ensure that our entrance was slick and efficient. There were naturally strict rules regarding privacy and she explained that we were not allowed to hang through windows to take photographs of members of the Royal Family as they moved about the grounds. We naturally would have loved a photograph of the Queen strolling through the gardens with her corgis. We enjoyed supper at the Palace with Kitty on several occasions.

What excitement one evening, when from Kitty's bathroom, as I leaned over the washbasin, I caught a brief glimpse of a very young, still single and very attractive Princess Diana popping in for a visit and then on another occasion we spotted Prince Andrew driving in through a side entrance.

What intrigued us greatly was the toilet paper in the Palace bathrooms. It was marked with the Royal Coat of Arms. We kept a few sheets from Kitty's staff toilet as treasured bookmarks for many years because it was quite unique. It was shiny and very slippery and resembled tracing paper. It was housed in a flat little box with a slit on one side and individual folded sheets popped out as you gave a gentle tug. The toilet paper became a fascinating little souvenir because each sheet was stamped with words to the effect that it remained The Property of Her Majesty the Queen! I read recently that the Queen takes her own special toilet paper with her wherever she travels and I understand that her preferred brand is called Andrex, but back in the 60's, she used Izal which we were told was very strong and medicated. Apparently some families still treasure letters written on durable Izal toilet paper by their family members who were World War 2 soldiers or prisoners of war.

Soon after Gwen had retired from her lecturing position, she enjoyed taking her overseas visitors on wonderful sight- seeing outings while she was their generous hostess. One memorable excursion with Gwen which is indelibly etched in my mind was the time she took Jessie and me to the Chelsea Flower Show. Enthusiastic crowds jostled us on the Bickley station in Kent and when the train glided to a halt, most of the carriages appeared to be jam- packed already.

Gwen, Jessie and I were separated as we boarded the coach. Gwen was completely uninhibited and suddenly remembered I had told her the week before, how my mom made her own ice cream. From the far end of the packed carriage came the beauuuuuu-tifully enunciated words, "Coooo-ey Ruth darling! I say, can you call out your dear mother's favourite vanilla ice cream recipe? "

Was my face red! Jessie was strap- hanging in the middle of the carriage and she blushed on my behalf. I was so embarrassed as I bellowed from the other end…. " Ideal milk, Orley Whip, condensed milk, vanilla essence…"

Back came Gwen's response, "I say dear, would Ideal milk be the same as evaporated milk? What's Orley Whip? Do we have Orley Whip in the UK?

I very much doubt it dearie. It's rather amazing but you really do have some wonderful new things in Africa, don't you darling! Can you suggest a substitute?"

Gwen had delved in her handbag and was scrawling notes on the back of an old church bulletin as the train swayed from side to side. By now she had a captive audience as I started to explain the method part of the ice cream recipe. Jessie and I suddenly noticed that others in the carriage had pricked up their ears and were also scribbling down my Mom's ice cream recipe!

Was I grateful when we finally reached our destination!

Attending the Chelsea Flower Show was a wonderful experience for us as South Africans. The show was first held in 1912 and has attracted visitors from all over the world. It is held for five days in May and is the world's most prestigious flower show. We had been told that the Queen is Patron of the Royal Horticultural Society and we secretly hoped we might just catch a glimpse of her viewing the exhibits because we knew she had expressed appreciation for our stunning South African proteas.

What a thrill it was to hear in 2018 and 2019 that the Kirstenbosch Botanical Garden exhibits had again been awarded gold medals! Their 36th and 37th gold medals in the 44 years that South Africa has been exhibiting. The head designer, Leon Kluge and his construction Team brought great honour to our country for their 2018 unique display incorporating the colourful artwork of the gifted crafter, Elmon Muringani, who depicted rural and informal township dwellings in the midst of the fauna and dazzling flora.

In 2019 Kluge's design depicted a 3 meter tall slate mountain, with one side representing Table Mountain and the other side, the Magaliesberg. There were cascading waterfalls and rivulets, colourful Ndebele hats and an abundance of glorious proteas, arum lilies, restios and fynbos. He chose the very apt title, Mountains of Abundance, for his eye- catching exhibit.

After we left the Chelsea Show, Gwen decided to redeem the half hour spent on the train from Victoria to Bickley by doing her Keep Fit exercises. She started by sitting bolt upright and stretching her neck and making herself as tall as possible, then she swung her head in all directions, which caused the tightly packed passengers squeezed in alongside her, to duck and dive out of her way. After that she let her head and arms drop forward and for the next five minutes she circled her head round and round and rolled her eyes in all directions. Jessie and I held our breath fearing Gwen might become so dizzy that she would topple right out of her seat. Next in her gym routine, she started raising her legs, one at a time and pointing her toes skywards and rotating each foot from the ankle, as if stirring a giant caldron. Passengers on all sides were hugely amused but Gwen persevered, completely oblivious of the embarrassment she was causing us when she showed too much leg or lacy petticoat.

She was pretty well out of steam by the time our train reached Bickley but fortunately it was only a short walk from the station to her home on the corner of St George's Road West.

Gwen was very dramatic and amused us no end one sparking Saturday morning. We dressed warmly and she drove us into the lovely Kent countryside in her spanking new racing green Triumph to pick black berries and to enjoy a wayside picnic. Seated on her tartan rug, Gwen suddenly spotted a friendly jersey cow lumbering by. It stopped in its tracks to stare at us as we sipped our tea. "Oh do look girls," she said excitedly. "Look at that beauuuuu-tiful brown cow! Isn't God amazing to have created a walking dairy on four legs! Look at that gorgeous pink udder, swaying gently from side to side and bursting with glorious rich, creamy milk for our good health and enjoyment! How absolutely splendid! Wouldn't it just make topping Devonshire cream to serve with our jam scones!"

After two weeks of relaxing in holiday mode at Gwen's lovely home, Jessie and I felt it was time to look for a temporary job seeing the stamps in our passports restricted us to unskilled labour. Our plan was to work for a while and then travel to Europe, using the money we had earned. We were longing to dip into Jessie's informative paperback handbook titled "Europe on $5 a Day" to see if it really was possible to find basic, clean accommodation at that price.

At 5am on a very chilly, dark January morning, Jessie and I set off on foot to Bickley station. Our final destination was Earls Court where we would queue with dozens of other eager work seekers at a recommended Recruitment Agency. We had a long journey ahead of us. From Bickley we headed by train on the South Eastern line and passed through 9 stations before we reached Victoria rail station. We were astounded to see so many very early morning commuters travelling into London on a punctual, spotless and comfortably warmed train.

Then we had our first exciting experience of using a tube train. I love the way our Afrikaans friends call it a "moltrein" (mole train) because of the way the trains burrow their way through dark underground tunnels at high speed. It's amazing to think that as the oldest Underground network in the world, London has 11 Underground Lines, covering 402 kilometers, connecting more than 270 stations, handling up to 5 million passenger journeys per day!

As 24 year olds, Jessie and I felt like real country bumpkins being first timers in London, but folk were extremely helpful in directing us to the District Underground Line to take us to Earls Court. There were important things for novices like us to get into our heads....Stand to the right on the escalators.

Check that you are on the Right Side of the Tracks for the Direction you wish to travel. Mind the Gap between the train door and the platform. Stand Behind the Yellow Line and make space for passengers surging out of the open train doors or you will be flattened!

It was a humbling experience standing in line with some obviously very cold, needy, hungry and desperate job seekers. This experience made us feel so grateful to have permanent teaching posts waiting for us back home. Here were folk willing to do anything, just to have a roof over their heads and to be able to put food in their stomachs. We waited patiently until we were shown into a small, dingy office and given the choice of working in a supermarket, a battery factory or a sausage producing warehouse. We accepted the challenge of becoming shelf packers at the Co-Op Supermarket in Downham, a district of south east London, within the Borough of Lewisham. It was largely a working class area, with many struggling families resident in the sprawling Downham Estate nearby.

Thinking about President Donald Trump's Mexican Wall of Separation on the southern border of the United States, reminds me that travelling on the Catford bus to our new jobs at the Downham Co-Op very early one morning, we met a friendly and well-informed London lecturer. She was fascinated to hear that we were from South Africa. She was very disturbed by what she had heard about the cruel policy of "Appartight." (Apartheid) She related a sad story about a massive seven foot high brick wall with chunks of broken glass embedded along the top, which had once been erected by wealthy residents in the very area to which our bus was taking us. The affluent folk had strongly objected to the idea of a 600 acre Estate with 7 000 new homes being built for poorer residents moving from far less attractive urban areas which were considered to be becoming too densely populated. Those who lived in the wealthier private homes in the tranquil, rural area of Bromley, wanted to prevent the working class citizens from gaining access to their "top drawer" suburb. This happened in the 1920's but sounded to Jessie and to me as unjust at the apartheid government's policy of group areas and Bantu homelands.

Being unpackers of goods and shelf fillers proved to be a novel experience and not as simple as it sounds. We had to wear "sensible" black lace up shoes and blue overalls with "Co-Op" printed on the back. We started the day by ripping open heavy cartons in the massive store room, then we dived into the boxes up to our necks, hauling out all kinds of exciting goods from mouthwatering Chocolate Shreddies, Honey Monster puffs to Jaffa Cakes and Jammie Dodgers and then to less enticing household requirements like fly swatters, household bleach, cockroach bait, ammonia, mouse traps and prickly toilet brushes built for exploring tricky S- bends!

Our floor manageress was a kind -hearted lady called Daisy, who lived in the nearby Estate. She even invited us to supper one night and said we were the very first Africans she had ever met and seemed to find us and our accents rather intriguing! Her little boy of six obviously did too and got a hefty kick under the table from his dad for leaning across the table and saying to us in his Cockney accent, "You two laaidies talk funny!"

Having been shown how to rip open cartons using our fingers like claws, we had to load the unpacked items into shopping carts and wheel them to the appropriate aisles. Daisy said Jessie and I would be in control of the Breakfast section as well as the Kitchen and Bathroom cleaning departments. A rather interesting Combination! Daisy handed us each a hefty metal gadget which she explained was used for stamping price tabs onto items. She spoke in a strong cockney accent and called the device her "plonker!" We had to look up prices in a catalogue and ask her for help if any items were unlisted. "No guessin' please, you African lie-dees," she insisted. We soon realised that our South African accents were totally foreign to Daisy, who could not understand why I was fair-skinned and asked me twice if my parents were missionaries in Africa! I discovered there was only one way I could get Daisy's attention from across the aisle when I was energetically "plonking" prices on items on top shelves whilst perched high on my ladder. I had to do my best to sound cockney and would then call out, "Die- zee."

That worked wonders and she would spin round immediately. So from then on, I answered to the name "Rothe," Jessie became known as "Jussay" and Daisy knew we needed help if we called out "Die-zeeeee!"

Accents can prove troublesome….One irate shopper swore at me, using unrepeatable cockney swear words because I apologised that we didn't stock the product she had requested. Whilst looking at buckets and mops she asked for "Spushall Kai" without telling me it was a breakfast cereal. How would I have guessed she wanted Kellogg's Special K on her breakfast table! When the furious shopper eventually located it all by herself a few aisles further along, she returned and bashed me on the nose with her Family Size 18 oz box letting out some choice expletives to register her displeasure at my incompetence. Thankfully none of my school pupils ever resorted to that form of revenge!

Having tried our hand at being industrious Co-Op carton un-packers and shelf fillers from Monday to Saturday, for a whole month, Jessie and I discovered to our dismay, that by the time government tax had been deducted and we had paid into the benevolent fund and the staff tea fund, our weekly take home pay amounted to the princely sum of £8.50! This barely covered our bus fare and the £3 we wanted to give Gwen, our generous hostess, as a small token of our appreciation.

So bright and early on the very next Monday, Jessie and I braved the cold and undertook another pilgrimage into London to the Recruitment Centre at Earl's Court hoping that our newly acquired supermarket skills would help us advance up the industrial ladder!

Inside Buckingham Palace. A Royal visitor arriving

30

PROMOTED TO A STRIPPER IN LONDON!

Things were definitely looking up! We were beginning to figure out the London Underground map. We remembered how to find our way to the Industrial Personnel Employment Agency. This time we were offered mugs of coffee by some charitable lady volunteers wearing bright yellow aprons. I think the helpers were called Sunbeams and they did help to lift our spirits as we queued alongside hundreds of despondent looking job seekers. Jessie and I were beginning to feel like old timers and we passed the time helping foreigners fill in their application forms. There seemed to be more enticing opportunities available to us this time. Rather than work in a butcher shop, a fish mongers or a hardware store, we opted to try our hands at biscuit making at Mac Farlane Lang and Company, part of United Biscuits, which by 1969 had just been hailed as the largest biscuit manufacturing company in Europe.

The prospect of being part of a team which produced chocolatey delights like Yo Yo's, Taxi wafer bars and the popular Mc Vitie's favourites such as Chocolate Digestive biscuits, chocolate Swiss rolls and fruity flavoured jam tarts was an exciting one. There was just one snag...we had to rise even earlier on these frosty mornings because there was an extra leg to our journey. After our train ride to Victoria and the Underground hop to Earl's Court, we piled into a coach with our fellow biscuit makers and were delivered to the factory 40 minutes later. We left Gwen's cosy home in the darkness at 5.30 am and returned after dark at 8.30 pm. There were more blue overalls waiting to be worn in our new job and even worse, we were given black hairnets! Not the invisible kind either. These ones had thick black strands and an elastic band which left a dent in your forehead. I felt as if I had a fishing net thrown over my scalp. Our floor manager told us bluntly that they were compulsory in order to "keep dandruff off the biscuits! "

On our first morning we were given an introductory talk on hygiene and cleanliness and were shown a trestle table with a rather frightening display of items which had been found in cakes, puddings and biscuits. One might possibly lean too far over the dough or icing and lose a button, a hair clip or even a contact lens, but how could any worker not miss his or her dentures, glass eye, hearing aid or wrist watch! Of course there were other intriguing little exhibits too like glass beads, lockets, cockroaches, dehydrated mice and whiskers, but let's not spoil our tea time!

We didn't let on to the hygienist that we were school teachers. We played along and were rewarded with vouchers for free cookies and pies at the factory shop for being able to shoot up our hands and obediently wait our turn to answer questions like, Why is it important to wash your hands and how often should you bath or shower!

To start with, our eye-hand co -ordination skills were put to the test by seeing whether Jessie and I would be able to grab a single non-stick wax lining from a box of linings and pop them speedily, only one at a time, into greased baking pans travelling towards us at high speed on a conveyor belt! The baking pans then continued merrily on their way and whizzed straight towards George from Jamaica. He was controlling a huge machine which aimed jets of thick sticky fruit cake mixture through shiny nozzles into our lined tins. Then on they travelled until they disappeared into cavernous ovens. Some two hours later, out would come a long line of fruit cakes bursting with nuts and candied peel and with an irresistible aroma which rekindled all our favourite Christmas memories.

George's tall, dark friend, Amos, also hailed from Jamaica and we met during a lunch hour over coffee and spaghetti in the smoke-filled canteen. After three weeks at the factory, Amos invited me to quit my factory job and go and live with him on his parents' Jamaican sugar cane plantation!

Amos operated a fascinating machine that turned out hundreds of decadent looking chocolate Swiss rolls. The lightly baked chocolate sponge cakes, warm and still unrolled, smelt enticing as they moved swiftly along the conveyor belt. Gleaming nozzles positioned up above, generously squirted luscious dollops of artificial cream onto the cakes. A wooden "paddle" would then spread the cream lavishly and the cakes would travel on towards an ingenious mechanical arm which would deftly roll each cake at high speed.

Before long Amos' delicious looking chocolate creations had been baked, cooled and machine wrapped in glistening cellophane.

One afternoon without warning, Amos' machine suddenly emitted some weird glug-glug, gloog – gloog sounds and then ground to a deathly halt. It had stopped squirting cream and had to be temporarily switched off. He said he had cleaned the nozzles earlier so suspected an unforeseen blockage somewhere. The next moment we saw that Amos had stripped off his vest and was covered in white foam, from his waist upwards to under his arm pits. His head and torso were deep in the cream vats. Before long he jubilantly held up some twisted strands of hessian fibre which must have worked loose in a bag of sugar or icing. Deftly flicking off the frothing cream, Amos pressed the starter button and in no time at all, his machine leapt back into action. Out popped more and more chocolate Swiss rolls. No cream had been wasted! Ever since 1969 I have chosen to eat jam Swiss rolls instead!

Some tasks in the factory were tedious like standing for hours on end to decorate cup cakes with Smarties or Jelly Tots or holding a long stick like a blackboard ruler and shoving the cup -cakes back into line if one rebel cookie popped out of the oven rather haphazardly.

Promotion could be earned quickly. Jessie and I enjoyed our next new challenge of making Mc Vitie's jam tarts. They smelt delicious as they came from the oven and had tasty fruity fillings which also plopped in from nozzles situated up above. We learnt to grab six tarts at a time as they flew past us on the belt and then with a swift flick of the wrist, we swished them into separate little compartments. Further along another worker would drop in a piece of waxed cardboard to separate the layers and her co-worker would flick another six tarts into position, then the compact double decker would travel off in a different direction to be neatly boxed. In the beginning it was tricky trying to grab all six tarts in the correct order when working at such high speed. We would often get jam squished under our nails or splattered all over our faces. If our timing was not perfect, the tarts would fly across the floor and disintegrate making a dreadful mess. It was at times like these, that I longed to be back in front of my blackboard! I realised afresh that I would far rather be working with impressionable young minds which I could challenge and mould than be handling sullen, inanimate little blobs of dough!

I had an amusing experience when a very badly behaved class of rowdy 10 year old East Enders came on a factory visit. All they wanted to do was rush about hoping to grab free chocolate biscuits and cake. Their elderly teacher was struggling to control them, then in desperation she looked in my direction, clapped her hands and yelled, "Come here boys and girls. I want you to watch this clever factory lady. You can see she's been making jam tarts for years. Watch how quickly she moves her hands and gets all her jam tarts into their correct little spaces. If you are good, she may even allow you to taste one."

Further promotion came swiftly at the biscuit factory and within a week or two Jessie and I found ourselves moving to more challenging departments! We made chocolate Yo- Yo biscuits and decided that the mint ones were definitely our favourites. Then we learnt how to operate the machine churning out chocolate wafer biscuits called Taxis which reminded us of our tasty South African Kit Kats and it wasn't long before we were entrusted with producing Mc Vitie's very popular

Chocolate Digestive biscuits and our take home pay shot up to £12 a week!

Which reminds me, that I was delighted to hear that these delicious biscuits, first created in 1892 by a young baker, named Alexander Grant, came out tops in a recent poll as the UK's favourite biscuit.It was fascinating to learn at the factory how this famous Digestive biscuit got its name. Because the biscuit recipe required quite a high baking soda content, it was believed that it would help those who suffer from post- dinner digestion!

Mc Vitie's has also been in the news this year for having created a limited edition " transatlantic " digestive biscuit with a scrumptious chocolate fudge brownie flavour as a special treat for guests at the Royal wedding of Prince Harry and Meghan Markle. I was told that the Queen never leaves home without her favourite chocolate digestive biscuits!

The factory offered interesting incentives like a free hairdo if you were not absent for a certain period of time or you were awarded free cakes or pies from the factory outlet. Quite honestly having been face to face with cakes and tarts all day, Jessie and I had absolutely no desire to look another pie in the eye, even if it was for a reward. But I do remember taking Gwen an Apple Crumble tart which cost only 8 pence and turned out to be a very respectable and scrumptious discounted Reject!

I had a heart-stopping moment at the end of my 6th week at the biscuit factory. I felt all alone now because Jessie had left on the overnight coach to visit a South African friend who was living in Edinburgh.

Having clocked in on time, with only 3 more credits to go until I earned my next free raspberry crumble, I reported for duty in my freshly laundered Monday morning overall and wearing my very visible black hairnet! My jovial department manager was Bob from Birmingham. He reminded me of Humpty Dumpty with his ample belly and cheerful red face. He had a delightful accent and said everything was "loev- ley" and he was just "popping oopstairs."

I was enjoying making Chocolate Digestives and was beginning to feel it was my new Calling in life! So it came as a huge shock when Bob broke the news to me that a brand new challenge was awaiting me. He announced that having successfully completed my first six weeks without being absent a single day, I had been promoted to Chief Stripper! While I was still catching my breath and searching for words, Bob continued......"You see that great big pile of boxes my love, go and wait behind them. I'll be with you in a jiffy and in just two ticks I'll show you how to strip! "

In case any of my past pupils are rolling their eyes and gasping in horror at the thought of Miss Taylor stripping behind a pile of crates in London, let me put your minds at rest. A stripper in a biscuit factory is a male or female who works at high speed, remaining fully clothed, stripping off appropriate lengths of very durable, adhesive duct tape to seal cartons as they whizz past on a rapidly moving conveyor belt! Apologies if I disappointed you!

A friend sent me an email this morning entitled Very Punny. It shows humorous signs displayed by the Indian Hills Community Centre in Colorado. Have you seen this one?

ELECTRICIANS HAVE TO STRIP TO MAKE ENDS MEET!

Last week I spotted this headline on a lamp post in Pinelands as I drove to our local shopping centre. It came from the front page of one of our Cape Town newspapers called The Voice and immediately it struck a chord with me.

JOB SEEKER FORCED TO STRIP

I couldn't help wondering whether the successful applicant became a professional sealer of biscuit or chocolate boxes! Perhaps someone who bought a copy of that newspaper will be able to satisfy my curiosity! All I know is that becoming a stripper in London helped me get to Europe on a shoe string budget.

Ruth as a factory worker, with bucket and mop

31

EUROPE ON A SHOE STRING

$\mathcal{T}$hose who travelled in the late 1950's and 1960's will remember a wonderful paperback book called Europe on $5 a Day which was first published in 1956 by an American ex G.I. member of the armed forces, named Arthur Frommer. The book was aimed at proving that with careful planning and budgeting, it was possible to cover the cost of your food and lodging for $5 a day.

Jessie and I had managed to live frugally thanks to Gwen's generous hospitality, so with our South African savings intact and armed with Jessie's paperback version of Europe on $5 a Day, a sleeping bag and a small rucksack each, we set off from the UK to explore Europe on a shoe string. We encountered exciting experiences all the way. Before leaving South Africa we had joined the Youth Hostel Association and discovered that throughout Europe clean, basic accommodation was available at a fraction of the price you would pay for a hotel room. Some hostels expected you to help with simple chores like sweeping the rooms, making coffee at breakfast time or mopping the bathrooms and kitchens. In exchange you received a steaming enamel mug of coffee and a whopper of a doorstep of fresh crusty bread and mixed fruit jam to see you on your way each morning.

In several of the hostels we had to share dormitory accommodation and we met folk from every strata of humanity. We did not appreciate it in Salzburg when the hostel supervisor marched into our girls' only dorm at crack of dawn demanding that we abandon our snug sleeping bags and head for the luke warm showers. I imagined our Hostel Supervisor, Herr Heinrich, to be rather like one of the Nazi camp commandants at Dachau or Auschwitz!

There was snow on the ground outside and yet he wanted us to vacate our dormitory by 8am. He kept barking "Aber Schneller! Aber Schneller!" in guttural tones, to make us go faster but of course we all slowed down and took refuge behind our towels. We thought it was despicable when he marched up and down yelling instructions while supervising the girls' ablutions. All that he was missing was a whistle and a sjambok! (type of leather whip.)

Later on when I read books written by courageous prisoners of war like the heroic Dutch lady, Corrie Ten Boom, who endured so much ignominy and brutality at the hands of her Nazi captors, I was actually grateful to have been given a very small taste of the daily humiliation she and her fellow women prisoners were forced to endure.

I'll never forget what happened in Athens. Jessie's wavy chestnut hair and my blonde hair was quite obviously not a common sight and attracted a fair amount of male attention. After a meal out, we found ourselves being followed back to our accommodation at night. As 25 year old females travelling alone, this proved unnerving. On one occasion we were distressed to discover that the door of our budget hotel room had a broken lock so we felt extremely vulnerable. At bedtime we piled all our luggage against the door. Jessie had a delicate little alarm clock which rang shrilly if bumped, so she perched it on top of the pile hoping we would be alerted if anyone tried to gate crash in the middle of the night. We both slept fitfully, jumping at the slightest sound. Isn't it unnerving the way floor boards creak by themselves and bath water from upper storeys makes belching noises in the drainage pipes whenever one stays in an old building.

On our second night in Athens we were followed back to our hotel by two decidedly dodgy characters. There was no elevator in the building and we realised we would be outrun if we tried to make it back to our 4th floor room, and in any case, the lock on our door was broken. So instead we tried to put our pursuers off the scent by ducking into a toilet on the second floor. We were huffing and puffing as we locked the door and crouched in the dark. We held our breath and kept dead still for 10 minutes. It seemed an eternity….

Then hearing no footsteps, I whispered to Jessie, "Take a peep through the key hole." She rose slowly to her knees and put her right eye to the keyhole. She gave a horrified gasp and slid down onto the floor. She had expected to see right down the lit passage to the staircase at the far end. Surely the coast would be clear by now? But instead she looked straight into a great big pair of dark brown eyes peeping at us through the keyhole!

A word of caution! Beware of hanging your hand-washed undies on a nifty little wash line you might locate strung across the bath in your Greek or Italian hotel. I did just that with my "smalls," and in no time at all, I heard loud shouts and a scurry of footsteps pounding down the passage towards our room. There was no time for a polite knock. The bathroom door burst open and was flung wide. Bare in mind (intentional misspelling!) that hotel and guest house proprietors have a key for every door! Through the steam rushed a very large, breathless, red-face Greek gentleman hugging a first aid- box to his chest. His face was not red from embarrassment but rather from attempting to take the stairs three at a time. He clutched at his heart and in between panting for air, he let out a torrent of Greek words. There wasn't time to decide whether to take refuge under the soapy water or to leap out and grab my towel from the back of the door. The situation grew worse. The proprietor was joined by a chamber maid and a waiter who rushed in with a stretcher. It suddenly dawned on me.....

This was no wash line. It was an emergency cord to be tugged in the event of a hotel guest suffering a heart attack or experiencing a "funny" turn in the bathroom. I assure you I did not find the experience funny at all and I slunk back to our room with a very red face.

I recall another embarrassing bathroom experience in a budget hostel in Milan. The communal bathroom was on the top floor and had only two small cubicles with bath tubs. Both were cramped and dingy with a musty smell.

Only one had a door with a rusty bolt. There was no hook on the back of the door and nowhere to place one's clothes. Not having slippers, I wore my flip flops to the bathroom. I laid out my pyjamas and toiletries beside my bath towel. This bathroom featured a unique arrangement. When one pulled out the bath plug, the soapy water was intended to gush out through the hole and onto the floor directly beneath the bath. It was then meant to drain through a vent, just like one finds in the base of a shower, to be carried away in drain pipes.

256

After a tiring day of sightseeing and walking for miles in a very busy, noisy city, where the exhaust fumes and pollution left us with very grubby necks and collars, it was good to relax in a hot bath before flopping into bed. I liked to pull out the plug and lie back, enjoying the warm water for as long as possible. On this occasion I noticed the water was draining very slowly. What had happened was that the vent under the bath had become clogged with soap and grease and matted hair and had obviously not been properly cleaned for months. I heard strange gurgling and bubbling sounds and peeped over the edge of the bath tub. I was alarmed to see my blue flip flops bobbing about merrily. My pyjamas and clean towel were awash but worse still, my soapy bath water was escaping under the door. I imagined a repeat performance where the bolted door might be kicked open and in would rush a valiant band of rescuers. I grabbed my drenched towel and tried to flee to the safely of our room along the passage.

Too late….the Boss and his cohorts were already on their way. By now my bathwater was forming rivulets down the stair case. I was actually very thankful that I couldn't understand Italian!

Wherever Jessie and I travelled in Europe we found the local folk most helpful and encouraging. Our paperback gem provided a wealth of useful and fascinating information. We soon learnt that one can find comfortable, clean accommodation in what is described as a "Pension." This has nothing to do with what we oldies look forward to receiving at the end of each month, although it didn't take me long to discover when I stopped teaching, that there is nearly always more month than Pension! In Europe a Pension offers similar accommodation to a Bed and Breakfast establishment. Many families convert one or two rooms in their houses into tourist friendly accommodation providing a comfy, homely atmosphere at an affordable rate. Having tried several European youth hostels, we enjoyed the greater sense of peace and privacy these private homes offered. It was also a joy getting to know the local folk in charming little Swiss and Austrian towns and villages. The pensions offered delicious continental breakfasts of freshly baked bread or crispy rolls, cheese and jam, with our favourite choice being the Swiss black cherry. There was always freshly brewed coffee on the hob.

Duvets were still unheard of in South Africa in the 60's, so it was a novel experience being introduced to them when we stayed in pensions in Switzerland and Austria. They were genuine duck down duvets which puffed up all around you and made you look as if you were snuggling into a great big marshmallow. When we stayed in a charming little chalet with a Swiss family everyone gathered in the kitchen where they had a great big gleaming cast iron Esse stove which burnt wood or pine cones. At night time our friendly hostess warmed our beds with cotton bags resembling large bean bags or "Huggies," which were filled with dried cherry pips. These were warmed in the oven and retained the heat beautifully. We decided they were as effective as hot water bottles and there was no fear of them exploding or leaking!

No one had warned us that unlike South African trains, most of the sleeping trains in Europe had unisex carriages. So it came as a rude awakening, just as we were tucked up on our bunks and drifting off to sleep, in our sleeping compartment described as a Couchette, when a crowd of jubilant male hikers burst in on our female tranquility. Showing no embarrassment at all, they started undressing in front of us. Using our best school marm tones we explained that regretfully this was a ladies' only compartment but to no avail. They were rugged Italian mountain climbers heading for the Jungfrau Joch, with plenty of testosterone and no inhibitions at all. It soon became quite clear that they did not understand our South African English.

On another occasion two very shy girls aged about 20 climbed aboard and made their way into our sleeping compartment. Jessie and I often found it useful being able to chat to each other privately in Afrikaans. The polite new comers obviously thought we were foreign tourists with a limited English vocabulary, and spoke very sweetly to us in pigeon English and to each other so that we would understand them for the next three hours. When it was time for them to leave the train, they were joined excitedly by three American friends from another carriage and we heard them say in broad Southern accents how good it was to be able to talk proper English again having been "cooped up with two foreign girls from Africa who could hardly speak a word of English!"

Jessie and I must have looked like lonely, abandoned waifs when we reached München and sat sharing a sandwich and sipping a cardboard mug of tea. It was freezing cold and we had pulled on all our warmest pullovers under our coats. Munich is not only known for its sausage and beer! It is the beautiful capital of Bavaria and is a wonderful city to explore because it is home to numerous museums, art galleries and inspiring centuries-old buildings in traditional German architecture. We had been told not to miss visiting the world's most famous fairy tale like castle, Neuschwanstein and the beautiful old town hall where the popular glockenspiel show with its melodious chimes re-enacts fascinating German stories from as far back as the 16th century. Then of course one would never be the same again after touring the Dachau Concentration Camp which is only 10 miles northwest of Munich.

As we sat on a cold metal bench thumbing through Europe on $5 a Day, we began to feel rather forlorn in this, the third largest city in Germany, where prices in the central area were seemingly well beyond our budget. Neither Jessie nor I speak German and after 6 unsuccessful phone calls from public booths to hostels and pensions, we were beginning to feel despondent.

Suddenly as if heaven-sent, two dear old German nuns with angelic smiles strolled by then stopped dead in their tracks. They turned back and were obviously concerned about our welfare. They spoke very little English but gathered that we urgently needed to find accommodation before nightfall. Afrikaans sometimes comes in handy when you travel. When the more senior nun used the word "bleiben" a couple of times I guessed it could mean "stay," like the Afrikaans word "bly" so our eyes lit up and in unison we both replied with a hearty "Ja! Ja! " as we had heard Germans saying in war movies! Sister Emilia scribbled an address on the back of an envelope and told us to jump on the Strassenbahn (a tram) to reach what we thought was going to be an affordable guest house or Pension.

We got off to a bad start because having bought tickets from a vending- machine, no one told us that you must first slide them into a slot on the tram to get them validated with the date and time. A very masculine looking fräulein tram conductor with whiskers sprouting on her chin thought we were trying to cheat the system. She bellowed at us harshly in front of all our fellow commuters and demanded that we climb off the tram at the next stop. Thankfully a kind old gentleman who understood English sensed our distress and bewilderment and came to our rescue.

It had been a long, tiring day for us. When we finally reached our destination, darkness was falling and we were grateful at the thought of having a warm bed and a roof over our heads.

But this was no guest house or pension. Convinced that we were desperate, penniless young ladies, all alone in a strange City, the dear kind- hearted old nuns had directed us to the inner city Bahnhof Mission, close to the Central railway station and similar to a Salvation Army shelter for the homeless. It was probably the equivalent of The Haven Night Shelter we have in Cape Town. There seemed to be foreigners from all over the world milling about in the entrance and clamouring for accommodation. There were screaming babies crawling about in wet nappies. There were weary unwashed bodies stretched out on every available inch of floor space. Some had covered their faces with hats or scarves to avoid the bright light. Others were grunting and snoring loudly under sheets of newspaper. We seemed to be the only two English speaking visitors. This was definitely not the sort of hostel we had expected, but by now it was pitch dark and freezing cold outside. There was still snow on the ground. We realised there was no way we could leave at this late hour and expect to find comfortable affordable accommodation anywhere else.

A tall, officious woman wearing men's lace up shoes and with her hair scraped into a straggly orange pony tail told us to follow her to the woman's dormitory. She warned us to keep an eye on our luggage so Jessie and I shoved all we could into the bottom of our sleeping bags and slept in several layers of clothing. I must say it was a novel experience sleeping with a camera in my pillow case and my toes curled round my passport and travellers cheques! There was no heating in the dorm so we were thankful for the extra layers of clothing. We had top bunks allocated to us. The girl below me had been working in a strip tease club in Istanbul and had arrived in Munich in search of greener pastures, while Jessie's downstairs neighbour was a Muslim new comer from Morocco who understood very little English and had no knowledge of German. She too was a desperate job seeker. There was no privacy in the communal bathroom, with an open row of showers and toilet cubicles without doors. The supervisor told us we would be called for interviews with a social worker first thing in the morning. We decided to save our ablutions until we reached our next hostel and hoped to make a speedy getaway at daybreak. Neither of us could understand why as holiday makers we needed to be helped by a German social worker when the hostel was packed with so many genuinely needy and unemployed people.

As you can imagine neither of us enjoyed much sleep that night. We felt we needed to keep an eye on our luggage. No windows were allowed to be opened and there was a nauseating smell of sweaty bodies and stale cigarette smoke. Girls seemed to be coming and going to and from their late night shifts at all hours. Many coming in late would still have to make up their beds. Others would scratch noisily in their bundles of luggage, flash their torches or rustle packets of sweets. A greasy smell of fish and chips seemed to hang in the air all night. We imagined our mattresses to be snug winter havens for legions of fleas, bed bugs and lice!

It was a relief when dawn finally broke but then another shock awaited us. Jessie and I had decided before turning in for the night, that we would wake early, settle our bill, forfeit our mugs of breakfast coffee and doorsteps of bread and slip out quietly. However, we had scarcely pulled on our clothes when we were summoned to an interview in a cheerless little office. A large sign on the door read SOZIALARBEITER. Knowing that "Aarbeid" means "Labour" in Afrikaans helped us to figure out who we were about to meet. Here we were questioned by a very large lady, presumably a Social Worker, who asked us to remove our outer layers of warm clothing, and before we could object, she had a tape measure in her hands and strode forward to measure our girth. As she patted our tummies she said words which sounded like "Bup- ee, Bup- ee. Wann? Wann?" We guessed she was saying "Baby Baby…When? "

Suddenly the truth dawned on us. The dear old nuns who hastened to befriend us at the airport as we sat muffled in our woolly layers and sharing a sandwich, must have thought we were young pregnant immigrants, desperately in need of a warm place to lay our heads.

Sensing our embarrassment, the social worker seemed to thaw somewhat. Without actually understanding all that we were saying, she suddenly yelled rather triumphantly,"Ja! Ja!" She realised when we produced our South African passports and air tickets, that this was a case of mistaken identity.

We felt like imposters as we signed out having paid a mere fifty cents for our overnight stay. The whole experience was intimidating but served as an eye opener to us. We came away feeling deeply humbled and very mindful of our many blessings. The whole experience left us with a greater appreciation for the wonderful work that the Salvation Army and similar faith– based organizations are doing, to uplift the poor and the homeless and to restore a sense of dignity and self -worth as they focus on providing health, healing and wholeness.

Alpine thrills. Igls, Austria

Sleeping in the berghaus, Jungfrau Joch

VW Beetle in the Ice Palace

The Berlin wall from the west side

32

JAMBO! JAMBO! HAKUNA MATATA!

*A*n exciting country to visit which should feature high on everyone's bucket- list is Kenya. If you remember the name Jomo Kenyatta you will remember to call the country "Ken- jah" and not " Keen- jah" as the old Colonialists used to call it. The locals all refer to their country as KEH-NYA and prefer you to pronounce it that way. Jomo Kenyatta was the first Prime Minister (1963) and President (1964) of a unified and independent Kenya. I discovered on my first visit there in the mid 1990's that his real name was actually Kamau Ngengi. However, he chose the word Kenyatta which is the Kikuyu word for the ornate belt he wore and Jomo means burning spear.

My three week long holiday in Kenya was action- packed from start to finish and was probably one of the most memorable adventures I have ever had.

I travelled on my own from Cape Town and landed in Nairobi after dark. Did you know that the name Nairobi comes from a Maasai phrase meaning "Cool Water" because of the refreshing Nairobi River which flows through the City. Because of its lovely soothing meaning, "Nairobi" has become a popular name for little Kenyan boys and girls.

Shortly before my visit, there had been a serious crime wave and ruthless criminals had been placing rocks and planks embedded with sharp spikes, across the airport off ramp. My Kenyan friends had advised me not to delay my departure from the Jomo Kenyatta International so I had decided to travel light with just one small, compact suitcase in order to speed up my exit through Customs.

Upon arrival, I had rather an alarming welcome to Kenya. As I grabbed a trolley, or what my American friends call a luggage cart and loaded my baggage, I noticed a chopped off chicken's head staring me with glazed eyes and a wide open beak as if pleading for help, (It definitely was not squawking Welcome to Nairobi!) and alongside the head, lay a separate pair of feet lying loose in the bottom. I certainly did not want to be arrested for smuggling or dealing in animal parts for muti, (medicine) so decided to hand the bits and pieces in at the Lost Property counter. The lady serving there rolled her eyes and told me that someone must have slipped the forbidden articles out of their luggage at the last moment, realising that fresh produce like that would be forbidden in the country to which they were travelling. She then smacked her lips excitedly and said the beak and feet had been intended as a gift to make someone a delicious dinner time snack called Walkie Talkies! I have since heard that our own Xhosa people call them "amanqina enkukhu " and regard them as a special treat when marinated and grilled or when cooked in a pot, accompanied by cubed potatoes, chopped onions, tomatoes, green chilies, black pepper and a little spice or curry. A Johannesburg friend told me Walkie Talkies are called "Runaways" by their locals! They are regarded as a healthy food because they are high in protein and low in carbohydrates and kilojoules. The beaks are not very meaty, so are used more for flavour and nutritional value in a pot of stew.

My friends had arranged that for the sake of safety, I should spend my first night with the Hillmans, very hospitable friends of theirs who lived in Nairobi. I was amazed to find that the family had a guard house at the entrance to their property and that besides having very stout burglar bars on all the windows, even their roof and chimney are protected by lethal looking barbed wire. I wondered what the Hillmans told their children when they showed concern for Father Christmas who would have a supreme battle trying to make a stealthy entrance via the chimney without being shredded on his way down!

I had come to Kenya primarily not to stay in a 5 Star hotel or to visit a luxury game reserve but rather to visit my missionary friends and to experience day-to-day life amongst the people with whom they were working. My first week was to be spent way up North in Kapsowar, almost on the Ugandan border, where my Welsh friend Sue, was Matron at the local hospital. She had learnt to speak the Kalenjin language in order to be able to converse with her staff and patients. The town had experienced troubled times because of ethnic clashes in 1992 and 1993. The conflict was primarily over land ownership amongst the Kikuyu and Kalenjin communities. Sue had actually hidden in her broom cupboard on one occasion when trouble flared and protests close to her home became particularly violent. A large number of Pokot tribesmen had acquired sophisticated weapons, especially guns and were using them to rob the Marakwet of their property. Thousands of cattle had been stolen too. Pokot terrorism was being blamed for causing the looming famine in the Keriot Valley because the Marakwet were too fearful to work on their farms.

Very early the next morning Mr Hillman kindly took me to the taxi rank in the downtown area of the city. I was to travel on the Leopard Express to Eldoret from where my friend Sue would fetch me in her 4 X 4 and drive me over some hair- raising mountain roads to her home close to the Mission hospital in Kapsowar. My heart sank when I saw the Leopard Express. It was a decidedly clapped out geriatric leopard which should have been let out to pasture long ago. It was an ancient Peugeot with bald tyres and with 3 rows of well- worn passenger seats. I noticed there were springs protruding and chunks of padding were popping through the greasy upholstery. There was a fuzzy strip of shocking pink material stretched across the dashboard, below which hung a placard saying I LOVE SMIRNOFF! Then in the top right hand corner of the windscreen I spotted a reassuring little sticker declaring "In God do I trust."

I just prayed that Solomon, the affable driver of the Leopard had not been imbibing Vodka before our early morning journey! We took off about an hour later as we waited for all three rows to fill up, then when we were full, we piled in three more late arrivals! There were 13 of us aboard when our driver finally gave a very loud blast on his hooter and set off for Eldoret, waving merrily to all those still queueing for taxis. He apologised that his window did not stay up by itself because the winding device had failed. He made us all very nervous when he drove with his left hand on the wheel and kept trying to shove the glass on the driver's side back into place using his right hand.

I had a very large lady sharing not only my my seat, but half of my lap as well. Everyone was friendly and jovial and before long there was a wonderful spirit of Ubuntu on board. (A feeling of well- being and good neighbourliness) The warm-hearted and hospitable passengers all started to pass around their food and cold drinks. One young man shared his entire bag of oranges and soon I felt myself diving and ducking to miss the pips which were being sucked and then spat out in all directions. It was humbling being the only white passenger aboard and to be welcomed so warmly. I was quite literally being embraced and accepted unconditionally by complete strangers in such an open-hearted way. I fell in love with Kenya and the Kenyan people from day one!

The distance from Nairobi to Eldoret is about 310 km but we took 5 hours to complete the journey with frequent stops along the way for passengers to clamber our, stretch their cramped limbs and relieve themselves right beside the taxi! Then there were more stops for those wanting to stock up on refreshments. Much of the route was scenic as we followed the escarpment and wound our way through the breathtaking Rift Valley. A beautiful sight as we approached Nakuru and looked down at the lake, was to see hundreds of exquisite pink flamingos sunning themselves. At times the road became very treacherous. Back in the mid 90's it was still single-carriage all the way to Eldoret. Our taxi was stopped several times for various traffic infringements and I noticed how often money was passed to officials for bribes. My fellow passengers explained that this was all too common in Kenya and the money which changed hands so swiftly for all manner of traffic offences was nicknamed "chai money" which could be translated as money for tea.

It started to rain heavily and we passengers became very anxious when Solomon continued to steer his old vehicle with only his left hand. He insisted on holding up the window alongside him with his right hand while negotiating hairpin bends. At the same time he managed to wave enthusiastically to all and sundry. As soon as he returned his hand to the steering wheel, the window dropped open again with a loud clunk and the driving rain blew straight in at us. Our driver swerved all over the slippery road, often taking wild chances and overtaking slower vehicles on sharp bends and blind rises. We dodged deep potholes and bounced over speed humps and experienced numerous heart- stopping moments as our driver ventured far too close to the edge of the highway which plunged hundreds of feet down into the Rift Valley.

Then suddenly as we rounded yet another hairpin bend, a tragic sight met our eyes. A lorry had slammed into an innocent cow meandering across the road. Instead of slowing down, our driver simply picked his way skilfully between the mangled remains of some poor local farmer's prized animal.

This horrifying sight upset us all and remained in my mind for a very long time.

Upon arrival in Eldoret, it was a huge relief to almost roll out of the Leopard Express. I was so stiff from being cramped for more than five hours that I wondered if I would ever be able to stand up straight again. It was a great joy to be met by Sue, who has remained a very special family friend ever since we first met in 1979. Sue had travelled nearly 80 km from Kapsowar on some very rough, corrugated roads littered with huge boulders, to come and fetch me from Eldoret. By now it was mid-afternoon and we were both ravenous so we popped into Sizzlers Steakhouse for a late lunch. It was here that I was introduced to my very first Kenyan long drop loo inside a restaurant! It took more getting used to than the one at the Nairobi airport. It requires a very special level of agility to use a long drop toilet without a seat, when your legs are feeling wobbly having survived for five hours in the back row of a cramped taxi under a layer of fellow human beings.

Ablutions over, we made our way into the packed restaurant teeming with animated locals who were all tucking into their appetising Sizzler lunch time specials with tremendous gusto. We were shown to a shared round table made of carved indigenous timber where we perched on tall backless stools resembling giant sized cotton reels and enjoyed a Sizzleburg Special with chips. I seem to recall that my hamburger filling was juicy warthog. It tasted rather like barbecued pork but was a little more on the wild side, having a slightly stronger flavour.

One needs nerves of steel to sit back and enjoy the Kenyan roads although I understand there have been huge improvements in recent years, with a double carriage way in place now, which must make driving so much safer.

It was lovely to arrive at Sue's comfortable little home before darkness descended on the Keriot Valley. Her view was across a small coffee plantation and there were bright red hibiscus bushes and vibrant shrubs growing in her lush garden. I was touched by the warm welcome I received from the hospital staff and the local villagers who had been told by Sue that I had travelled many, many miles from a faraway country to come and visit their country. Some had lovingly brought, from their own meagre resources, generous gifts of melons, eggs, pumpkins, rice and fruit and one dear old granny even offered a live chicken until we explained tactfully that it would not manage to survive the very long aeroplane journey back to Cape Town! I saw immediately how much they loved and respected Matron Sue, calling out to her, "Muttron, Muttron!" as we toured the hospital wards.

Sue and her incredibly committed team had dealt with some intriguing and very challenging medical emergencies. A local man had been involved in a tribal faction fight with bows and arrows and arrived at the hospital with a very long, lethal- looking arrow poking right into his head. He had never travelled in a car before, so Sue calmed him and helped him settle in the front passenger seat. While she ran to fetch her car keys to drive him to a City hospital, her patient decided to experiment with the window winder. He soon discovered much to his dismay, that if he closed the window, there wasn't room in the vehicle to accommodate the arrow, so using his bare hands, he snapped off part of the shaft which was protruding from his skull. This made it much harder for the surgeon to remove the arrow head and the splintered shaft and it was nothing short of a miracle that the young man survived to tell the tale.

Many of the local folk still practise craniotomy, meaning that if someone suffers a bad headache or feels a throbbing pain in the head which could in reality be from a fever, he/she immediately suspects that the problem has been caused by an evil spirit or demon inhabiting the victim. These superstitious folk believe that an evil spirit is pounding relentlessly on the victim's skull and demanding to be let out. They hasten to the rescue and very often a sharp piece of tin can or a dirty axe or pen knife, or even a very sharp pointed stick, is used to bore a hole in the sufferer's skull. One can imagine how disastrous this procedure is when performed under unhygienic conditions and without using any form of anaesthesia to nub the pain.

Having left the wound open for a while to drain and supposedly to allow the evil spirits to make their way out, the gaping hole is then plugged with a dollop of thick, sticky mud or animal dung. Many promising young lives have been lost tragically because infection, dirt and maggots have entered the wound.

A dear little boy arrived at the hospital with a substantial portion of his skull missing after having had his suspected evil spirits released. Potent antibiotics were immediately administered and his young life was saved in the nick of time. For future protection he was fitted with a tough, resilient cycling helmet to guard the vulnerable portion of his exposed brain. As his head grew, he would need to be fitted with bigger and bigger cycling helmets.

What a blessing his parents had sought timeous medical intervention and his precious little life was saved.

While I was staying with Sue,I met a brave lady who lived way down in the Keriot valley. She had been collecting firewood when she was bitten on her right hand by a puff adder, a venomous and very dangerous snake. Although they move slowly, puffadders are highly aggressive and have a swift, accurate bite. The venom is cytotoxic, and as it spreads it causes necrosis which may lead to gangrene.

To prevent the poison from spreading, the lady's anxious husband had grabbed his machete (a broad blade used like an axe) and hacked off her arm at the elbow. He then bound the stump in old rags dipped in paraffin and the courageous lady hiked all the way up the steep valley to the hospital for help. A skilful surgeon straightened the jagged stump and administered life- saving antibiotics. On the days which followed, I saw a miracle happening in the hospital ward, before my disbelieving eyes. As if making up for the lost portion of her right limb, the lady's left arm started to grow and grow, enabling it to stretch far and wide and transforming it into a versatile and unique part of the lady's anatomy.

It was fascinating to see ladies collecting piles of silky textured leaves and making them into neat bundles which they laid out for sale. The leaves reminded me of those on our own beautiful Silvertree which is an endangered plant species. It is part of the Protea family and is found in a small area of South Africa's Cape Peninsula. The Afrikaans folk call it Die Witteboom (White tree) because of the light, silvery sheen on the leaves and we even have a railway station in Cape Town named after the tree!

I wondered if the ladies were going to grind the leaves into a type of snuff or dry them to make a health tea or roll them into cigarettes for the locals to smoke, as an alternative to cannabis!

I was astounded at Sue's explanation. This type of tree is known in Kenya as the Toilet Tree and believe it or not, many of the locals queued to purchase piles of these soft, downy leaves to use as a substitute for toilet paper! I was even more shocked to learn that in the drier, arid areas certain tribes like the Maasai, actually use pebbles as toilet paper. In our own country it has been upsetting to hear that some very poor families resort to collecting old telephone directories so that pages can be ripped out and hung on spikes in their toilets to serve as toilet paper.

Whilst in Kenya I heard a delightful story about a group of philanthropic American visitors who couldn't bear the thought of the Maasai having to use pebbles because they had no toilet paper. Upon their return to their homeland, the kind hearted and generous spirited tourists despatched a load of Kleenex tissues to Kenya to be freely distributed to those deprived of basic necessities. The tissues were flown in just in time for Christmas. The local Maasai people were delighted to receive free jumbo- sized boxes of pastel coloured tissues but felt they were far too beautiful to be wasted in long drop toilets. Instead they decorated every acacia thorn tree in sight with pastel pink, yellow, blue and lime green tissues and said it was their BEST Christmas ever!

A new and rather frightening sight for me was to see tribesman from groups like the Pokot walking around armed with bows and arrows for their protection. Some tribes use venom from deadly snakes on the tips of their arrows to protect themselves from hostile, marauding tribes. Another intriguing fact was to discover how instead of using a retail brand of Sun Screen to block out the Equator's searing Ultra Violet rays, the Pokot people cover their bodies with a thick layer of mud mixed with blood! The blood helps the mud to adhere to their skin and stops the mud from cracking. An added blessing is that this mixture serves as an excellent insect repellent too!

While I was staying with Sue I found that all my hand washed underwear was turning pale beige, a pretty cappuccino colour! This was because the natural water contains a high percentage of iron and in some areas no chlorine is added to the water, so it sometimes squirts out of the taps looking rather like Pepsi or Coca Cola!

On my first Sunday in Kapsowar, Sue and I were sitting quietly in church watching folk of all ages drift in from the nearby villages. Some of the more mobile patients had also gathered in the little hospital chapel. We were greeted with happy smiles and cheerful banter.

Church time on Sundays was obviously a very special time of meeting together for praise and worship for everyone. But not having watches or clocks and being accustomed to watching the sun's position in the sky, many worshippers drifted in late. I had been warned that church services often continue right up until lunch time. Just as we stood to sing the opening hymn, two nurses burst in on the packed congregation. They charged down the aisle and headed straight for Sue yelling, " Muttron, Muttron, Come quickly. We need you now! Lady giving birth to twins! "

Sue grabbed my arm. We clambered over our tightly packed fellow congregants and sprinted towards the operating theatre. We hastily dragged on freshly laundered theatre gowns which were neatly stacked on a chair close to the door and covered our shoes with protective cotton booties.

Sure enough, there was a beautiful wide-eyed young Kalenjin woman lying on the operating table. She looked no more than 20 or 22. She was obviously in great pain and was pushing and heaving for all she was worth. It was a case of all hands on deck and we had to act swiftly. I was happy to help where I could even if it meant just monitoring the blood pressure of the young mother-to-be. Sue explained her cause for concern. The hospital obstetrician was on weekend leave and the slim patient had a very narrow pelvis.

A tragic phenomenon occurs in Kenya where female circumcision is still practised by many tribes. At a tender age, possibly between 11 and 15, this unfortunate young lady had been forced by family tradition to endure what is often a traumatic and even a life- threatening procedure, where some of her external genitalia had been cut away. This primitive surgery is not performed under anaesthetic in a sterile operating theatre or by a trained surgeon skilfully using a scalpel. Instead the procedure is usually done by a local woman, in poor lighting and on the dirt floor of a hut. After that the unfortunate young lady would have had her vagina sewn closed with elephant grass or reeds, to help her to "remain pure" for her husband.

Invariably this female mutilation causes tremendous pain and bleeding and results in serious complications in later life, and particularly when giving birth. So on this occasion the hospital team had no option but to perform an urgent Caesarean Section to save the life of their patient and the precious, fragile lives of the tiny twins.

Cries of joy rang out in the theatre when two healthy little babies were successfully delivered. The young doctor in charge immediately offered a prayer of thanksgiving. The proud new mother was overwhelmed when a sturdy little boy and a petite baby girl were handed to her for a quick cuddle before they were whisked away to be washed. It was impossible to hold back tears and I shall never forget the Kalenjin lady's beaming face and her beautiful smile of gratitude when the perfectly formed little twins were returned to her, looking as if they had been polished from head to toe.

After lunch the off duty hospital staff planned a relaxing Sunday afternoon forest walk. Before setting off I was introduced to Joseph, a tall warrior-like figure who was armed with a very large lethal-looking bow and an impressive quiver of arrows. He immediately displayed his precision and accuracy in archery by taking aim at a poor defenceless little field mouse scuttling under a bush about 30 metres away. This horrified me as an animal lover but Joseph explained that he needed to be on target because from time to time, one might encounter bandits lurking in the forest. They might jump out and rob hikers. This was a Sunday afternoon stroll with a difference!

On another little amble through the local settlement we met a dear old lady affectionately known to the locals as the Spider Woman. Her particular skill was being adept at successfully extricating spiders, ticks, beetles and any other "goggas" or foreign bodies like beads, match stick heads or mielie pips, causing pain or discomfort if lodged in auditory canals! Spider Woman had a unique method of removing the offending creature or object. Instead of using a syringe or a teaspoon full of warm olive oil, she chose to gently pour in some warm sweet coffee. After a gentle soak, the old lady would then fish about in her patient's ear using a wire coat hanger which she bent into a formidable hook to suit the size and shape of the ear. She worked from her little hut and had an impressive array of extricated items displayed on her doorstep, hoping to attract potential patients to her practice! She charged one shilling a visit and seldom lacked patients.

I was intrigued by the names of some of the items available in quaint little roadside stores in Kenya. When I needed to purchase a new roll of underarm deodorant, I was offered two enchanting fragrances, Paris moon or Cream Soda! I thought I would be adventurous so I settled for Cream Soda. When I returned home after my holiday, Desi, one of my staff colleagues said as I walked into the staff room, " Mmmmm, whose brought a cream soda! I haven't drunk one of those for years!"

The roadside adverts on huge billboards grabbed my attention too....

ARE YOU HAVING AN AFFAIR?
WE WILL CATER FOR IT.

Warning on an OMO WASHING POWDER BOX.
Use detergent with caution or it will devour your undergarments.

SWEET AND QUICK
Pull yourself out of the miseries of a sore throat,
coughs and hoarse voice.
Chew the sweet DESEPT TABLETS.
THEY WILL GIVE YOU QUICK RELIEF
PLUS A SMOOTH VOICE.

BRITA WHYTE TOOTHPASTE.
GIVES YOU BIG STRONG WHITE TEETH.
BETTER FOR BITING.

Instruction printed on an aerosol can of insect repellant in our hotel room.

DEPRESS PROTUBERANCE ON CANISTER TO ACTIVATE THE REPELLANT SPRAY MOST CONSCIENTIOUSLY THEN AIM WITH PRECISION AT OFFENDING INSECT MENACE AND YOU WILL BE REWARDED.

Then in a printed hotel brochure placed in every bedroom.

IT IS NOT ALLOWED IN KENYA TO DRESS TOPLESS

And here is one of my favourites…

PLEASE DO NOT FEED MONKEYS WITH FRUITS IN THE DINING ROOM. REMEMBER MISCONCEIVED LOVE OF ANIMALS MAY END CATASPROPHICALLY.

One cannot visit Kenya without taking a ride in a Matatu. You do however need to have nerves of steel. A matatu is a Kenyan taxi and you see them everywhere. They are either the size of a minibus or of a larger bus. A matatu is the most popular form of transport in Kenya.Before you actually see it, you will know that a matatu is heading your way because you will hear the beat and throb of blaring music coming from its "boombox." You will be fascinated to see passengers clinging to the roof of the taxi and surrounded by bulging bags of shopping, suitcases and often a crate or two of squawking hens or doleful ducks.

Nancy's little corrugated iron house in Sajiloni

A Kenyan long drop toilet

33

FROM STRIPPER IN LONDON TO UNDERTAKER IN KENYA!

*M*y first week in Kenya was just an initiation period and a gentle warm up for more drama to follow!

Sue had arranged to take leave from the hospital for the remainder of my holiday and we had an exciting schedule planned. We set off bright and early the following week in her sturdy 4x4 vehicle to tackle some hair- raising roads. Our plan was to visit our South African friend, Nancy who worked amongst the Maasai people in Sajiloni, a tiny settlement in an arid area close to Kajiado. Nancy had given up her teaching post and a comfortable little flat in Durban and was teaching literacy to the herd boys and training the Maasai women to earn a living by doing beautiful beadwork so as to create key rings, necklaces, beaded pens and mats to sell to tourists. Nancy was the only white person for miles around and had moved into a Maasai settlement to live cheek by jowl with the locals so that she could become fluent in their language. The men from the local church community had built her a one room rectangular corrugated iron hut which sat on a cement base. The floor was roughly laid and sloped badly to the left hand side of the hut but Nancy always looked on the bright side and said cheerfully, " Whenever I drop anything I know exactly where to find it because everything rolls or bounces in that direction!"

Nancy explained that in her little village, which was no more really than a very large kraal with a number of scattered huts, it was considered very rude and anti- social to lock one's door. As their local dearly loved missionary and hands-on lady, Nancy seemed to be expected by her neighbours to be available at any time of the day or night, to solve any problem or fix anything that broke. Her door had a flexible hinge made from a piece of rubber tyre so if anyone so much as tapped at the door, it swung open and in came a cluster of locals accompanied by dogs, cats, chickens and from time to time, an inquisitive goat!

Because white folk are somewhat of a rarity in Sajiloni, our arrival on Nancy's doorstep caused a major stir. I was obviously the first person they had seen with blonde hair and the children clustered round to pat and stroke my head with their hot little hands. Some even tried to pull strands of my fine hair to see if mine would spring back and form tight little curls like theirs!

We noticed that the ladies of the village had long dangling ear lobes and we learnt that this is a traditional Maasai form of ear piercing, considered to be very appealing to the men folk and it usually becomes the vogue when the ladies enter adulthood. This special effect is created by first slitting the ear lobes. Then to acquire a good stretch, a beaded weight, a circle of wood, an empty film canister or a small Vaseline bottle, is hung in the ear while it is healing, so as to create the drooping loop. Some of the men have ear piercings too and prefer to have beaded adornments. Sometimes beaded wire or string is looped through the rim of the ear and for a more dramatic effect, the entire centre part of the ear may even be removed.

The Maasai love bright colours and many choose to wear red because they believe that it frightens lions away. The men often wear a red robe which they call a shuka. The woman wear colourful clothes decorated with bright beads. They explained to us that the beads speak to them and each colour has a meaning e.g. red for bravery, white for the rich milk from their cow, blue for the azure sky and the rain, green for the plants, yellow for warm hospitality and black for sorrow and hardship.

Something that fascinated me no end was to see happy little groups of Masai boys returning from their initiation ceremonies which are intended to mark their passage into manhood. In order to keep their painful, fresh wounds clean and germ free while they healed, the young initiates would cover their genital areas with brightly coloured plastic yoghurt tubs strung round their waists on leather thongs. The yoghurt tubs seemed to bob up and down in unison as the boys jogged back to their villages. Many of the proud young initiates were herd boys who had been taught to read and write by Nancy.

Supper with Nancy was also a novel experience for me because she served us some rather greasy tasting goat stew. It was accompanied by ugali which she explained was a mushy mix of porridge made from maize flour and chopped spinach. I found it quite salty and chewy and it reminded me of coarse mashed potato. In South Africa maize porridge is called "mielie pap" or "phuthu" and it is a popular staple food for many of our people. Many find it delicious served at barbecues with meat and gravy or with a spicy mixture of tomatoes, onions and often beans and this township favourite is known as Chakalaka!

Nancy had borrowed sleeping bags for Sue and me to use for our Sajiloni visit. We wondered how on earth we would clear the line-up of spectators without offending them. We hoped to get enough privacy and standing space in her little house to be able to unpack, change, lay out the sleeping bags and climb into bed. Because Sajiloni was experiencing a serious drought, all water had to be recycled. Nancy's "bathroom" was a simple wooden cubicle with standing space and a shelf to hold a large washbasin and a jug. One could only have a little strip wash in the basin and the water would then be used for rinsing the dishes, washing ones' clothes or watering her few little succulent plants. Her long drop toilet was close by and some of the elders at the local church had presented her with a box- like toilet seat as a birthday gift.

Nancy warned us not to visit the toilet alone at night but to wake one another, flash our torches and make a noise, because of the presence of cheetahs and leopards prowling in the vicinity. We also had to step very carefully and be on the lookout for snakes.Nancy had already had to deal with 3 black mambas in her house! And there we were preparing to settle into our borrowed sleeping bags and doss down on her cement floor.

We slept fitfully on the hard floor with the smoky smell of the sleeping bags strong in our nostrils and trying not to imagine that a black mamba was slithering across our backs. We were filled with admiration for Nancy who had left home and loved ones and sacrificed so much to serve the Maasai people with such love and selfless devotion.

The next day was a most interesting day of visitation where Sue and I learnt so many fascinating things about the Maasai people.We saw a very striking young lady who was brightly clad and adorned with a most beautiful beaded collar. She was accompanied by quite a large entourage of maidens. As she walked, she let out the most heart - rending wails. We presumed she had lost someone very dear to her and was on the way to a funeral. Quite the contrary! She was about to acquire a handsome young Maasai husband and was en route to a wedding feast. She was crying great big crocodile tears to reflect her sadness in leaving her parents' home and to express deep gratitude for her fine upbringing!

We visited a number of delightful old folk living in huts made with a neatly constructed framework of sticks and poles and covered with animal skins to keep out any rain. We had to bend almost double to enter through a very small opening and wondered how on earth old folk with arthritis and rheumatism managed to stoop so low. There were no windows and smoke escaped through a tiny hole where the poles met in the centre. Nancy explained that the entrance was designed to prevent large animals like cows and camels from wandering in to escape the heat. There were no windows in the hut so as to keep the heat, dust and snakes at bay!

I had an embarrassing experience upon entering the first hut. It was very dark and smoky. I felt my eyes burning, causing tears to stream down my cheeks. Sue and I had been warned to enter slowly to become accustomed to the gloom.

Then one feels around gingerly for a cool spot on the ground before plonking down in the dark. This is because the Maasai folk light little fires inside their huts for cooking, making chai (tea) and for warding off wild animals. Hasty visitors have been known to settle themselves on the smouldering embers which don't always glow in the dark.

I thought I was being extra cautious and lowered myself gently in the dark feeling certain I had selected a cool spot and had avoided having roast rump! From under me came a smothered screech then a loud cackle, followed by much mirth. In the dark I had unwittingly sat on the lap of a visiting granny who had walked for 5 km to have afternoon tea with the visitors from afar. I asked Nancy to offer my sincere apologies in their language, but there was so much laughter and frivolity that I don't think the old lady even heard!

Fortunately she seemed to think it was a huge joke to have been nearly flattened. Several speeches of welcome followed our arrival then hot sugary chai was brought to us in used jam tins which served as mugs. We were rather horrified to see how the "mugs" were being polished in time for our arrival. Two Maasai ladies were aiming their saliva into each tin, adding a good handful of coarse sand then making a paste to scour the mugs until they gleamed. We hoped that the boiling hot water used to make the tea would effectively deal with any bacteria. The Maasai brew was made with three generous pinches of leaf tea, four teaspoons of sugar and a little squirt of goat's milk stored in a dried gourd.

After much chatting and interpretation by Nancy whose knowledge of their language impressed the old folk no end, we moved to the next little cluster of beehive huts. This time we were informed that there was a special birthday celebration in progress and we were offered a drink from a gourd being passed round from hand to hand in the darkness of the hut. Because it is considered rude to reject a gift or a kind gesture, Nancy suggested that we keep our upper and lower teeth pressed tightly together and pretend to take little sips in the darkness. We hoped that our lip smacking and grunts of approval would sound convincing!

This time I was going to make quite certain that I did not land on anyone's lap or find myself sitting astride a pet goat or sheep in the smoke-filled hut. I headed for the central pole which is rather like a main tent pole supporting the roof. I grabbed it with my right hand, peered through the smoke and took note of the lie of the land. As I settled into a gap between a visiting dog, three hens and two elderly neighbours, I wondered what on earth the local folk used to treat their poles. This was definitely not creosote. It felt moist and slippery and I dug deep into my pocket for a tissue before accepting the gourd from our Maasai hostess. As the cold liquid moistened my lips I realized this was not anything I had ever tasted at any other birthday celebration. I remembered Nancy's tip about clenched teeth and gratefully passed it on to the next party goer! I felt even more grateful when I discovered afterwards what was in the celebratory drink. It was not quite our kind of pink milkshake! It was a mixture of sour milk with a touch of ox blood, a generous squirt of camel urine and had been stirred with a charred stick to give the brew a unique woody flavour!

As for the stickiness on the central pole in the hut….. the less one knows about that, the better! The smoky atmosphere causes eyes to water and noses to run, so the best place to run to when you want to give your hand a quick wipe, because you don't possess a handkerchief, is to the pole! On my very next visit I went armed with a travel pack of Wet Wipes!

Nancy told us a hilarious story about what happened when she returned to Kenya with a brand new set of dentures after holidaying in South Africa. The villagers commented on how well she looked and admired her beautiful broad smile. She owned up and admitted that she had returned with a brand new set of teeth. They found this concept hard to grasp so Nancy described them as "Duka" teeth (shop teeth!) and explained that they were made specially to fit her mouth by someone called a Dentist who is like a Tooth Doctor and she had to buy them! They then asked all kinds of questions which resulted in her having to demonstrate to her Maasai neighbours how she was able to pop her dentures in and out. You can guess what happened next….they all wanted a turn to wear her shop teeth and there was great mirth and frivolity as the duka teeth were passed round her circle of admirers!

After a very happy time of socialising, it was time for Sue and me to attend a little afternoon service for ladies at the local Bush Church. This proved to be another memorable occasion. Ladies of all ages drifted in and out. Not having watches, they seemed to arrive when the sun told them it was time to gather, or when they heard singing in the distance. Nancy played her guitar and led them in singing Maasai choruses, before asking me to bring a greeting from South Africa. She then held the little congregation in suspense as she told them an exciting Bible Story in their own language. She used brightly coloured Sunday School illustrations on large flip charts and there was much ooh-ing, ah-ing and clicking in agreement from the onlookers.

I was fascinated to discover that the little Maasai babies were wearing no nappies. (diapers) Instead, the moms seemed to be mindful of their bodily needs and from time to time would hold them out over a dusty patch of soil and allow them to make little puddles. They would then be given a gentle swing in the breeze to drip dry! During the service some of the women would breast feed their babies then stretch their legs onto a friend's lap for an outdoor pedicure where their toe nails were cleaned using brutally sharp acacia thorns.

I was deeply moved to see these generous ladies who are so impoverished, sacrificially placing their little coins in an offering bag to help less -privileged villagers. I was suddenly reminded of the poor widow mentioned in the Bible who sacrificially gave all she had, which was one small coin called a mite. A few of the grannies dozed in the afternoon heat, oblivious of the flies which buzzed around their eyes and lips. Some younger ladies used porcupine quills to check each other's hair for fleas or ticks. There were two rather hectic dog fights during the little service and this disturbance caused several of the sleeping babies to start crying. This immediately prompted some of the older ladies to yell at the dog owners. Nancy very wisely played a few chords on her trusty guitar, announced it was time for more singing and everyone settled down again. It certainly was a Women's Auxiliary meeting with a difference!

It had been a very long, hot day for us, full of new and exciting experiences. It was hard to believe that only ten days ago I had been teaching History to my grade sixes back in my classroom at Pinehurst Primary! I knew how much they were going to enjoy hearing all about my Kenyan adventures.

It was almost dusk by the time we arrived back at Nancy's little corrugated iron home perched on a crooked concrete slab. We were longing for some Ceylon tea out of China mugs instead of scrubbed jam tins.

"Oh no," said Nancy as she parked her trusty vehicle. "There's a whole Maasai delegation waiting on my doorstep. I wonder what's up!"

All too soon we found out....

As we stepped out of Nancy's sturdy old pick-up truck after a bone - rattling journey home, we realised that something dramatic had happened.

A dead body was draped across the threshold of her little house. There was much wild gesticulating and loud chatter and wagging of fingers in progress. Nancy greeted the gathered throng in Maasai and asked them to sit down quietly and explain exactly what had happened. So many were all trying to yell out explanations at once that she resorted to Teacher Tactics asking them how many ears she had. When they bellowed "Two!" she said that unfortunately one ear worked better than the other so it would be a good idea if she only listened to one person at a time. That seemed to work fairly well; although many villagers were whispering their own versions in the background.

One kindly old lady decided to step forward and very discreetly flicked a tattered garment across the poor deceased gentleman's nether regions, but without actually going too close.

Apparently this very ill middle aged man had been an outcast from a nearby village. He had come to the Sajiloni settlement hoping for a warmer reception and for some kind folk to offer him shelter. However, he had walked many miles in the hot sun. Regrettably he had not been made to feel welcome at all and only survived for a day or two. Much of the hostility he received could be blamed on ignorance and superstition. Nancy managed to establish that the man was probably suffering from the HIV virus and was in a weakened state before he set off on his long hot journey by foot.

Now that he had succumbed to the illness, no one was prepared to take responsibility for him, fearing that they too would be smitten with AIDS. The elders of the village made it quite clear to Nancy that she should accommodate the corpse for the night because the Big God she serves would look after her and not let her catch his sickness! Nancy explained that she had two visitors staying with her and that all the floor space in her tiny house was being used. Some villagers peeped in to check for themselves. Our unrolled sleeping bags were right up against the wall on one side and the door on the other. We promised the villagers that we would make a safe place for the body outside. By now it was becoming very smelly having lain in the hot sun all day. The onlookers rolled their eyes disapprovingly and shouted unanimously, "No! No! Not outside! The wild animals will devour his flesh and the spirits will be angry."

We had to do some quick thinking….

Nancy came up with an excellent plan of action. We three women would carry the body to a safe distance from her house, cover the poor lifeless man with a tarpaulin stored in Nancy's truck. We would pin it down with heavy boulders hoping that the jackals and hyenas would not be able to dislodge them and tug at the body. For extra protection we covered the entire mound with branches stripped from the surrounding acacia thorn trees. We assured all the onlookers that we would pray and ask our God to look after the man's body all through the night. Then another bright idea came to Nancy. She filled a lantern with paraffin and strung it up in the thorn tree right above the man's body, feeling optimistic that wild animals would be frightened off by the flickering flame.

Sue and I woke at first light and headed straight down to the tree. Amazingly enough the little paraffin lantern had burned all night. The boulders were still in place and the dead body appeared to be intact.

Our prayers had been answered and the local folk were going to be very relieved to think that evil spirits had not been let loose in their village. It saddened us greatly to discover how many people are gripped by fear and held in bondage because of age-old superstitions passed on generally by word of mouth from one generation to another. Nancy knew of some Maasai folk who would not allow one to take photographs of them because they believed that the camera would capture part of their souls, so for safety we always asked permission before taking a photograph.

We swallowed a hasty breakfast because the tropical sun was rising and the odour from the putrefying corpse was nauseating. It had dawned on us at midnight that Nancy, Sue and I would have to get used to the idea of becoming voluntary undertakers! If we transported the body to the Central Police Station in Nairobi the police would surely arrange a decent pauper's burial.

Whilst visiting Nancy and travelling about with her in her faithful old bone shaker of a truck, Sue had left her 4X4 vehicle parked at Mayfield, the Nairobi guest house belonging to the African Inland Mission. Nancy had very kindly offered to take us back to Nairobi after our Sajiloni visit, so it made sense for her to undertake only one journey to the Capital, seeing it was 70 km each way on very rough roads. We wrapped our luggage as best we could with protective plastic sheeting before laying the emaciated body across our suitcases. Not having an air freshener, we resorted to using my entire aerosol can of Elnett hairspray to make the atmosphere in the cab slightly more bearable. We drove all the way with the windows wide open taking in huge gulps of fresh air and hoping that we did not encounter any roadblocks or bandits with bows and arrows, who would jump out and slow our progress.

Upon arrival in Nairobi, we received some very startled looks from the top brass at the Police Headquarters when we three maidens asked for help in carrying a corpse into their yard.

As we saw the body being rather unceremoniously deposited under an overhanging tree, we drove away with heavy hearts. It was incredibly sad to think that this poor unfortunate man had not one relative or friend in the whole wide world who was prepared to stay by his side and ensure that he received a gentle and dignified send off.

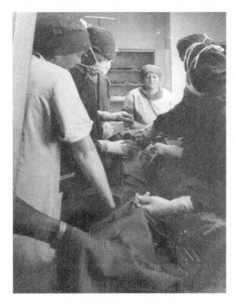

Ruth monitoring blood pressure during a Caesarean delivery in Kapsowar

Nancy's ablution block in Sajiloni

34

BLACK MAMBA UNDER MY BED

*A*fter a good night's rest at the Mayfield guesthouse Sue and I set off bright and early the next morning to drive the 273 km up north to the Lake Baringo district where we were to spend a couple of nights with her UK missionary friends, Michael and Joan. We hoped to see some beautiful birds near the lake and an added bonus would be to encounter some crocodiles and hippos. It was extremely hot so we were delighted when soon after our arrival Michael and Joan took us to enjoy a refreshing swim at the Lake Baringo Country Club. Thereafter Joan suggested we unpack and have a little rest before supper. We were thankful for this suggestion as the 43 deg. Celcius temperature had left us both feeling limp.

I am suddenly reminded of two courageous South African ladies, Lorna Eglin and Betty Allcock, who served so faithfully as missionary teachers on the far side of Lake Baringo until they were almost 70! How I admire them for coping with the loneliness of singleness in far-flung arid regions, the primitive living conditions they endured and the intense heat, not to mention the deadly snakes and wild animals!

Sue and I had flopped onto our beds and had actually drifted off for twenty minutes. Dusk was closing in as Joan came to call us for supper.

As she reached the bedroom door she flicked on a switch and a solar-powered lamp cast an ethereal blue-ish glow across the room. I sat up and stretched and was about to step into my sandals when Joan screamed, "Ruth! Black Mamba! Don't move!"

I cast my eyes down and looked straight into the evil challenging eyes of the mamba, which was not pitch black as I had imagined, but rather an oily looking sombre shade of brownish- grey. It's the inside of a mamba's mouth which is apparently jet black but thankfully this black mamba's mouth was still closed!

Sue sat bolt upright. Her eyes were like saucers. She pressed herself flat against the opposite wall and remained dead still. I froze momentarily then standing on the bed to stay clear of our unwanted intruder, I looked around desperately for a weapon. All I could see was my flimsy little bright pink folding umbrella. Having been told how mambas move at lightning speed, rear up high and attack with aggression, striking repeatedly as they inject potentially lethal venom into their victim, I realised my hand -bag size pink umbrella from China would be utterly useless.

At that moment, Joan's husband Michael, having heard her scream, came to our rescue bringing with him his son's cricket bat which was a far more formidable weapon. Michael was accompanied by his brother who was visiting from Canada. With hearts pounding, Sue and I were told to keep our eyes on the mamba as we backed out of the bedroom as calmly as possible. Michael had obviously experienced close encounters with deadly black mambas before. The two brave brothers exercised great patience as they waited at a safe distance for the full length of mamba to slither from under my bed. Then before it sought refuge under Sue's bed, the men pounced, aiming for its head with the cricket bat. We were amazed at the power in its lithe, muscular body as it reared up high and thrashed about in an effort to escape the lethal blows.

Having made quite certain that the black mamba was dead the men burnt its remains in an outdoor brazier containing hot coals which

Michael called a "jikka." This they explained was advisable just in case the snake's mate returned in the night to look for it!

That night Sue and I wet our bath towels, rolled them into tight sausages and shoved them into the gap under our bedroom door, for fear that any other reptiles or nocturnal creepy crawlies might choose to explore our bedroom.

We had been warned that we were in black mamba territory. Joan had told us how snakes quite often enter houses to escape the heat. They slither over the cool tiles and hide out in cupboards and have even been known to slip into travellers' suitcases where they find comfort between cool silky underwear!

But to have an 8 foot black mamba come out from under my bed and slither across my flip flops as I was about to step into them, on my very first night at Lake Baringo was more of a travel adventure than I had bargained for!

An overnight train journey from Nairobi to Mombasa proved to be another unforgettable experience especially when the front coach of our express train was derailed when we struck a hapless elephant crossing the railway line at 3am!

Sue and I had reported to the train station at 7pm in good time for our departure at 7.30pm. We had read on Trip Advisor that departure times can prove troublesome if one has a tight schedule in Mombasa. We soon discovered that the overnight train from Nairobi is often delayed or even cancelled. A whole hour after our scheduled time of departure, a very polite announcement was made~ first in Swahili and then in English~ "Ladies and Gentleman, we humbly apologize that due to unforeseen expectations beyond our control, this train was unable to depart at 7.30. We therefore ask you to help us by being patient so that we can prepare to depart as soon as our circumstances permit!"

Well, thankfully our circumstances eventually permitted! We were finally on our way just before 10pm.Fortunately we had enjoyed a supper before leaving for the station so we decided we would head straight to bed. There were six of us in our second class compartment but only Sue and I had bought bedding tickets. We opted for the top two bunks because the four Kenyan ladies said they preferred to sleep in their seats. It amazed us the way they covered their heads with their brightly coloured Kangas (wraps) , which we discovered could be used as head- wraps, robes, skirts, beach sarongs or even as towels. They snuggled into their Kangas and then gently rocked themselves to sleep with the rhythm of the train and managed to remain upright all night.

A very efficient young bedding steward made up our beds and then told us to lie down so he could "enclose us for the night!" He pulled a stretchy piece of netting across our bunks to stop us from falling out! Sue and I felt as if were trapped in hammocks or were peering out at each other through high slung volley ball nets! We were both exhausted after a long hot car journey from Sajiloni and an emotionally draining day fulfilling our responsibilities as voluntary undertakers. Added to that, was our late departure from Nairobi.

Using the toilet on the train proved a daunting experience. I had no idea that long drop loos existed on Kenyan trains! Sure enough there was no toilet seat, just a round hole in the floor! It reminded me of a port hole and was covered by a metal flap on a strong spring which was operated by pressing a pedal with the ball of your foot. As you peered through the hole, you saw the blur of railway track whizzing below you at a terrific speed.

Going to use the toilet at the far end of the carriage was definitely not for passengers having a faint hearted disposition. To start with, one needed an adventurous spirit to negotiate the corridor as the train lurched round bends in the track. In fact the entire operation required tremendous co-ordination, precision and agility. You had to get the timing perfect so that the pressure exerted by your foot on the spring, kept the flap open for just long enough. Our express train was hurtling along in an attempt to make up for lost time as it steamed up hills and swung through deep gorges. It was very difficult to balance in mid-air without having the security of a toilet seat under one, just in case you needed to make a forced landing. The next challenge presented itself when it was time to carefully aim the toilet paper through the aperture in the floor without the tremendous draft blowing it straight back at one with a mean vengeance. Ducking and diving was essential so it was important to maintain one's balance whilst demonstrating extreme agility and stamina!

We dropped off to sleep very quickly and slept soundly until just before 3am. There was a tremendous thud and the brakes of the train squealed in anguish. Sue and I were almost rocketed into orbit before the train ground to a rather abrupt halt. There was complete silence for thirty seconds, then as passengers were woken violently, we very quickly realised that our train had met with a major mishap. There was a babble of voices and a pounding of footsteps. We un-entangled ourselves from the protective netting, scrambled down from our top bunks and peered out into the darkness. Everyone seemed to be racing to the front of the train to see what had happened. We saw little pin pricks of light puncturing the inky darkness. Before long dozens of local villagers had hastened from their beds and were threading their way through the dark bushes and were soon thronging the railway track. Sue picked out a few Swahili words she could understand and relayed the tragic news....

The front part of our train had slammed into a very large bull elephant as he nonchalantly lumbered across the tracks. In no time at all, a huge excited crowd had gathered and the villagers were wielding razor sharp pangas (machetes) to cut the unfortunate animal into large chunks. They then ferried large chunks of elephant meat into their settlements. We were told by a fellow traveller that Kenyans consider elephant meat to be a delicious delicacy and we recalled having seen smoked elephant meat for sale in the Nairobi market.

It was a joy to eventually arrive in Mombasa seven hours late; with the dining coach having run out of food and water. There had been much shunting back and forth of railway coaches, as we waited for a replacement steam engine.

Kenya's coastline has some of the most beautiful, dazzling, unspoilt tropical beaches in the world. I marvelled at the blinding white powdery sand and the turquoise water. Our hotel was on Diani beach and was called The Two Fishes because it was managed by a Mr and Mrs Fish! The beach was dotted with waving palm trees and seemed to stretch for miles on end. There was a beautiful swimming pool which terminated in what was called a Wet Bar at the end closest to the dining room. It was a delight being able to keep cool under the tropical sun as we remained in our swim suits to sip freshly squeezed fruit juice while relaxing on submerged bar stools. Since then my husband and I have encountered similar Wet Bars in Zanzibar, Seychelles and Thailand and have decided it's the perfect way to chill!

Diani beach has a beautiful coral reef lying fairly close to the shore line. Sue and I hired the services of two delightful Kenyan brothers who offered snorkelling trips out to the reef on their wooden dhow. Nothing was too much trouble for the affable brothers who had broad grins and smiling eyes. They supplied snorkelling masks and flippers or fins, as they are sometimes called and assured us they had been soaked in baths of salt water and were germ free! This was my very first snorkelling experience and it proved to be one of the most memorable highlights of my Kenyan visit. The reef was breathtaking in its unspoilt beauty and Sue and I felt as if we were swimming in an aquarium.

Multi -coloured fishes of all shapes and sizes swished past us as we gently flippered our way through the shimmering turquoise water. We marvelled at the perfection of Creation as exquisite iridescent bright blue miniatures darted past our masks and hid in the forest of waving fronds.

Our relaxing and rejuvenating week at the coast passed all too quickly. We hired heavy old-fashioned bicycles from an old man in a shack near the hotel and explored the surrounds.

When we returned to our hotel room we discovered that an inquisitive little trio of grey vervet monkeys had squeezed through our open window and were exploring our bedroom. They had already tucked into our bananas and scratched under our pillows. We arrived back just in time to stop those nosey little intruders with their white- fringed black faces, long white cheek whiskers, nimble little black feet and black tipped tails from plundering our supply of cashew nuts.

Another unforgettable holiday experience was our camel derby, where for forty minutes Sue and I enjoyed a grandstand view from the backs of our obliging and docile beasts. When we tugged on the reins a little too enthusiastically their faces contorted into wide grins showing huge yellow teeth that looked as if they could do with a good flossing! We could think of no better way to explore the long stretch of pristine powder- white sand.

Diani Beach undoubtedly has great appeal not only to beach lovers and water sport enthusiasts but for honeymooners, hikers, families, nature lovers, back packers and party poopers!

Once back in Nairobi, there was just time for one last taxi ride on a matatu. My Kenyan friends told me that "tatu" means three in Swahili and it is considered that there is always room for three more passengers aboard a Matatu. I also heard that the taxis usually have three rows of benches. Yet another explanation was that back in the 1960's the fare was usually paid in three coins. The matatus are privately owned mini buses and are frequently overloaded. Quite often, excess commuters and luggage gets hoisted up onto the roof. I was fascinated to see intrepid passengers, young and old, perched up high, clinging to their luggage and even clutching prized hens and goats!

The matatu drivers seem to follow their own set of traffic rules and I found I did an awful lot of praying and nail biting between destinations. My hair raising journey to Eldoret on the Leopard Express had helped to initiate me somewhat.

Desmond.

The matatu was taking us to the most popular Nairobi under cover market where I was hoping to buy some of the beautiful, vibrant coloured hand- made baskets and bags to take home as gifts. The skilful art of weaving, dyeing and grass- rolling has been passed on from generation to generation within Kenyan families. The Kenyan ladies use strands of sisal grass, doum palm, palm leaves and the fibres of banana leaves to weave exquisite baskets and bags of all shapes and sizes. They use natural dyes made from vegetable juice, tree bark and crushed roots to create eye-catching colours.

On the last night of my Kenyan adventure Nancy joined us from Sajiloni and before Sue drove me to Nairobi airport, we enjoyed a farewell meal together. It was a rare treat to dine at the world famous open-air Carnivore restaurant in the Langata suburb of Nairobi. On travel websites and in tourist brochures the Carnivore is aptly described as "The Ultimate Beast of a Feast!" As we entered through a tropical garden, a tantalising smell of barbecued meat greeted us from a giant roasting pit and I was overwhelmed by the selection on offer. The meat was being barbecued on glowing charcoal and the restaurant which first opened its doors in 1980, offers customers An Eat-All- You-Can Buffet. We were fascinated to flip through the Visitors' book and to note how many rich and famous celebrities from all over the world had chosen to enjoy an Out of Africa meal at The Carnivore.

To start with, the three of us shared a generous and intriguing meat platter with all kinds of exotic sizzling meats and sausage we had never encountered in a restaurant back home, or had ever dared to sample. Each sliver of meat was carefully labelled with a little tag attached to a toothpick. I was game to try everything on offer, which included rabbit, puffadder, crocodile, ostrich, hartebees, elephant, kudu, camel and springbok. A little white paper flag was placed on our table and while it stayed aloft, handsomely dressed and extremely attentive waiters kept offering us fresh hot meat. Whenever you needed time to recover, you simply tipped the flag sideways. Think of it as signalling, "I *surrender!*" We thought this was a very helpful and novel arrangement.

We were positively groaning by the time the evening was over and with our tums full of delicious Nyama Choma (barbecued meat) Sue and Nancy delivered me safely to the airport for my homeward flight. Friends who visited the Carnivore in recent years reported that the menu was much "tamer" now because in 2004 the Kenyan government imposed strict rules on the sale of game meat. However, tourists can still tuck into succulent barbecued slices of chicken, lamb, beef, pork, ostrich and if they're adventurous like I am, they can sample a succulent chunk of flame- grilled crocodile!

You will be delighted to know that in her popular Channel 4 series, Food Unwrapped, the English TV presenter and journalist, Katie Marie Quilton, shared the exciting news that crocodile meat is now regarded as a Super Food! It is apparently low in cholesterol, full of protein and is packed full of Omega -3, the "good" fat, which we are told can lower your risk of heart disease and stave off arthritis, depression and even dementia! So Golden Oldies let's watch for Crocodile steaks coming to our tables!

Catching a ride in a Kenyan Taxi

Ruth with the Maasai Lady

35

I LOVE AMERICA AND HER PEOPLE!

*O*ver the years I have had the joy of travelling to the United States of America on four separate occasions. Each time I have found the American people to be warm- hearted, hospitable and extremely generous.Back in the 1960's and 1970's I found they did not know much about our country, South Africa.

When I announced that I was from South Africa, the response was usually, "From which country in South Africa?"

Being pale and pink, with blonde hair, and having been a teacher for 38 years, I was often asked if I had been sent as a missionary to Africa! Some folk event asked if my mum or my dad was black and how come I was so pale! We South Africans do not particularly like our own accents yet it was great being told in America that I had "such a cute British accent!" Strangely enough, the Brits ask if we are from Australia! I was even asked to read a TV weather bulletin in Atlanta because the producer thought I had a "neat" way of talking!

In more recent times we received puzzled looks when I opened my mouth and spoke with a Cape Town accent and my husband joined in the conversation with his Lancashire accent!

Having given talks in Sunday Schools and at an elementary school I was asked afterwards by the children during Question Time, "M'am, How come you are wearing regular clothes?"

I must have been a huge let down....It turned out that they fully expected me to have arrived from Africa sporting a skimpy grass skirt and draped in beads and with not much else for the sake of modesty! I was frequently asked if I had ever encountered lions or tigers on my way to school and there was huge disappointment when I explained that I would have to visit a zoo to meet a tiger who had been imported from India!

One very friendly jet setter from Chicago started telling me all about her recent Amtrak vacation where she had travelled 3, 000 miles by train from coast to coast. She suddenly stopped in her tracks and apologised profusely saying, "Ah, I'm sorry honey, I forgot.....You're from Africa. Now let me explain what a train looks like! "

I was fascinated by the names of some of the American churches we passed as we travelled.

There was the Morning Glory Fellowship, the Bright and Morning Star, The Four Square on the Word Church, The Abundant Life Church, The Brand New Church, The Cathedral of Faith, The Champions Centre and the Strict and Particular Saints! Many American churches have such a large membership that they are spoken of as Mega Churches. I was told of one church in Houston which has about 43 500 weekly visitors attending its various services and programmes. It is a familiar sight to see advertisements outside American churches.

WE HAVE THE BEST CHOIR IN THE DEEP SOUTH. BERTIE JONES, THE BEST SOUL WINNER IN THE SOUTH. COME IN AS A SINNER AND LEAVE HERE AS A SAINT.

When attending an American church, visitors are often asked to stand up and are warmly welcomed with hugs and handshakes by those sitting close by.

Several times we were told it was a "joy and privilege for them to have real live Africans worshipping in their service." A number of churches even laid on a delicious Sunday lunch for visitors, which we regarded as a wonderfully hospitable gesture.

Remarks were made like, "Coming from Africa you must be absolutely loving all the exciting new experiences like driving on fast highways, eating ice cream, waffles and pancakes and drinking Starbucks!"

It became quite a common occurrence to be asked if I knew someone's neighbour's brother's second cousin Maud who had gone out to Africa and had settled just to the east of Cape Town, or had I ever met their late uncle Fred's son Claude from Baltimore, who was working on a mine somewhere in Africa. At times it was even suggested that these USA citizens now living in Africa would be very touched if I could personally drive over one Sunday afternoon and drop off a little gift brought all the way to Africa from their loved ones back in the States. It did sound like a loving and thoughtful gesture until they brought along the addresses. I discovered that Maud was living in Harare in Zimbabwe and Claude was a mining engineer in Witbank, Mpumalanga! I guess these cities do appear to the east of Cape Town on a map.

Witbank is much closer than Harare, but would require a drive of 958 miles (1542 km) from Cape Town, so it was hardly an enticing destination for a Sunday afternoon jaunt! I wonder how Claude is managing to pronounce the new name for Witbank with his Baltimore accent? Witbank is now known as eMalahleni!

On subsequent visits to the USA I have taken postcards and travel brochures of Cape Town, showing our beautiful Waterfront, The University, Table Mountain with the cableway ascending, shopping malls like Canal Walk and modern, upmarket homes. I observed that many folk were dumbfounded and simply could not believe that this was Africa!

I love the way the Americans express themselves! Honk your horn (Press the hooter)

Have you seen my Doo Hickey? (Thingamabob!) How ya all doin'? The response? I'm doin' good!

Don't be fooled as I was, when visiting in the Deep South. As my friend and I were about to leave a Supermarket, the friendly lady at the till said, "You'll all come back."

I replied, "No, actually we're leaving tomorrow and will be flying to Seattle." She smiled again and as I went on my way, she promptly repeated, "You'll all come back"

So we went on our way realising it was a lovely Texan way of saying that she hoped to see us again!

Instead of saying Press the button in the elevator. Just say "Mash 'em!" Change your flat means Change the punctured tyre.

Did you know that in America an Undertaker is a Mortician? A baby's pram is a buggy or a stroller.

Curtains are called drapes and a tap is a faucet.

A baby's dummy is referred to as a pacifier. An exhaust pipe is a tail pipe. Male travellers carry their money and documents in bum bags. Ladies call them Fanny Packs!

We put jam on our toast but Americans spread jelly on theirs.

We carry handbags but they refer to a bag as a purse and a purse is a wallet! Their biscuits are called cookies and their scones are referred to as biscuits.

It's unusual to find teaspoons in coffee shops or diners. We were always given little plastic or wooden sticks to stir our beverages. We were never given tea in a tea pot. You must request hot tea or you will be given iced tea. You normally receive a tea bag and boiling water and brew your own tea.

There's a knack to squeezing a tea bag with a plastic stick! In hotel rooms, a kettle is referred to as a hot pot!

An airport official at Washington Dulles International Airport said rather impatiently, "Ma'am you gotta be outa ya cotton pickin' mind!" when I asked him where I could find a trolley. My friend, Pat, and I needed one to ferry our luggage to the taxi. He went on to chide us, saying "Ma'am, surely you realize, this ain't no rail road. This be an airport!" It suddenly dawned on us....

A trolley in America is a tram or a street car. What we should have asked the airport official for was a "luggage cart!" We got it right the next time!

The Americans are great at providing excellent service delivery. Even when you mingle with thousands of other guests visiting Disney World, you get the feeling that you are special and that they are there to serve only you and to provide you with an unforgettable experience. We never saw one scrap of litter on the ground in Disney World. Workers with brooms and scoop-like devices worked tirelessly to keep all the theme parks in pristine condition.

Not once did we encounter a toilet which had run out of paper. Toilet paper was supplied on huge reels, such as the ones which hold fire hoses. As the toilet paper diminished, a back- up reel miraculously appeared. Many toilets are self- flushing, being activated when pressure is released on the seat.

Some cubicles even have an automatic means of releasing a puff of air freshener. We enjoyed the toilets which had musical seats or toilet rolls which played cheery little tunes as you tugged at the paper. We also noticed wherever we went, that the toilets have a large gap under the doors. This safety feature provides sufficient privacy, yet enables a little child to clamber out, should the door not open for some unforeseen reason.

We thought it was great the way hotels and motels advertised their rates and occupancy in flashing neon signs to save you the hassle of finding parking and going into a hotel, only to be told that all the rooms had already been taken. Americans often choose to have celebratory meals at popular hotels and we were fascinated to see that they are far less reserved than we South Africans are. We saw delightful banners displayed which announced to passers-by that

LORDY, LORDY, OUR MAUDIE'S FORTY!

CHEERS PERCY AND AGNES! FIFTY YEARS OF MARITAL BLISS. DON'T RUN OUT OF STEAM!

MIX, MINGLE AND MOVE YOUR FEET. BERTIE AND STELLA AWAIT YOUR COMPANY.

Americans are tolerant folk and are far less inhibited than we South Africans are. They accept people of all shapes and sizes. I noticed in Disney World that no one stared or passed unkind comments even at morbidly obese folk.

Because of their acceptance of all shapes and sizes, one frequently sees outsize folk confidently stepping out in shorts or tight pants and snug fitting T shirts to enjoy a day in one of the theme parks or even to parade in swim suits at one of the Water Parks.

It was difficult, however, to smother a giggle when I saw an extra -large lady who was touring with a gospel choir from Jacksonville. She was wearing a tight- fitting shocking pink T shirt with the words " I'm all out for Jesus!" emblazoned across her ample bosom in luminous lime green!

I noticed an excessively obese lady browsing in one of the 250 shops in the Florida Mall, the largest mall in Orlando. She was discreetly being shown a range of tent- sized dresses and smocks. Instead of being humiliated by having to select a garment off a rail marked XXXX LARGE or GIANT SIZE, that range of outsize garments was politely marked 'OUR COMFORTABLE RANGE.'

I would love to return to that store one day. The prices were enticing and best of all, my day was made when the helpful assistant sent me away from the MEDIUM rail where I was bargain hunting. "No ma'am," she said gently." That's not your range. You head down to the right. What you're looking for will be in the petite range!" Oh to be petite again! Florida is the place to shop ladies!

It's hard to be disciplined about eating habits when enjoying a holiday in the USA. Meals are made to look so tempting and their portions are extremely generous. In Disney World we noticed that many visitors were chomping enormous hickory smoked turkey drum sticks. These looked and smelt enticing so we bought one each to nibble for our lunch in Magic Kingdom. We soon discovered that each leg actually provides enough succulent turkey flesh to satisfy a family of four.

Many American families choose to purchase take-always or take-outs all year round. Ready- made TV dinners are popular and make catering so simple. As summer approaches, folk collect Vacation Vouchers allowing for discounts at " Eat all you Can buffets" with free refills of cold drink or "pop" as fizzy drinks are often called, or "Four eat and pay for Two." Meals are made to sound so affordable like your Breakfast buffet for only $3, 99!

I caused a stir when I made a milk tart for an American friend who was hosting a dessert and coffee evening. When she told her guests that I had made a South African tart, they were wide -eyed and hugely impressed! They gathered round to peer at my pie and said incredulously, "Wow! How neat is that! You made that pie from scratch?"

Dessert evenings are very popular in the States and one often finds the hostess serving a great big slice of chocolate, red velvet or caramel cake with a generous dollop of ice cream or whipped cream. In the summer one can purchase delicious frozen pies and tarts bursting with strawberries, blueberries or cherries which are ready to thaw and bake in the oven, so you don't ever have to make anything from scratch if you don't feel like it!

Americans love ice-cream and we all remember Barack Obama telling us that his favourite flavour was the Classic Mint Chocolate Chip whereas Donald Trump's hot favourite remains cherry vanilla. I read somewhere that on average an American eats 22 litres of ice cream a year! Now here's great news for those of us in the Comfortable Range. A company called Breyers has come up with a real Winner called Double Churned Light which is advertised as 98%

fat free and without sugar, yet it's even creamier because of the churning process.

One is spoilt for choice when it comes to choosing an ice cream parlour in the States. We were intrigued by some of the unique flavours on offer like Butter Pecan, Cucumber and Lime, Rocky Road, Cookies n Créme, Cookie Dough, Cherry Garcia, Butterscotch, Chocolate Fudge Brownie, Orange Marble, Coconut Rum and Bailey's Irish Cream!

I wish I could have captured the expression on Joe's face when he asked for an ice cream at a kiosk in Typhoon Lagoon, one of Disney World's water parks we thoroughly enjoyed. Joe was struggling to make up his mind because he had reached the front of the queue and was suddenly confronted by a board listing 50 tantalising new flavours which had not yet reached Africa. Sensing Joe's predicament, the lady behind the counter said cheerfully, "Sir, I recommend you try a garbage pail" then she hurriedly added,"There go two garbage pails now."

As Joe looked up, I could almost see his eyes stretching to panoramic mode. Two very large ladies, definitely belonging to the Comfortable Range, virtually rolled away from the ice cream parlour carrying mounds of vanilla ice cream piled high in colourful kiddies' plastic beach buckets or pails. Through the middle of the ice cream mountain in each pail was a Chocolate Flake as we call them here. The entire mound was decorated with chopped nuts, multi- coloured Sprinkles and glacé cherries. To top it all, a kiddies' beach spade was impaled in the ice cream. Before the ladies had even reached the shade of their beach umbrella and had flopped back into their recliners, they started scooping out heaped spade fulls of the yummy looking soft serve ice cream and shoving it down their throats with relish.

Suddenly our thoughts turned homewards. We pictured the excitement and joy a disadvantaged township family would experience should some kind benefactor deliver a garbage pail ice cream to their front door as a rare and unexpected treat for 6 family members.

We spent a glorious, carefree day splashing about in sheer abandonment in our swimsuits at Typhoon Lagoon having stowed our clothes and valuables in lockers strategically placed. Somehow a wonderful tropical beach atmosphere has been created with real beach sand, palm trees, beach chairs, waves and even the odd sea gull circling and swooping overhead. Legend has it that years ago a massive storm carved out the bay and created Typhoon Lagoon leaving relics such as a battered ship, shipwrecked items, odd surf boards and sun bleached skeletons.

Americans are so good at organising and everything they plan seems to run like clockwork. Typhoon Lagoon offers fun for young and old. Joe and I took advantage of the free transport offered from our hotel to the Park. We started our day at Castaway Creek where we hopped into great big tubes and floated gently for more than 600 meters round the entire Park. There were entrance and exit points along the route if you felt you suddenly wanted to hop off to buy a can of pop or a garbage pail ice cream or to attempt another ride. The raft rides were particularly exciting, especially those with fast moving rapids and bumps. I was reminded of the many happy Saturday afternoons I had enjoyed bouncing down the rapids in the Mooi River with the Treverton boarders.

We were intrigued by the name Humunga Kowabunga and were told it was an exciting five- storey body slide in the pitch dark. After whizzing down at break- neck speed from a dizzy height, I landed upside down and back to front as I splashed into the pool at the bottom, losing my sun hat, dark glasses and ear rings! But Americans seem to think of everything and there was a diver on duty, all set to take the plunge and rescue any submerged person or property.

Having caught our breath, we decided to take a more tranquil scenic ride down Mount Mayday. We noticed that life jackets were freely available in select locations and there were vigilant and experienced life guards on duty at all the rides. Food and drink was not allowed to be consumed in the water or on the rides. The food and beverage kiosks had delightful names…Leaning Palms, Happy Landings, Typhoon Tilly's, Lowtide Lou's and Let's Go Slurpin'!

Wherever we went in Disney World we were impressed by the efficiency, the caring hospitality, security, cleanliness and user-friendliness of the Theme Parks. I have had the joy of visiting Disney World on three occasions and each time there have been new innovations and more and more exciting things to see and do. In fact one could almost spend a week just exploring EPCOT. Disney World is not only about Mickey Mouse and Donald Duck.

Sadly many adults avoid visiting Disney World because they think it's merely a kids' paradise. We were delighted to discover the "Fast Pass" system which hadn't been introduced on my first two visits. It's a wonderful way of making quite sure when you purchase your tickets that you avoid standing in long queues.

The most memorable part of our day at Typhoon Lagoon was undoubtedly the time we spent in the Wave and Surf Pool, the biggest in North America. Imagine the thrill of enjoying a real surfing experience without having to go to the ocean. At intervals an enormous 15, 24 metre (50ft) wave would build up and then come crashing down. It was great to surf in with the power of the generated wave, propelling you to the shore at lightning speed. But for those swimmers who preferred a tranquil wallow, it was relaxing to wade in the shallows and enjoy bobbing about in the smaller breakers which rippled gently towards the golden shore. It gave us great pleasure to see adventurous little tiny tots shrieking with joy as they tottered away from the encroaching waves which seemed to be gobbling up their little toes.

Americans the world over seem to demand first class service. They are probably more outspoken than we are about expressing their dissatisfaction when service is shoddy. Good service keeps customers happy and makes them feel that you care about their well- being.

I loved the way we were often treated upon arrival for supper at a popular restaurant. Our surname was recorded on a clip board and we were then shown to a comfortable area to enjoy a cold drink or watch TV while we waited. We then sat up and leapt into action when we heard the following announcement over the intercom....

"Calling the party of Stott to table number 16. Welcome to the Snack Box. Kindly proceed to your table. "

A friendly hostess would then step forward and hasten to show us the way. She immediately provided us with a free jug of iced water or iced lemon tea and a menu. The attentive service was nearly always impeccable.

If you ask for a toilet or cloakroom in the USA, don't be surprised if you receive a puzzled look in return. They have some delightful names for their toilets besides usually being referred to as the "Wash room." They may point you to a Comfort Station or a Rest Room. Joe and I had an embarrassing experience in a very large departmental store where he made the mistake of asking a shop assistant where he could find the men's toilet. It might have been his Lancashire accent, but she looked completely nonplussed. When Joe provided a few more clues, the dear lady said at the top of her voice in a delightful Southern drawl, in front of a number of fellow shoppers, "Oh Sir, now I get ya! You wanna use the potty! Follow me!"

Our minds boggled. We both imagined her hauling out a chamber pot from behind the haberdashery counter! Surely she didn't expect Joe to hide behind a clothing rail to use it in private. It therefore came as a huge relief when the helpful assistant led us to a gleaming porcelain toilet, perched on a raised platform and hiding behind a burgundy brocade curtain in the far corner of the store.

"There you are Sir," she pointed, "Make yourself at home and by the way, there's no charge for using our potty!"

We live and learn!

When we returned to our tour bus after a 90 minute break for lunch and some exploring, we couldn't make out what language our guide was using to muster the passengers. As folk gathered at the given time, she was bellowing enthusiastically words which sounded like, "J'eet? J'eet? " We were mystified.

Then in the next breath she yelled lustily "Jaw pee? Jaw pee?" Fortunately an amiable Texan was on hand to interpret for us. Apparently our tour guide was merely checking that all her passengers had sufficient time to enjoy their lunch and visit a Washroom (or a Comfort Station!) and she was yelling,

"Did ya eat? Did ya eat? "

She followed up by being very practical. "Did you all pee? Did ya all pee?"

Back in the day, before digital cameras hit the scene, we bought rolls of 35mm plastic film in plastic or metal canisters and threaded them into a spool in our cameras to take still photographs or slides. I recall that most of my slides were Kodak, Fujifilm or Agfa. When an entire roll of film had been used, you either mailed it away, or took it to a pharmacy to be processed and made into slides or photographs. Slides were usually returned to you within 10 to 14 days, mounted in plastic or cardboard frames and which had to be viewed in a hand held slide viewer or a projector.

What sadness when several reels of my slides were returned to me having turned pale pink, bilious yellow or violent green. I was told that the x-ray scanning machines at the airport were to blame and that I should have known to put my camera and canisters in a protective lead -lined pouch. It broke my heart to see that the spray thundering over the Niagara Falls had turned bright pink with splotches of mottled green detracting from the inspiring beauty of one of the most spectacular Natural Wonders of the World. Sadly Emerald Lake in the Canadian Rockies was no longer Emerald. It was returned to me as Lake Vermillion! Thankfully the next time I visited, I was able to capture the lake's sheer emerald beauty on a memory card in my digital camera.

I received some strange looks when I took three canisters to a pharmacy in Seattle which offered a 24 hour colour printing service. I greeted the assistant and said, "May I hand these spools in for developing?" The lady seemed nonplussed then suddenly the penny dropped and she said triumphantly,"Ah, you wanna turn in your rolls?"

It's such a joy nowadays to travel with a compact digital camera which can take underwater shots and has the ability to store hundreds of happy holiday photographs on one tiny memory card.

Mind you, if that lady in the pharmacy made the same offer again, I would jump at the opportunity of being able to turn in my rolls!

Especially my tummy rolls!

Ruth driving Colin's new Ford Mustang in Arizona

Scrambling for moon dollars at the Houston ticker tape parade

36

BRIDESMAID IN THE ROCKIES

*A*nyone who has seen the movie Sleepless in Seattle, made in 1993 and starring Tom Hanks and Meg Ryan will appreciate what a beautiful city Seattle is. Its nickname is the Emerald City because not only the city itself, but all the surrounding areas, are filled with lush green vegetation all year round. Our Seattle friends told us that Seattle usually gets rain or drizzle on about 150 days of the year! Some patriotic folk consider Seattle to be the Coffee Capital of the World. It certainly was an exciting experience for Joe and me to be introduced to Starbucks by my Seattle friend Janet.

The enticing selection on offer proved mind boggling. Being blonde, I felt I should be loyal seeing that so many demeaning jokes are made about blondes. Should I be tempted by a Starbucks "Blonde Doubleshot" or a "Blonde Vanilla Bean Coconut milk latte" for starters? Perhaps I should ask for something different and daring like "Pumpkin Spice Chai tea latte,"or "Maple Pecan Latte" or an "Iced Salted Caramel Mocha" w, Georgiahich sounded mouth -watering. Janet suggested I be really daring and sample one of Starbuck's brand new drinks called a "Frappuccino." Well, after sipping one "Double Chocolaty Chip Crème," I was well and truly smitten for the rest of our stay. Seattle is definitely an ice cream and coffee lovers' Paradise!

Janet has been a wonderful family friend for forty years ever since my mother's attention was drawn to her attractive Seattle accent in an elevator in the busy City Centre of Cape Town. She and her husband were touring South Africa with a group from the United States. My mother was very gregarious and made wonderful friends all over the world. When she died at almost 84, she still had the names of over 400 friends on her mailing list. Many of them tell me how much they miss her friendship and her cheery annual newsletters. Mom always had a soft spot for Americans. One of her favourites was Neil, a charming young man from Atlanta Georgia. Neil visited South Africa with the Agape Musical Group and became like a foster son to our mom when he extended his stay for further studies in Cape Town. Later on mom enjoyed wonderful hospitality from Neil's mom, Cleo, in Florida USA, and they struck up an enduring friendship. Mom derived great pleasure from offering hospitality to foreign visitors to our shores and loved showing them parts of our beautiful City which are not always included in tour itineraries. In return for mom's genuine, caring friendship, my brother and his wife and Joe and I have been the recipients of incredible love and warm hospitality from our mother's wide circle of overseas friends whenever we too have travelled abroad.

It was on my very first trip to Seattle that I had an unforgettable experience as I travelled by car across the Canadian border with Janet and her husband Victor. They had very kindly invited me to accompany them on a five- day trip to enjoy some of the most spectacular parts of the Rocky Mountains. We headed north to Alberta and in the picturesque little town of Canmore, we found a delightful Bed and Breakfast which resembled an Alpine chalet. It was called "Jac n Sarah's" and would serve as a perfect home base while we explored the magnificent Banff area, just 26 km away. This area boasts incredibly beautiful landscapes, lush green forests, towering snow-capped mountain peaks, un-spoilt natural wilderness with abundant wild life and exciting well- marked hiking trails. Of course there were reminders wherever we looked, that we were entering Bear Territory!

Having experienced an eye -ball to eye -ball encounter with an inquisitive, meat -seeking bear at our tent flap in the Smoky Mountains on a much earlier trip to the States, I felt better equipped to ward off any unwelcome advances. I had been warned not to wear perfume or hairspray, not to attempt to scramble up a tree if pursued and to carry a noisy rattle or a tin of marbles to give the bear a sudden fright! But would I have the courage to look the bear in the eye, back off slowly and talk gently to him so that so that he would grasp the bare facts! I was a human and spoke a different language. If that approach failed, would I have the courage to lie dead still, roll up into a tight little ball and play possum while he circled and sniffed at me!

We received a warm welcome from our B&B host and hostess. Having enjoyed a cup of tea with them, Janet and Vic settled into the downstairs room and I was given what was called their Skylight Room. I had to scramble up a wooden ladder into the loft which afforded magnificent views of the snow-tipped peaks encircling Banff National Park.

Down in the kitchen, Sarah was ironing what looked like a magnificent gold choir robe. Jac was polishing a pair of very smart shoes for her to wear and I noticed a snow white pair of silk stockings hanging up to dry. Sarah chuckled when I asked whether she was preparing for a special choral performance.

Instead she explained that she was a marriage officer and would be marrying a young couple from Winnipeg the very next morning. I could not think of a more beautiful and romantic setting than this for a bride and groom to seal their vows. I secretly wondered whether we would be allowed to hover nearby and witness this very special occasion.

That evening as we watched sunset from the balcony of the chalet, which Jac referred to as their "deck," the soon-to –be- married couple arrived to run through final preparations with Sarah. They introduced themselves as Bruce and Janet and immediately commented on the fact that I had a different accent to my Seattle friend Janet and her husband Vic. They became ecstatic when they heard that I hailed from South Africa and said what I had often heard before when visiting the USA. "Wow, that's amazing! You are the very first African we've met!"

After a friendly introductory chat all about Cape Town and my teaching career, we not only found ourselves being invited to their 10am wedding the next day, but as the overseas visitor from Africa, I was invited to be Janet's bridal attendant, ring bearer, photographer and witness to the fact that Sarah had joined them together in Holy matrimony!

There was just one major problem! I had no bridesmaid's apparel! We had travelled light and all my smart clothes were back in Seattle. Janet was warm-hearted and kind and put me at ease immediately. She explained that because of their rather impulsive and spontaneous decision to have a quiet, private wedding away from home, in a beautiful tranquil outdoor setting, she would be wearing a simple pure white cotton dress with sprigs of embroidery and Bruce would be in a smart new shirt and long pants. There would be no sparking sequined tiara, no veil, no flashy tie and no top hat!

There was great excitement the next morning as we gathered on the banks of the nearby Bow River. Victor and Janet sensed my excitement and they too seemed enthusiastic about attending the wedding. Our travel plans for that day were happily put on hold. I had washed and ironed my blue T shirt and decided to wear my blue, pink and mauve floral skirt. It was the only skirt I had brought with me on this 5 day trip and somehow I felt that an impromptu bridal attendant, photographer and witness all the way from the southern tip of Africa, would look more respectable in a skirt than in pants or jeans! Unfortunately the only shoes I had with me, apart from my trainers for hiking, were my flat beige slip on sandals called mules!

Sarah looked the perfect part, dressed to perform her legal duties as the couple's Marriage Officer. She cut a striking figure in her gold robe, white silk stockings and gleaming shoes. Jac set up a simple sound system and provided soft background music as I carried the wedding rings on a satin cushion and accompanied the young couple from their car. Janet looked radiant and her lovely dark hair shone in the sunlight. Her white cotton dress was simple yet stylish and was perfect for an outdoor wedding. Bruce looked dashing and boyish as he gently squeezed his bride's hand and led her to a grassy knoll where Sarah was waiting to perform the nuptials. The service was simple and deeply meaningful. I felt so blessed and privileged to have been asked by the newly- wed couple to play a rôle in their marriage celebration.

Sarah told us that Banff is a favourite and highly sought-after area for outdoor weddings and couples fly in from all over the world. She had already been booked to officiate at 15 weddings throughout the Canadian summer months. After the simple ceremony we were invited to share an informal wedding reception with some tasty eats on Jac and Sarah's wooden deck. Then Bruce and Janet said farewell and headed off to enjoy a peaceful honeymoon in the magical Rockies surroundings before setting off back home to Winnipeg to share their exciting news with family and friends.

We all felt we had been enriched by the experience and had made some beautiful new friends. We exchanged addresses so that I could mail them their wedding photographs. It had been such an unexpected surprise event for me and one which has remained an indelible heartwarming holiday highlight for me since the mid 1990's. So it came as an enormous shock, as you can well imagine, when as soon as we had waved farewell to the newlyweds, Sarah asked me how I would like to receive my payment for being their bridal attendant! Would I prefer cash or a cheque! I was speechless. I actually felt I should have paid the couple for allowing me the privilege of sharing the joy and excitement of their marriage day in such a magical setting.

However, Bruce and Janet were out of sight already. Sarah had been paid in full for the vital rôle she performed and insisted that I accept the $60 dollars they had so generously left for me.

I shall never forget what it was like to be an African bridesmaid in a skirt and sandals in the Rockies and to be paid for my services!

Wedding at Canmore in the Rockies

AUNTIE FOR THE FIRST TIME!

*N*ever underestimate what an immense joy and privilege it is to be part of a happy, united and caring family. This week I took my almost 94 year old Auntie Kay out to lunch and realized afresh how blessed David and I am to have had two grandmothers in their 80's, a Grand dad who reached his 90's, an Uncle who was still playing golf in his 90's and two Aunts in their mid-90's!

On the night that Stephen, my mom's first grandchild was born, we were at the Baxter theatre in Rondebosch watching an enthralling Agatha Christie play. My best friend, now my sister- in- law, Margaret, had gone into labour that morning. My mom was on tenterhooks and kept slipping out of the theatre to phone the Somerset Hospital for news. Then back into her seat she would scuttle and whisper, "The little head has just appeared!" Then one scene later, out she would go again. Generally speaking, the theatre -goers seated around us were long suffering and understanding because my mom had excitedly whispered that she was restless because she was about to become a new granny at age 66.

Only one heavily made up lady with bright mauve hair, overpowering perfume and crimson talons, kicked up a fuss. She herself was no saint and was causing a disturbance behind us by pushing her knees into the back of our seats and by rustling chocolate wrappers and smacking her lips with rather too much delight. At one point, she said in a very loud stage whisper to her companion, "Good heavens Maizie, what on earth's the matter with this woman?"

My breathless mom, now revelling in her brand new granny status, had just plonked down in her seat after finally hearing the wonderful, long-awaited news from the labour ward at the Somerset Hospital in Green Point. "It's a healthy baby boy and all is well! A mighty long labour but no need for a Caesar. And you are an Auntie now! " she whispered excitedly in my ear. I was naturally overjoyed to have become an Auntie and could hardly concentrate on the remainder of the crime thriller.

Thankfully interval followed soon afterwards, so after a few quick 'phone calls down in the foyer to share our exciting baby news, we could settle back in our seats and enjoy the second half of the programme, much to the relief of those seated around us!

Looking back now to 5 January 1983, when I became an Aunt for the first time, I realize that was undoubtedly one of life's most joyous experiences.

Being part of a close -knit family is a wonderful privilege and a blessing I shall never take for granted. My widowed mother and I shared the joy of baby Stephen Taylor's first nine months while my brother and his wife lived in an upstairs apartment in Dorp Street, Stellenbosch, a beautiful part of the town which is steeped in history. After that, we had to face sad farewells as the little family trio headed to England for a four year stay. As a past pupil of Rondebosch Boys' High School, David had been awarded a scholarship to complete a D.Phil. at Balliol College in Oxford.

I remember being able to buy a return air ticket to London for under R2 000 in the early 1980's. I had the joy of being able to visit my brother and sister- in-law on three separate occasions during their Oxford sojourn. I am so grateful that although distance separated us, I was able to experience their children's exciting developmental milestones.

My first niece, their eldest daughter, Kathleen, was born in Oxford, just before her big brother Stephen, turned two. My mum was also able to visit the family during those four years of overseas study. Much to our delight Margaret gave birth to a second son, named Ross who was born two years later.

To start with, Dave and Margaret rented a student flat in Summertown House, but as their family grew in size, they were able to occupy a rustic little cottage at the entrance to a farm in the charming village of Besselsleigh, just 7 km from Oxford. Stephen, Kathleen and Ross were all fortunate enough to spend their formative years growing up in the unspoiled Oxfordshire countryside. Here they experienced the joys of exploring country lanes, picking blackberries, snowy Christmases, log fires, roast chestnuts, building snowmen, shiny holly, Robin redbreasts, inquisitive little foxes and cute prickly hedgehogs.

It was wonderful having a base when I visited England in the July school holidays. I remember the time my Welsh friend, Sue, was on leave from her matron's duties at the hospital in Kenya and travelled up from her parents' home in Pembroke Dock to visit Dave and Margaret. She and I borrowed their bicycles and pedalled our way through the delightful little Cotswold villages.

We also had a wonderful friend called Bronwen Hughes who ran an excellent B&B in Queen's Road, Windsor. She was one of dad's founder pupils at Westerford and our family received the most warm-hearted and generous hospitality from Bronwen whenever any of us visited Britain. I shall never forget one embarrassing and rather painful experience I suffered when visiting Bronwen one July. I loved the long mild balmy summer evenings when it remained light until 10.30 pm. Bronwen had been blessed to have a twin son and daughter. Philip and Lee-Ann had turned 10 and were sporting shiny new bicycles. One glorious evening Bronwen packed a picnic supper and suggested we cycle along the picturesque tow paths along the River Thames. She too owned a bike and loved to cycle with her twins. She borrowed a bike for me from her neighbour and off we went. My bike had a basket on the handlebars so I was delegated to carry the picnic goodies and the flask of coffee for our supper.

To reach the tow path, we first had to pedal through a very busy part of town. It was 6pm and the roads were still congested. It was soon after I had noticed a road sign saying Bagshot 10 miles, that disaster struck! Before I knew what had happened, the saddle on my borrowed bicycle had collapsed under my weight and then seconds later, the entire bike seemed to fold! I was catapulted into the road and I remember crawling into the gutter on all fours as fast as I could, just as a huge truck thundered by, only centimetres away from my head.

Bronwen shrieked, "Oh no! I was told it was a folding bike but the old chap next door said he had tightened all the nuts."

Well, quite obviously some of the nuts and bolts had worked lose. Our sandwiches were splattered everywhere and the Thermos flask was shattered. We managed to salvage a couple of apples which had bounced to safely and two bananas which were partially recognizable. My knees and elbows were badly grazed from being flung onto the tar in a most unladylike fashion and I had wrenched my shoulder and neck muscles. Sadly our cycle ride turned into a gentle stroll back home with Bronwen's bruised and battered guest bringing up the rear. We had to settle for a picnic in her back garden instead of on the scenic tow path. Two days later Bronwen very kindly drove me to an excellent osteopath who managed to straighten me out and eased my pain by giving me some very effective clicks and tweaks.

A word of warning! If you ever borrow a folding bicycle check that all the nuts and bolts have been tightened and take a tool kit with you, just in case!

Here's another little travel tip....If you ever decide to journey on a long distance coach, slip a little torch (flashlight) into your handbag. You never know when it might come in handy!

After my visit to Windsor, I had the opportunity of travelling down to South West Wales to visit several lovely Welsh friends in the Pembroke area. They recommended I use an express coach called The Rapide, which I boarded at Victoria Coach Station at about 9am. After a journey lasting a little more than 7 hours, with only a few key stops along the way, we finally wound our way along a twisty road into Pembroke Dock.

The Rapide was a very comfortable double decker coach with helpful staff aboard who made sure that all the passengers were happily settled and well cared for. I was impressed by the way the elderly folk were made comfortable and carefully assisted as they clambered on and off the coach. A hostess circulated amongst the passengers selling refreshments. Being a very long journey, it was a relief to find that there was a toilet at the rear end of the coach.

I noticed that several passengers were queueing to enter it and then for some strange reason, they left the door slightly ajar. I supposed they might just be claustrophobic. I waited a while then shot to the back of the bus once the coast was clear. We South Africans are conservative folk so I decided I was going to close and bolt the door. Once inside the cramped space, I soon realized why my fellow passengers had been leaving the door ajar. I was plunged into inky darkness. It was quite obvious that the light bulb had failed. As the door swung shut, I had taken note of where the toilet seat and wash basin were, so decided to use the facility as quickly as possible and beat a hasty retreat. I heard voices in the aisle and knew that already another urgent queue was forming. I suddenly felt an enormous burden for blind people and tried to imagine what it must be like when one's entire world is as pitch dark as my stuffy little space had just become. That was when I made up my mind to pop into a Boots pharmacy as soon as the opportunity arose, to purchase a little flashlight to keep in my handbag.

I fumbled about in the dark and found the toilet paper and then located the basin and taps. But when travelling overseas it's always a challenge to figure out how to flush the toilet. In some countries there is a lever, some still have a chain suspended from a cistern up above, others have a button on the wall and there are some where you stamp hard on a pedal. In Disney World we encountered some amazing self-flushing toilets which flushed automatically as you stood up. This procedure was often followed by a quick discreet puff of air freshener as you vacated the cubicle.

But this was the first time I had ever used a toilet on a coach in Britain. As I groped about in the pitch dark I could not feel a chain or a lever or a pedal. Then suddenly.....success! Just to the right of the toilet and close to the washbasin, I felt a knob protruding from the wooden panel and pressed it as hard as I could.

Horror of horrors! A very loud siren wailed and the bus driver applied his brakes forcefully. In the darkness my fingers had strayed to the Emergency button. Cars hooted frantically. There were shrieks from the passengers. I could hear thuds as some who were queueing for the toilet staggered about as they battled to maintain their balance. Someone pounded on the toilet door and their frantic fists nearly sent me flying as I came hurtling out with a very red face. The Rapide shuddered to a screeching halt on the M4 Expressway as cars went whizzing by. Our coach driver spun round and looked somewhat perplexed but kept his cool. The hostess came charging down the aisle with a First Aid box yelling, "Are you all right dearie? Did you have a funny turn in the loo?"

I tell you it wasn't funny at all! It was hugely embarrassing. Everyone turned to stare. Some mumbled under their breath about foolish people who don't use their eyes! I apologized profusely and explained that I was a foreign visitor and hadn't realized that the bulb wasn't working.

The hostess looked very relieved that I hadn't fainted or had a heart attack in the toilet and sensing my shock and distress, she hastened to bring me a mug of very sweet tea.

Nowadays I never travel without a little penlight torch, just in case!

Soon after Dave's graduation and their return to Cape Town where he accepted a lectureship at the Denneoord Teachers' Training College in Stellenbosch, they welcomed baby Helen, who was two years younger than Ross. Mom and I were overjoyed to have the little family back in

South Africa and many happy jaunts were made to Stellenbosch to share birthdays and family Christmases.

But the years have rolled on and there have been numerous joyous and meaningful family events.

My four nephews and nieces spent many happy school holidays with me in my single years when I owned a duplex flat in Pinelands, an attractive tranquil suburb which has the distinction of being the first Garden City of Cape Town. Perhaps even more noteworthy is the fact that Pinelands is considered to be the first town- planned area to be established in South Africa!

The layout of our suburb was based on the revolutionary ideas regarding systematic and orderly town planning formulated by a gentleman called Sir Ebenezer Howard, so it is not surprising that many of our local landmarks are named after him. Sir Howard had grown up in England and had seen the grey dinginess of densely populated manufacturing towns. He set out his vision for planning more attractive towns in a series of books about Garden Cities. His dream was that homes and shops should be surrounded by attractive gardens and lush vegetation. Homes should have distinctive features and should replace drab tenement blocks. Houses should be built apart from factories and warehouses. Industrial areas should be easily accessible to workers.

It was actually a prominent South African businessman, Mr. Richard Stuttaford, remembered too as a farmer and later a City Councillor, who became gravely concerned about rapidly deteriorating urban conditions after the First World War. Many people had flocked to the cities because of the diamond and gold rush. Hundreds had died in the influenza epidemic and rentals had climbed steeply. Mr. Stuttaford met Ebenezer Howard and was impressed with his proposition and personally donated large sums of money for the transformation of Pinelands into a tranquil tree-lined Garden City with many thatched houses and beautiful gardens. Looking at our delightful suburb now, it is hard to imagine that it was once a sandy wasteland covered sparsely with wattle trees. Then tens of thousands of pine trees were planted in an effort to anchor the drifting sands from the Cape Flats.

Our school pupils in Pinelands listened with rapt attention to visiting speakers and historians who shared fascinating tales about our suburb. They were spellbound as they heard tales about a tribal chief called Langalibalele, who was imprisoned in this area, and about a thriving brick making business when a clay pit was discovered, a wood and iron hostel used to accommodate bubonic plague patients, a British Army base camp set up during the Anglo- Boer War (1898–1902) and camels being trained right here in our leafy suburb of Pinelands to fulfil postal duties in the Kalahari Desert!

That explains why certain property developers were mystified when the bleached bones of camels as well as hundreds of horseshoes and tent pegs were dug up at the time of foundations being laid. With the current problems we are experiencing with strikes and the slow delivery of mail, I wonder if anyone has thought of reverting to using camels in the South African Postal Services. Wouldn't it be exciting to see camels clomping round Pinelands bearing bags of Christmas mail! We might just receive our cards before Easter!

Life is full of happy surprises! Here my husband and I are, many years later, feeling privileged and blessed to be living in a delightful little cottage in the Pinewood Retirement Village where my mother became one of its first residents in 1995! My brother and his wife are still very happy living in Stellenbosch where thy lead busy, active and productive lives.

I am enormously proud of my nephews and nieces. Before they left their family home, Stephen, Kathleen, Ross and Helen all enjoyed their studies at Stellenbosch University and were actively involved at their church, sharing their musical abilities on clarinet, piano, trumpet and violin respectively and often in singing groups. Stephen, Kathleen and Helen all played hockey for South Africa at some stage. Kathleen played in the Beijing and London Olympics and in the Commonwealth Games in Melbourne and New Delhi and had the opportunity of playing professional hockey in Rotterdam.

Stephen gained a PHD and is an economist working at Strategic Planning in the Department of Basic Education in Pretoria, Kathleen is an Associate Attorney at a large legal firm in Cape Town, Ross is a Mechanical Engineer, at a company based in KwaZulu-Natal and Helen has just completed her PHD as a Rhodes Scholar at Oxford and returned to South Africa to take up a challenging legal position in Johannesburg. It was exciting to reach Great Aunt status six years ago when Ross and his wife welcomed Thomas and then his little sister Zoe just two years later.

But now it's time for Great Auntie Ruth to become a medium- size Auntie again, so I'll close this chapter and jog down to the treadmill! Yes, we old timers have a real gym in our Village and it's waiting for me!

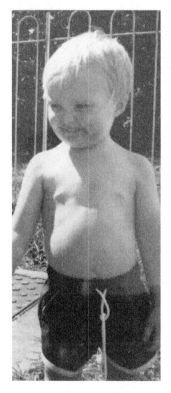

My mom's first grandchild, Stephen

My eldest nephew, Stephen, with his sister, Kathleen

My younger nephew Ross, wife Jess, and children, Tom and Zoe

My niece, Helen, with my brother, David and his wife, Margaret at Balliol College Oxford

My niece, Helen in court attire

38

NELSON MANDELA'S 100TH BIRTHDAY

*O*n Wednesday 18 July 1918 and 100 years ago, our beloved Nelson Mandela, affectionately known to us as Madiba, which was his clan name, was born in the little rural village of Mvezo, close to Umtata.

Today would have been his 100th Birthday. I pen this chapter in honour of him as we commemorate his life and thank God for the amazing gift Madiba was to our world.

He was the first black president of South Africa (1994 to 1999) whose courageous struggle against South Africa's apartheid system of racial segregation and cruel discrimination turned him into a greatly revered global icon. It also earned him a joint Nobel Prize with his predecessor Mr F.W.de Klerk, for working peaceably together to end apartheid and to lay firm foundations for our nation to enter a new era as a democratic South Africa.

In honour of Nelson Mandela's Centenary, I would like to share the story of yet another dramatic Rescue, but not from a cave or a tsunami, but rather from the Jaws of Death! This story also has a happy ending and I know it would make Madiba's heart rejoice as it did our family's hearts.

I think my story would bring a beautiful smile to your face, Madiba.

I can just picture it. Your smiles were never forced. They were spontaneous and genuine. I know how much you loved children and enjoyed cuddling babies in your strong arms.

Before we left Sea Point to move to Stellenbosch for my dad to complete further studies through the Afrikaans medium, and when I was still a tiny tot our family was blessed to have the services of a most loveable and hardworking 30 year old household helper called Edie Nombewu. She lived on our property and became a dearly loved and valued member of our extended family. Sadly our finances and student-style lodging on a farm in Stellenbosch didn't permit Edie to move with us. I believe my little brother David and I cried our eyes out when the time came to hug Edie goodbye.

However our beloved domestic helper was able to read and write and a most wonderful thing happened. Edie loved to read the newspapers and always tried to keep abreast of current affairs. Quite incredibly her eyes had spotted an article in the Cape Argus announcing that our dad was to become the founder headmaster of a brand new co-educational high school called Westerford. In an amazing way our beloved Edie managed to track us down and once again offered to become our live-in domestic helper. What rejoicing there was when she rejoined our family in Rondebosch and Edie remained with us until she went on pension at the age of sixty.

My dad had bought my grandparents' delightful little double-storey house in the mid 1950's when they decided it would be wise to scale down and move into a two bedroom apartment all on one level. They were only a few blocks away from us, in close proximity to the Rondebosch station and the Fountain shopping Centre on the main road. It was a joy and enormous privilege for David and me to grow up with our granny and a grandpa living a mere five minute walk away.

Our new home was called The Little House and was number 14, the very last one at the end of a narrow, tranquil oak- lined street. Because our road was a cul de sac, with a spreading oak tree at the end, very little traffic, apart from our visitors, moved up and down the road and our widowed mom remained in that house for more than 40 years until mid- 1995!

It was an enormous blessing to be surrounded by caring, warm-hearted Rondebosch neighbours. On one side we were bordered by the Lilacs school Hostel which housed boarders from Rondebosch Boys' High School although it was situated alongside the Prep School. Behind us lived Mr Gerald Shaw and his delightful family. Gerald was the enlightened political editor at the Cape Times. The Doyles lived opposite us and were a kindly old couple who had resident boarders and like my grandparents, the homely Doyles had enjoyed living in that tranquil leafy haven for many years.

Then all of a sudden, into our quiet little cul de sac and into number 12, the double- storey house alongside ours, moved two political stalwarts and activists, leading members of the South African Congress of Democrats, Comrades Ben and Mary Turok. Ben had been a leading trade unionist and in the mid 1950's he had already been served with a banning order. He faced a treason trial and Ben and Mary had both spent time in prison for their courageous efforts to aid the illegal ANC.

We were in for exciting times. We first realised our new neighbours were liberal- minded folk when our domestic helper rushed in breathlessly and told my mom she had been coming up our road from the shops and had greeted our new neighbour who was mowing his lawn. "Good morning Master," she said in a friendly tone. He smiled back and his warm response was, "Hello. I'm not your Master. Please call me Ben." Of course this was all very new to her in the Apartheid era, and she was not quite sure how to respond.

The very next week my mom happened to spot Mary Turok slipping into our garden after dark and hiding sacks containing banned literature under our hedge. When my mom went and confronted her, Mary shared news that they were expecting a raid by the Special Branch Police and would be grateful for our family's co-operation. So mom and Mary formed a great alliance. We would gladly allow them to hide their books in our garden and our lips would be sealed should the Special Branch head our way.

The Special Branch Police raids were frequent, cruel and unexpected. They were usually carried out under cover of darkness and often late at night. We would hear the police vans screaming up our quiet little dead end road.

Crude Afrikaans commands were barked in exasperated tones as the police burst in on the privacy of Ben and Mary's family home, where they often warmly welcomed like-minded comrades all striving to achieve freedom, fairness and social justice.

We would switch off our lights and David and I would peep through the curtains in my upstairs bedroom window. The policemen were ruthless in their raids. We would hold our breath and pray that no one would be hurt. Bright torches were beamed into their eyes and flashed in all directions. The garden at number 12 was tramped through and searched thoroughly. We watched and waited in suspense. Mixed race couples were cruelly wrenched apart and carted off in police vans for breaching apartheid's wicked Immorality Act which was only repealed by Mr P.W.Botha in 1985. It was tragic that many loving young couples had to flee overseas or cross our borders into Botswana or Zambia to marry a partner from another race group.

We were happy to discover that the Turoks' banned books were never unearthed or confiscated from under our hedge. We greatly admired the Turok family's courage and followed Ben's long and distinguished political career as an ANC veteran member of parliament for 20 years. He was imprisoned for 3 years for his fearless stance against Apartheid. Prof. Ben Turok was a key figure in the Freedom Charter process and was greatly respected for speaking out fearlessly against ill-discipline, reckless spending and corruption in government circles while he was co- chairman of the ethics committee. Ben always joked that when the calendar rolled round to 26 June, he enjoyed a double celebration. Not only was it Ben's birthday but also the day on which the Freedom Charter was adopted in 1955.

Ben was born in 1927 so he certainly earned his retirement. Over the years he achieved 3 degrees in Engineering, Philosophy and Political Science.

In recent times he had served as director of the Institute for African Alternatives and editor of the journal, New Agenda. His quiet presence and wise counsel is greatly missed in government.

IN MEMORIAM

My brother and I were greatly saddened to hear of Ben Turok's death on 9 December 2019 at age 92. He will be greatly missed by his wife Mary and his 3 sons and grandchildren.

The 1970's were soon upon us and continued to be troubled times. Edie had been joined at her little home in the township of Gugulethu by her niece, Elsie, the daughter of her dead sister. Elsie arrived from the Eastern Cape with her diminutive infant, Edie's great nephew Samson. Elsie was anxious to find urgent medical assistance for her desperately ill little baby son. Her common law husband, Mazena, worked as head gardener at the home of the American Ambassador in Brooklyn, Pretoria and visited her every Christmas. Elsie had produced 14 babies and sadly only five of the infants had survived.

The townships were troubled places in the 1970's and white folk were often fearful of entering these areas. Yet our intrepid mom often took Edie home after a week's hard work. It had always been our family's policy to allow her to spend time resting and seeing her family during weekends. Edie had mentioned in passing that her little great nephew was a sickly child and could not seem to take milk from his mother's breasts.

Upon dropping Edie at her home, my mom asked to be introduced to Elsie and baby Samson and was appalled by what she discovered. Elsie herself was seriously malnourished. Her own milk had long since dried up. She was as thin as a rake and had travelled for three days all the way from the Ciskei to Cape Town, hunched in a third class carriage with wooden seats. Elsie had only a sandwich and a small bottle of water to sustain her. She spoke isiXhosa and Afrikaans and sadly had never learnt to read or write.

Elsie's last- born bouncing baby boy had ironically been given the name Samson because he was a hefty, robust little chap at birth, having weighed in at nine pounds! My mom battled to hold back her tears as she was introduced to baby Samson. Elsie was holding a fragile, emaciated little waif who at seven months weighed 2kg less than he did at birth! We decided to call him Sammy which sounded like a more appropriate, diminutive form of Samson. His real Xhosa name was Mzikayise, meaning "House of my father" but great Aunt Edie wanted him to be called Samson because of his sturdy appearance at birth and in memory of her late brother whom she said had died whilst working in the depths of a diamond mine in Kimberley.

Elsie had arrived in Cape Town at the height of the most inflexible apartheid regime so that there was every likelihood of her being jailed if she was found in the City environs within 72 hours of her arrival. She was so desperate to see her beloved Auntie Edie again and to get urgent medical help for her baby that she had risked hiding in Edie's little township house for five days before my mom rushed to the rescue.

Realising that Sammy was desperately ill, instead of driving straight home, my mom took Elsie and baby Sammy straight to the Red Cross Children's Hospital in Rondebosch. After very thorough screening tests, the verdict from the team of doctors' there left my mom reeling. Not only was Sammy dying of starvation because his mom's breast milk had dried up, due to Elsie's own malnutrition, he was also suffering from kwashiorkor, caused by protein deficiency (which explains why his hair had an orange tinge) as well as marasmus, rickets, recurring pneumonia, gastro- enteritis, meningitis and encephalitis!

A gentle lady doctor drew my mom aside, explaining that marasmus is a form of severe malnutrition which is why little Sammy looked emaciated and was lacking in energy. He had arrived at our home clad only in a grubby vest and a sodden diaper. Elsie had wrapped her precious little bundle in a very old, threadbare striped towel with a deformed looking dummy tied to a frayed piece of string round his stick-like little right wrist. He barely had the strength to push the flattened dummy in and out of his parched mouth.

Sammy's wobbly head appeared to be top heavy on his scrawny little frame and he stared at the medical team through huge brown eyes as if pleading for help. My mom could see how moved the doctors were as she explained how little Sammy had unexpectedly, and only in the last few days, become a Heaven-sent, precious part of our lives.

The medical team lovingly warned mom not to become too attached to the little mite because his chances of survival were very slim. But our indomitable mom always rose to a challenge and refused to give up hope. She mustered the support of all the faithful prayer warriors she could think of and our friends the world over, joined our family in praying for a miracle for this precious little life which we believed had been entrusted to our care.

The Red Cross Children's Hospital was very short of beds at the time, but an elderly little Jewish lady doctor found Sammy a cot in a side ward known as the "drip room." For a whole month he spent three days each week on a drip containing glucose. After that my mom pleaded to be allowed to take Sammy home to give him intensive nursing to the best of her ability. Fortunately the Medical Superintendent had given Elsie a permit to stay for three months while her baby received medical attention.

By now the Christmas holidays had arrived and I was home from Treverton for five weeks and was able to share the nursing duties with mom and dad. I shall never forget the night I came home to discover that I had become a foster sister at age 30 to a darling little Xhosa baby. My good friend Margaret, who later became my sister in law, was head of the music department at Rustenburg Girls' High School and we had chosen to celebrate the start of the school holidays and my homecoming, by going out to enjoy supper at a Sea Point steak house.

As Margaret dropped me back home, we heard the pitiful cries of a tiny baby. Initially we presumed there was a stray kitten prowling in our garden. Then an incredible sight met our eyes as we pushed open the front door and entered my parents' lounge.

In the space of a few short hours it had been transformed into a cluttered, colourful, chaotic nursery! There was my mom in a plastic apron in the midst of it all. We stepped over a bright blue baby's bath parked in the centre of the carpet and clambered over piles of cascading nappies, a plastic bucket and a heap of fluffy pastel-coloured blankets. Margaret inadvertently stepped on a plastic duck hidden behind a bucket. The flattened duck let out a muffled death rattle rather than a welcoming quack!

To greet my mom and dad we squeezed past a table full of baby soaps, shampoos, cotton buds and Wet-Wipes, tripping over teddies, rattles and teething rings as we walked. Dad was sitting on the sofa, surrounded by chaos, gently rocking baby Sammy and grinning like a proud new grandpa. Beside my mom we spied a large cardboard carton bursting with neatly folded baby clothes ~ blue, yellow and white, just perfect for baby Sammy. What a wonderful God- given donation this was. It transpired that our good friends, John and Disa Gibbon, had heard of the unexpected arrival of Sammy and had generously come to the rescue by parting with all the items their last two babies, Jeremy and Murray had used throughout their toddler years.

John Gibbon had been one of my dad's right hand men on his staff at Westerford before leaving to become the Principal at Sea Point Boys' High. After my dad's untimely death in October 1976, Dr John Gibbon returned to Westerford and took over the reins as the new Headmaster and led the school very ably until his retirement in March 1995.

Imagine my amazement upon being appointed to serve on the Staff at Pinehurst Primary in Pinelands in 1982, to discover the two delightful little Gibbon brothers, Murray and Jeremy in standards two and four.

It was their baby clothes and toys which proved such a blessing to our little Sammy as he embarked on his Cape Town Adventure. What fine rôle models to our young people they have turned out to be! Both Jeremy and Murray followed in their dad's footsteps and proved to be excellent headmasters at their respective high schools in Pinelands and Claremont.

Soon after mom's visit to the Red Cross Children's Hospital, we discovered that Elsie had actually travelled to Cape Town from the Ciskei accompanied by another two of her surviving children! Sidney (known as Oupa) and Regina (called Miemie) had been smuggled into Edie's little home in Gugulethu. For fear of the Apartheid police finding them, they were kept out of sight and were being watched over by an older sister called Nompapi and a brother called Jeffrey. So now all five survivors of Elsie's 14 pregnancies had come to Cape Town illegally in a desperate search for a better life.

Elsie was penniless and was quite obviously totally overwhelmed by the whole situation facing her. She pleaded with mom to keep little Sammy at least until she had nursed him back to health. Elsie remained in Gugulethu and cared for Miemie and Oupa who could only speak isiXhosa. The eldest siblings, Nompapi and Jeffrey, had moved to Cape Town a few years earlier and had managed to find menial jobs. They promised to do their best with their limited resources to help support their mom and younger siblings by doing odd jobs.

And so it was that at age 58, our intrepid mom, chose to become a mother for the third time, knowing full well what could happen if she was caught hiding a black baby in a white area.

I am quite certain my mom would have found the inspiring words of our beloved Nelson Mandela compelling, "May your choices reflect your hopes, not your fears."

The driving force behind our mother's bold and selfless decision to attempt to save one precious little dying black baby and give him a fair start in life, was motivated by her fierce sense of social justice and her spirit of hope and optimism. She seized this as a God-given opportunity to make a meaningful difference, not just for little Sammy but for his entire family.

Baby Sammy Runeli aged 7 months and weighing only 7 pounds (3,175kg) and with very little chance of survival, moved into our Rondebosch home on Thursday 21 November 1974. He very quickly became a precious part of the Taylor family, with his doting Great Auntie Edie on the spot to help my mom and dad care for him. Our dad fully supported mom in her new rôle but being a dedicated headmaster who often arrived home in time for a late supper, he knew that mom would become Sammy's main Carer and was concerned that she would have to shoulder most of the load.

What about the Group Areas Act you may be thinking? Under the Apartheid government of South Africa this Act of Parliament assigned racial groups to different and separate residential and business sections in urban areas. This excluded non Whites from choosing where they would like to settle and precluded them from moving into certain areas restricted to Whites. Cruel Pass Laws made it compulsory for non-Whites to carry pass books if they wished to enter "white" parts of the country. A pass book was known as a "dompas" which literally means a "dumb pass." This draconian law was only repealed by President FW de Klerk as recently as 1990.

Would we be able to nurture a little Xhosa baby in Rondebosch without upsetting less liberal- minded neighbours in our area? How would the authorities deal with our family if they found out what my parents were doing? Could my dad lose his headmaster's position? We realised the penalties were stiff, with a jail sentence being a frightening possibility.

It's at times like these that one acts according to one's inner convictions and listens to the voice of one's conscience. As a family we knew exactly how a God of love who created all men and women equal in His sight, would want us to treat one of His precious little people.

My foster brother Sammy's next few months were critical. It was a long and arduous road to recovery. His progress seemed so slow. He cried incessantly and didn't even favour us with a little smile. After frequent visits to the Red Cross Hospital he was nearly eight months old but severe spinal curvature prevented him from making any effort to sit up or be propped up with cushions. From the start Sammy was allergic to cow's milk so the hospital advised us to feed him every four hours from a bottle of formula made from soya beans which would provide our little waif with a rich source of protein. Today of course there are mixed feelings about the health benefits of soya products but little Sammy tolerated it well and he soon began to gain weight very slowly. To start with, the poor little fellow was too weak to suck the teat on the bottle. We had to use a syringe to drop tiny amounts of formula onto his pale and anaemic looking little tongue.

There was great excitement when just before he turned nine months, we managed to capture Sammy's first coy little smile on camera. At nine months he also managed to sit upright with a strong hand supporting his lower back. There followed many sleepless nights while Sammy was teething or suffering from a fever or diarrhoea. Because of his shaky start in life and having been deprived of nutrients for his first seven months, all Sammy's developmental milestones were delayed.

What jubilation at 18 months when he held my dad's finger very tightly and took his first wobbly little steps. He adored my dad and called him "Uncle," which he pronounced "Onkel." He loved to wait near the front door for him to return from school. Then he would try to carry dad's briefcase and using all his might, it would be dragged down the passage and into the study. We often caught Sammy climbing into dad's shoes or sheepskin slippers and shuffling towards the full length bedroom mirror where he would assume a hilarious ballet- like pose with his hands on his hips.

Mom and Dad realised it was essential for Sammy to become fluent in his mother tongue, so in spite of all the unrest in the townships, either our mom or dad would take Sammy back to Gugulethu every Friday to spend time with his mom and his Xhosa speaking family. He would then return to my mom and dad for special nurturing and medical care during the week.

Sammy was only 18 months old at the time of our dad's untimely death and missed him dreadfully. It was heartbreaking to see the little fellow waiting in vain at the front door night after night for his "Onkel" to return from school. His coming into our lives in such an amazing and dramatic way, helped to fill an enormous vacuum in our mom's life after dad's death because up until then, Mom had been involved in so many aspects of school life at Westerford. But now Sammy's needs and those of his extended family in Gugulethu occupied a great deal of her time and attention.

He was growing stronger and becoming more and more adorable. He had an irresistible smile and a warm, endearing little personality. Everyone who saw little Sammy was instantly drawn to him and asked to pick him up for a cuddle. Our friend Marge hugged him and said, "Sammy, you are so cute, I could just eat you up!" His sensitive little dark brown eyes grew as big as saucers and he clung onto her and pleaded, "No, no, no, please Auntie don't eat me!"

When Sammy was just three my mom took him on holiday and drove all the way up to Mooi River in Natal to visit me while I was teaching at Treverton. For safely sake on the long journey, mom was accompanied by Tinus, a young university friend of my brother's, who was his early twenties. Sammy had a great time visiting me at Treverton and the school boys let him sit on their horses and bounced him gently on the trampoline.

I travelled back home to Cape Town with mom and Tinus at the end of term and clearly remember a difficult situation we encountered when we tried to find accommodation in the Orange Free State. It had been a long hot drive from Mooi River and mom's old model car did not enjoy the luxury of air conditioning. We stopped outside the Philippolis Hotel and immediately spotted a glaring sign above the main entrance stating WHITES ONLY or BLANKES ALLEEN in Afrikaans, followed by the words RIGHT OF ADMISSION RESERVED.

The cruel and heartless Separate Amenities Act No 49 of 1953 forced racial segregation in theatres, movie houses, hotels, restaurants and even on beaches and in buses and trains. It aimed at eliminating all contact between whites and other race groups. We could not bear the thought of little Sammy being turned away or publicly humiliated by a callous hotel manager.

Mom hit on a great plan of action to smuggle our little black baby into a Whites Only hotel in the heart of the Orange Free State, a fiercely Nationalist Party stronghold. Sammy loved it when Mom told him bedtime stories and his favourite characters were those in the Brer Rabbit Book by Enid Blyton.

She told Sammy to take a great big breath and snuggle deep into Tinus' sleeping bag and pretend he was Brer Rabbit hiding from the naughty Brer Fox. Sammy loved this exciting new game and with his sleeping bag slung over his shoulder and an armful of clothes, Tinus shot past the Manager's office, bounded up the staircase, two steps at a time and deposited his precious bundle gently on the bed. He whispered excitedly, "All right Sammy, you can crawl out now and take a big breath. Brer Fox is eating his supper downstairs!"

We ate picnic snacks for supper in our rooms, settled our hotel bill before bed time and decided to make an early morning departure to avoid any embarrassment at breakfast time.

Now to fast track Sammy's amazing progress and span the years right up until 2020 …..

He was a happy, healthy, fun-loving little chap all through his primary school years, most of which were spent in Gugulethu learning to speak Xhosa and bonding beautifully with his mom, his siblings and his beloved great aunt Edie. My mom did all she could to forge a strong bond between Sammy and his mother and he grew up calling her "Mama" and my mom "Auntie."

His weekends back in Rondebosch were always a special highlight and a comforting time for our widowed mom. Sammy was six when I returned from Natal to teach in Rondebosch. My brother, David, was teaching in Stellenbosch so we were both able to spend quality time with our little foster brother and we did our best to help care for his extended family too.

In his high school years Sammy preferred to be called Sam. He attended Salt River High School for two years then something momentous occurred!

History was made in South Africa on 9 January 1991! At long last the integration of public state schools was initiated when thirty- three formerly all-white schools opened their doors to pupils of colour. Sam was overjoyed when Dr John Gibbon accepted him into standard eight (grade 10) at Westerford. This was made possible thanks to a bursary awarded by Caltex and our mother's willingness to make financial sacrifices on Sam's behalf. He made wonderful friends at Westerford, took part in the drama production of West Side Story and became the 1st team hockey goalie, accompanying the team on an exciting sports tour to KwaZulu-Natal.

At the end of standard eight, Sam had the wonderful opportunity of travelling to Britain, Germany and Switzerland, where he learnt to ski. This holiday of a lifetime was made possible thanks to the generosity of our very kind German friend Klaus whom my Mom had first met in an elevator in Cape Town! He was a young single fellow doing temporary work in Cape Town many years ago. My mother's friendly encounter and her offer of South African hospitality led to a life- long friendship with Klaus and his family.

Having matriculated at Westerford in 1993, Sam took a "Gap Year" and worked as a volunteer youth worker at the Scripture Union in Rondebosch. He attended junior and senior boys' camps, served as camp cook and as a dedicated leader at the Fresh Air Camp at Froggy Pond in Simonstown where he helped under privileged children enjoy an unforgettable seaside holiday.

Then while employed in the Unit Trust department at the head office of The Old Mutual in Pinelands, Sam experienced a genuine Calling to train as a policeman at the Police College in Graaff- Reinet. His heartfelt desire was to serve his country. Dave and I travelled up to attend his passing out parade. How we wished our dear Mom could have been with us to share this proud moment. Who would ever have imagined that this tall handsome policeman was once the malnourished little waif, with little chance of survival, who was entrusted to our family's care in 1974.

———————

But it's now 2020 and since his graduation, Sam has gone from strength to strength. Having first served at Wellington in the Boland, in the Cape Winelands where he became fluent in speaking Afrikaans, he was then transferred to the Woodstock Police Station in Cape Town. It was there that he met his Xhosa wife, who had moved to the Western Cape from East London.

Sam is a detective now and he and Melissa are happily married. Sam has fathered two happy, healthy little boys and our family is helping to educate his first born son who is in grade 8 this year. We are grateful to God for the privilege we enjoyed of being able to help raise Sam through very turbulent times in our country. We rejoice now as we see him serving his country and its citizens with courage and dignity. What a proud moment it was for our family to see Sam being awarded well-deserved service medals at a recent police parade.

After his retirement at age 70, having served as the head gardener for the American Ambassador, Sam's dad Mazena, moved from Pretoria and joined Elsie in the family's little Gugulethu home. Then just 5 years ago, after a life lived to the full, Mazena slipped away peacefully at the age of 90.

Some years ago, our family was given the opportunity to purchase dear old Auntie Edie's rented 2 bedroom council home for the family to enjoy a measure of stability and security in Gugulethu.

Sammy's mother, Elsie, turned 86 and pressed on valiantly in spite of suffering from diabetes, thyroid problems and failing eyesight. Sam has been an exemplary son in the sacrificial way he has supported his

family. Sadly he has had to bury his older sister, Miemie, and his brother, Jeffrey, in the last 10 years and then just a year ago, a much loved old uncle.

I know Madiba would be immensely proud of Sammy for having overcome so many seemingly insurmountable hurdles in his young life. I can imagine the tall, handsome statesman stooping to admire Sam's medals, giving him a firm handshake and saying in his unique inimitable way "Well done, young man.

I am proud of you! Keep up the great work. Our democratic South Africa needs more chaps like you!"

Rest in Peace dear Madiba. How our country misses your cheerful, gracious presence, your spirit of tolerance and forgiveness and your wise words.

It's now some months since I wrote the chapter in honour of Madiba's Centenary. Other chapters have been added as vivid memories have flashed back.

Much has happened since July 2018. We returned to Thailand in March 2019 for another happy reunion with our many special friends who live in the Land of Smiles.

Sadly Sammy's beloved old mother, Elsie, was recently laid to rest in her 87th year. We salute him for his selfless love and devotion to her.

As the 2019 academic year drew to a close we received heart-warming news. Sam's firstborn son, Siphe-Okuhle Noel, who has proved to be a promising little student ever since he entered grade 1 in 2013, heard that he had been accepted to enter grade 8 at Westerford in 2020 for his high school education!

So our family is rejoicing in the knowledge that our long and happy association with Westerford will continue at the school our dad, Noel Taylor, founded back in 1953!

May I conclude by leaving my readers with this inspiring challenge from Nelson Mandela. It was a call he made in 2008 for the next generation to become leaders in addressing the world's social injustices.

Sam aged 18 months with foster uncle Noel

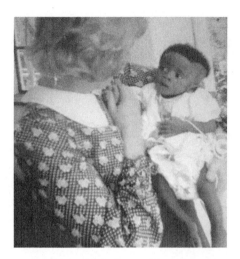

Ruth and Baby Sam, aged 7 months

Sam (right), the detective, honoured at a medal parade

Sam's son, Siphe Okuhle-Noel accepted for Westerford in 2020

*"What counts in life, is not the mere fact that we have lived.
It is what difference we have made to the lives of others that will
determine the significance of the life we lead."*

ACKNOWLEDGMENTS

- My heartfelt gratitude goes to our Heavenly Father who guided and guarded me as I travelled thousands of kilometres.
- Sincere appreciation to our many good friends who encouraged me to put pen to paper and share my life's adventures and travel experiences.
- My dear husband Joe inspired me to write my memoirs in secret as a surprise for his 90th birthday.
- My beloved parents Noel and Muriel Taylor passed on their love of adventure and travel and faithfully hoarded all my letters, postcards, pamphlets and travel notes for many years, hoping I would write a book one day.
- I am grateful that I was taught by excellent Geography and History teachers who instilled in me a love for our own wonderful country and a burning desire to explore other continents.
- A heartfelt thank you to our good friend and fellow resident, Desmond Martin who painstakingly drew the delightful illustrations for my book.
- I am most grateful to Greg Davies, a talented past pupil of Pinehurst, who designed the eye-catching cover for my book

and helped me tremendously with the layout. I learnt afterwards that Greg has a fear of snakes, especially dangerous ones that lurk under beds!

- I thank Jerome Williams at Postnet Pinelands and Tanya Justus at Rozprint for their patient guidance and courteous assistance on many occasions as I prepared rough drafts.
- A sincere thank you to all my pupils and colleagues at Treverton, Rustenburg Girls' Junior School and Pinehurst Primary. You made my 38 years of teaching a joy and privilege. I miss you all!
- My heartfelt gratitude goes to loving friends and relatives all over the world who opened their homes and their hearts and offered me generous hospitality, delicious meals and who took me to visit beautiful places and meet interesting people.

As I type this, heart breaking news of the massive bomb blast in Beirut has rocked our world. My memory flashed back to December 1968. My travelling companion and I stayed in the heart of Beirut and spent Christmas with our missionary friends, Les and Agnes de Smidt.

I pictured the scene of utter devastation and as I thought of the hundreds of lives lost and the missing family members I wept with the good people of Lebanon.

Printed in Great Britain
by Amazon

60226730R00210